HOW WE WRITE

The Varieties of Writing Experience

HOW WE WRITE

The Varieties of Writing Experience

WRITE

HILTON OBENZINGER

THE "HOW I WRITE" PROJECT AT STANFORD UNIVERSITY

Earlier versions of chapters have appeared in Catamaran Literary Reader and XCP: Cross Cultural Poetics

Produced in the United States in 2015 by The "How I Write" Project at Stanford University

Hilton Obenzinger

531 Lasuen Mall

P.O. Box 20121

Stanford University

Stanford, CA 94309

ISBN: 978-1517152604

Manufactured in the United States of America.

Book design by Dennis Gallagher, Visual Strategies, San Francisco.

10 9 8 7 6 5 4 3 2 1

For Diane Middlebrook

Other books by Hilton Obenzinger

Beginning: The Immigration Poems, 1924-1926, of
Nachman Obzinger (curator and editor)

Busy Dying

Running Through Fire: How I Survived the Holocaust by
Zosia Goldberg

a*hole: a novel

American Palestine: Melville, Twain, and the
Holy Land Mania

Cannibal Eliot and the Lost Histories of San Francisco

New York on Fire

This Passover or the Next I will Never be in Jerusalem

Five on the Western Edge: An Anthology of Work from
San Francisco (coauthor)

The Day of the Exquisite Poet is Kaput

Thunder Road

Bright Lights! Big City!

A Cinch: Amazing Works from the Columbia Review
(coeditor)

CONTENTS

Introduction

In 2002, Hilton Obenzinger began a series of public conversations with colleagues at Stanford called "How I Write." These dialogues were friendly, informal, and interrogatory, built around the fundamental questions: When did you start to write? Who inspired you? Do you have a method? Do you have a time and place you choose to write? Do you ever get stuck? And so on. He asked these questions of historians, novelists, philosophers—many of the people we expect to be lifelong writers—but also of physicists, psychiatrists, mathematicians, and computer scientists. The evening conversations that grew out of these questions—usually with an audience of 50 to 100—were personal, often intimate, recalling memories from childhood or school days, sometimes eliciting surprising secrets or surprised recognition ("nobody ever asked me how I write") and immensely interesting to those of us who read, think about, and cherish the written word. Over the thirteen years of the series, Hilton talked to dozens, maybe hundreds, of his Stanford colleagues, and the fruit of those hours of talk is condensed here in this eminently readable (and well written!) book, *How We Write: The Varieties of Writing Experience*.

In 1837 the young Ralph Waldo Emerson delivered an address at Harvard known as "The American Scholar," which many regard as our national intellectual Declaration of Independence. It is framed by a question not unlike those that Hilton poses, although maybe more a marveling query than a direct question. He wonders how "raw" life and ordinary experience get transformed through the alchemy of writing into coherent constellations of thought. He put it this way:

> The theory of books is noble. The scholar of the first age received into him the world around; brooded thereon; gave it the new

arrangement of his own mind, and uttered it again. It came into him life; it went out from him truth. It came to him short-lived actions; it went out from him immortal thoughts. It came to him business; it went from him poetry. It was dead fact; now, it is quick thought. It can stand, and it can go. It now endures, it now flies, it now inspires.

It's a beautiful passage, and a little later in the essay Emerson goes on to say that writers are like silkworms; they almost can't help digesting the world, converting mulberry leaves into what Emerson calls "satin." And, he says, "the manufacture goes forward at all hours."

One consistent theme we find in the writers Hilton talked with is just this kind of night-and-day commitment, dedication, and—one might almost say—"addiction." Once one becomes a writer, it's hard to stop. They do not speak of it as "manufacture," but the word that recurs throughout these conversations is its simpler and more blunt Anglo-Saxon synonym: "work." And, not surprisingly, many of the writers you will encounter in this book tell us how *hard* that work is, the hours and months that go into a draft that is superseded, the years of research that get distilled into one chapter, and so on. Writers work, and they "workshop" their work, among their working colleagues. But somewhere along the line, "work" becomes "craft," and even in rare moments it begins to feel like play—effortless and exhilarating. And that is why writers go back and do it again and again.

Hilton's project over the past thirteen years has been extraordinarily generous. His purpose, he says, was to sustain "a community of shared inquiry and insights about the writing process itself." He succeeded marvelously, and in the process, celebrated his colleagues and returned a gift of gratitude to his university, filled with appreciation for the liberal life of the mind such an institution nourishes and encourages.

At one of the "How I Write" conversations a few years ago, we got Hilton to sit on the other side of the microphone where his colleague Kevin DiPirro could pose him the questions Hilton likes to ask his guests. Hilton is the author of close to a dozen books, including novels (*a*hole*), memoir (*Busy Dying*), biography (*Running Through Fire*), academic literary history (*American Palestine*), and the American Book Award-winning *This Passover or the Next I will Never be in Jerusalem*. He has a doctorate in Modern Thought and Literature from Stanford and a lifetime of experience as a political activist and freelance writer to draw on, so he had no trouble telling the audience how he wrote, and writes—working, crafting, and sometimes even making satin out of leaves.

This book we hold in our hands will be another in Hilton's bibliography, but although it is *by* him it is not *about* him. It is his tribute to friends and colleagues, and a celebration of the writing life that brought them—and now us—together.

Thank you to the Hume Center for Writing and Speaking and Stanford Continuing Studies for their loyal sponsorship of "How I Write" over all the years.

Charles Junkerman

Associate Provost and
Dean of Continuing Studies

Stanford University

Invitation

WRITING IS OFTEN seen, and is sometimes revered, as an isolated and even tortured endeavor. In *How We Write*, and in the "How I Write" conversations upon which this book is based, Hilton Obenzinger brings to light the details of authors' private writing lives. He at once reinforces and challenges what we know about the lonely "word act" of writing. In the early "How I Write" conversations in the Hume Writing Center's cozy basement room, Hilton invited a curious audience into an intense yet casual conversation, a conversation flowing as it might around a dinner table. This audience marveled at writers' revelations of their writing stories, and left inspired with insights and ideas to bring to their own writing practice. *How We Write* invites a new audience to dinner, to be similarly inspired and surprised by the twists and turns in the conversation and by the truths revealed.

Julia Bleakney
Director, Hume Center for Writing and Speaking at Stanford University

Renato Rosaldo

The "How I Write" Project

ON SEPTEMBER 26, 1996, Renato Rosaldo suffered a stroke. Within a couple of weeks, "Poems started coming to me," he said. "I was sitting there and these lines would start coming to me. I didn't know exactly what they were, and so I started writing them down because I thought I should do that." Professor Rosaldo is one of the world's leading cultural anthropologists, but he had never written poetry before.

His doctors told him that he would have to do not only physical therapy but also cognitive therapy, employing both hands and both sides of his brain. So although he was right-handed and it was only his left side that had been affected by the stroke, he would now try to use both hands to write. "And I thought, 'Well, a poem—that's something I've never done before.'"

As he began to write poems using both hands, Dr. Rosaldo drew pictures along with them. "On my fortieth birthday I [had] started painting and drawing. And I remember my first class, where they showed us a grapefruit and I drew a circle," he laughed. "But I had loved to draw when I was a kid, and I would just get completely absorbed in this. And so I [had] worked at that for quite some time—since I was forty. But the last thing I expected was for poems to start coming to me." He'd had no ambitions to become a poet. "It was just something that happened to me," he explained.

"I realized that if I write left-handed, things happen that don't when I write right-handed," he said. "Sometimes these things will come to me in Spanish and sometimes in English and sometimes both combining." He had grown up in Tucson in a bilingual family. "Sometimes I write a Spanish version first and then translate it, and then work back and forth." Writing took such a long time, the languages playing off of each other, that he would often end up writing parallel poems. "Even if I did a complete version in Spanish and then translated it, I think of them as written bilingually. And sometimes I have found that I don't want to get them to match, so I produce two versions because I feel that they are almost like two plants growing differently."

He described writing in this entirely new way, using two languages as well as both hands, as "almost like working two sides of a street." The English would lead him to make some changes in the Spanish, then the other way around. "It is hard to tell which one is leading and which one is following. It gets very strange. That's maybe because I grew up speaking Spanish with my father and English with my mother at home; and then there was a period where I lost my Spanish and got it back when I was still young." Working two sides of the street was not easy. "I guess that's the theme: hard work, patience, attention."

Despite the difficulty, Dr. Rosaldo saw writing poetry as deeply healing, and it brightened his day. In fact, he became addicted to the practice of poetry, finding that he couldn't stop. "When I don't write, my day is grayer," he explained. "The world just gets grayer." As he began his healing by means of poetry, he thought he would end up writing a book of poems called *Healing Songs*. But while the poems just "came to him," he also had to learn how to make them work—to craft them, take them seriously. He knew he had to revise his poems paying the same attention to craft as he would when revising his scholarly writing. But he also realized he needed help. "I can rewrite prose—I've worked at it for a long time. But I don't know how to even begin rewriting a poem. . . . I lined up somebody to be my poetry tutor because I figured I wouldn't try to play the violin without a teacher, and I thought it seemed like new terrain, so I knew I needed help."

Still, needing help "was a very strange feeling," Dr. Rosaldo confessed. After all, he was a professor—a seasoned scholar, not a novice—and he was famous in his field. "I was a veteran cultural anthropologist and an infant poet—a kind of helpless infant." His new situation really struck him when he went to a reading given by some well-known poets. "I went in and I realized I could walk freely in the room." Nobody stopped him, no colleagues crowded around him. "I'm in a place where I'm a complete nobody. This is terrific! Look at how easy it is to walk around!" In contrast, when he'd go to anthropology meetings, he would be lionized. So many admirers would crowd around him that "it was just very hard to get from one room to another. It made me wonder how a centipede walks."

In the poetry scene, he was alone, uncelebrated, naked, which was refreshing; but he needed help, needed a community—people who would respond to his work, give him critical feedback. He joined a poetry workshop that met every month in his neighborhood, and over the course of years of sharing his work he did learn to write poems. He ended up publishing a book, although with a different title, with considerable success: *Prayer to Spider Woman/Rezo a la mujer araña* received an American Book Award in 2004.

Renato Rosaldo told of his journey into ambidextrous, bilingual poetry during one of a series of public conversations on writing I've been holding at Stanford University since 2002. I thought it would be valuable to learn about how people work—all kinds of writers: those who produce fiction and poems as well as those who write lab reports, histories, computer science textbooks—the whole gamut. Professor Rosaldo's story was stunning—but it turned out that it wouldn't be the only time I would be astonished.

For many, it was exhilarating to talk about what playwright Amy Freed called "a chaotic and mysterious adventure." For quite a few, writing is simply an instrument, not the main focus of their work as chemical engineers or sociologists—even though everyone at the university, from math professors to musicologists, must write; even if it only means cranking out mundane, uncreative word-stuff like memos or grant proposals. While some professors are very aware of their own writing process, many said they hadn't thought about it in years or they hadn't really paid much attention to it. Some were startled: they told me no one had ever asked them about it.

I decided I would ask.

Here was a major university, with thousands of people involved in discovering, creating, debating, and imparting knowledge, burrowing themselves deeply in libraries and labs—and other than those people who take personal interest in or make a special point of studying writing, there wasn't much of a self-aware community of shared inquiry and insights about the writing process itself. By asking about it, I hoped one benefit would be to help cultivate that shared awareness, to foster a community of writers. Since the project began, the university's writing program has been revamped and reenergized, and the Hume Center for Writing and Speaking was established, where I taught honors and advanced writing. The Hume Center was where many of these conversations were held.

"How I Write" conversations were informal, with no pretense of plumbing the depths of anyone's scholarly expertise or of attempting empirical thoroughness. Rather, these talks probed what the writing part of these scholars' and artists' work entailed—whether their field was physics or anthropology or fiction—in an easygoing, meandering fashion. The first announcement summed up the goals:

> "How I Write" is a series of conversations with faculty and other advanced writers to explore the nuts and bolts, pleasures and pains, of all types of writing. While content is always an issue, the conversations will primarily focus on work styles, such as where, when, and how a writer composes, allowing us to examine habits, idiosyncrasies, techniques, trade secrets, hidden anxieties, and delights. We will discuss how a writer generates ideas, sustains large-scale projects, combines research with composition, overcomes various impediments and blocks, and cultivates stylistic innovations. Writing communities share experiences (even bad ones) so that all writers can learn and grow, and Stanford is an exceptionally rich community for gaining such insights.
>
> Join Hilton Obenzinger in a conversation on the techniques, quirks, and joys of advanced writers producing work in all fields and genres.

I really didn't know what to expect. I figured that I would hold the first few conversations with people with whom I had worked, colleagues who would feel at ease, and in that way I would discover what to ask and how to allow my guests to bare their inner writing selves with as little interference on my part as possible. I would invite writers to say anything they wanted at the outset, then we would engage in conversation, and finally I would open the floor to the audience to join in with their own questions or observations.

I got thrown for a loop. After just the first two conversations it became abundantly clear just how wildly different were the ways writers approached the "nuts and bolts, pleasures and pains," and everything else.

Mary Lou Roberts, a professor of French history who now teaches at the University of Wisconsin, is gregarious and voluble, and her conversation is frequently punctuated with laughter. I couldn't imagine anyone better to start the series. Early on in the conversation she described her writing process with an analogy:

I saw this painting a long time ago at the Museum of Modern Art in New York, and thought, "This is my writing process." It was five panels: the first was incredibly blurry, the second panel was a little clearer, the third was a little clearer, the fourth was crystal clear, the fifth had started to fade a little bit. To me it feels like I always know what I want to say instinctively, because when you research, you make choices—you read some things and not others. I tell my graduate students, "Don't think; just go on instinct," because I think it's a very underrated human resource. So I have an incredibly vague idea—and then, when I begin to write, slowly it becomes clear.

As part of this process of traveling from blurry to clear (and back to slightly blurry, but on a higher level), she would have to write prodigious amounts before she could figure out what she actually wanted to say. Consequently, she would toss out large quantities of writing. And this didn't come easily:

I've thrown out whole chapters—sad, but true. And it is a really unfortunate thing because I am a real type A personality. That was the single hardest thing for me to come to terms with: how much time you waste. You can't sacrifice quality by including something when it is wrong; you just have to realize that the path from A to Z is never going to be straight. The way my writing has changed is that it has gotten better—not just my writing, but my whole thinking as a historian. I've gotten a lot more patient, more tolerant of waste. Because of that, I think my work is better.

The audience gasped. Some were shocked at the notion that instinct could play such a major role in scholarly research. But many more groaned at the idea of throwing out whole chapters, pages and pages of precious work. Professor Roberts is a particularly fluent writer—the words come to her easily, and I could see students in the audience who were much less fluent shuddering at the image of themselves painfully squeezing out a few pages and then blithely throwing them away. Such self-immolation was inconceivable.

My next conversation was with David Abernethy, a political scientist, and his approach stood in stark contrast. While he had written many articles and two books years before, Professor Abernethy was only just coming out with *The Dynamics of Global Dominance: European Overseas Empires, 1415-1980* after years of not publishing anything. This book certainly had a major historical quality to it, but for a political scientist, the key word was "dynamics." Professor Abernethy was searching for patterns and models he could extract from all of the many different colonial histories, not from just the particular, individual characteristics of the histories of single countries such as New Zealand or Paraguay or Vietnam.

Interdisciplinary work has its difficulties. But I was more shocked to learn that *The Dynamics of Global Dominance* took fifteen years to write. "I decided to ask a fairly large and intractable question," he explained. "Why did people from a tiny part of the world (Western Europe) dominate so much of the world for half a millennium? I had a huge question, the answer to which, it seems to me, helps to define the modern world—so it was an important question." Certainly, he had a lot at stake, and a vast scope, but does that account for why it took fifteen years?

Professor Abernethy explained that he would devote himself to teaching and administrative work during the academic year, and he would only write during the summers and during bits of sabbatical time. It was a long haul, and he didn't publish articles in journals along the way as many scholars do. A lot of people in his field thought he was a completely unproductive scholar—perhaps one of those professors who get tenure and then rest on their laurels, cozy in their sinecures. But he was far from lazy. Several times in our talk he called himself a loner, and it seems clear that he insisted on following the Paul Anka/Frank Sinatra "I Did It My Way" school of thought. Yet, just as Mary Lou Roberts would allow herself to write at length until she understood what she wanted to say, Professor Abernethy had his own method for formulating his argument:

> The first seven or eight years were spent just doing research, asking the question, "How did Europeans expand in various parts of the world?"—and then the other side [of that question]: "How did these empires collapse?" Research is writing: you are always taking notes. In note-taking, I find if I carry out a dialogue or conversation with the writer, rather than passively recording what the writer said, I can present my own voice, use my own reactions, as the basis of what I write later on. My own device is parentheses: I am reading something, taking notes, add a parenthesis: "This is nuts," or "Greatest point I ever heard, but what about the other one three pages ago?" I am directly engaging the

author with parentheses. And the parentheses mean I know that I am speaking. And then I run through the parenthetical notes and that becomes, in part, the argument. So the process of seven or eight years of taking notes produced my own reaction, which I used later on. You start at some point after maybe eight or twenty years trying to write something up, a first chapter.

Once again, the audience gasped. Waiting to write, then actually writing the book after eight or twenty years? He was, of course, writing all along, producing his running commentary, growing his analysis. But he waited and waited, holding back before he actually began the book itself. He seemed to follow the dictum put forth by another professor: "Don't write until you see the whites of their eyes!"

There was more: after fifteen years, he had produced 1,100 manuscript pages, and his publisher told him it was unmanageably large. He needed to cut it. "So I spent fifteen years marching up the hill, and then another three years marching down. The book would not have seen the light of day had I not cut it by 30 percent or so. And the painful process of deleting words that took all those years to get on paper was pretty tough."

Eighteen years!

Perhaps I shouldn't have been surprised by David Abernethy's method of persistent incremental Talmud-like commentary or Mary Lou Roberts's easygoing, effulgent free-writing. But I was taken aback by how very differently they and others worked, and how strong-willed and idiosyncratic they could be about their writing process.

What I learned from all of the conversations is that the unexpected is a given in all aspects of people's writing and intellectual lives. Eric Roberts, a computer scientist, refuses to have a computer or even a TV at home; home is the place where he goes to read books, which line the walls. Eavan Boland, a celebrated Irish poet and director of Stanford's creative writing program, devours high-tech magazines, and for relaxation she writes computer programs. So much for stereotypes.

I was surprised in so many other ways: some people described how much they hated writing (or how much they suffered to make words work right); others revealed hidden disabilities; still others provided powerful and sometimes strange insights. For example, English professor Terry Castle, author of *The Apparitional Lesbian* and *The Professor,* responded that she wrote "very neurotically." As it turned out, a lot of faculty writers could say the same thing. But then she held up a sheet of paper with microscopic-looking scribbles—one of the sheets of paper on which she had written the first draft of her dissertation many years before. To my astonishment, the entire draft of her dissertation consisted of just seven such sheets, with tiny scrawls on both sides—the kind of writing someone would employ if they were copying the Bible on a grain of rice. She had little explanation for why she felt compelled to write in such "an imponderably tiny handwriting"—just that she had to write that way and that it worked for her. Then, in 1983, every professor at Stanford received a computer, and she left the world of Lilliputian script.

When I asked the late historian George Fredrickson to join me in a public conversation on writing, he was surprised at first. He volunteered that he had never thought much about how he wrote before. But then he told me that the best compliment he had ever received about his writing was when a colleague, after reading something he had written for *The New York Review of Books*, said, "You have a perfect expository style—because it is no style at all." By this, Fredrickson explained, his friend meant, "The reader isn't aware of how the article is written; it doesn't call attention to itself; the writing doesn't interfere; you just give the meaning." And this transparency, this "seeming absence of style," described his entire sense of writing. History as a discipline pays attention to quality prose—Herodotus and Edward Gibbon were literary masters, after all—but as do many other fields, it uses prose only as a vehicle to convey its task. Some fields, I learned, are entirely suspicious of good writing: many scholars and scientists, and even poets and novelists, are scornful of writing that they believe distracts from critical content by seeming to call attention to its own eloquence. In any "word act," for them, the juice is in the act—the word is only the peel.

I also learned that writing is vitally important at a university, no matter what your work may be. One conversation was with John Hennessy, an important computer scientist, successful entrepreneur, and, not least of his accomplishments, the president of Stanford University. He dispelled one of the myths of his own college days: "We had a notion that engineers had to know how to use slide rules or calculators or computers but not how to write. And that is the biggest falsehood you could possibly perpetrate on young people. I think writing and rhetoric (public speaking) are the two most valuable skills across any discipline in any field." This is a powerful endorsement for the importance of learning how to write. Perhaps it's obvious, but it was still good to hear the president of the university say it.

The title of this book is *How We Write: The Varieties of Writing Experience.* This is a book about "word acts"—a term akin to the linguistic term "speech act," which describes the ways speech is a performance, a form of intention and action, not merely a passive or descriptive utterance. Written words, of course, are acts on screens and paper as well—scripts for performance, if not the vocal performance itself. Writing can make things happen—whether a biological discovery, an epiphany in fiction, or a philosophical disquisition. The subtitle is a little tip of the hat to *The Varieties of Religious Experience* by William James. (In fact, James was at Stanford at the time of the April 1906 earthquake. Rebecca Solnit, one of the participants in this project, describes in her book *A Paradise Built in Hell* how James drove up to San Francisco after the disaster and returned very moved by the way people had come to each other's aid—by the deep altruism during crisis motivating survivors and not, as so many assumed, "the law of the jungle." This experience deeply affected his understanding of psychology and philosophy.) This book also examines experiences without judgment, as did James—although the comparison with his exploration of religious sensibilities shouldn't be regarded too closely: while there certainly may be "healthy minds" and "sick souls" involved in writing, that's not my main focus. Instead, I am struck with the same notion of the pluralist universe of multiplicity and diversity that excited James: with such a wide variety of attitudes and so many idiosyncratic practices, it's clear that there is no one way to write, no single type of word act—although there are patterns of concerns and practices.

As for creating a sense of writing community, after years of holding these conversations, faculty and students—and others around the world who have listened or watched the conversations on "Stanford on iTunes"— have at least gained a better sense that the process of writing, including their own, is worth examining. They may also believe that something can be achieved by sharing each other's experiences and methods. Beyond that, I've been able to borrow useful techniques and compelling experiences from faculty to share with students. For example, political scientist Terry Karl employs a technique to challenge her own assumptions, a way to test her hypotheses, honed under dangerous conditions during the civil war in El Salvador—and her approach can be reproduced (under much safer conditions) in college dorm rooms.

In addition to the many public "How I Write" conversations over the course of thirteen years, I've had many more private ones with poets, novelists, philosophers, social critics, journalists, and others; and I've worked with thousands of students writing short essays, extended research projects, sermons, scripts, personal statements, biographies, stories, business plans, fiction, poetry, and more. In other words, I have a lot of people talking in my head, a chattering archive that I bring to each topic—and so many of these voices are strikingly eloquent. When Pulitzer Prize-winning historian David Kennedy explained how he learned to write history, or when Tony Award-winning playwright David Henry Hwang revealed the process through which he created his hit play *M. Butterfly*, I didn't need to say much more. Of course, I shaped the conversation and the way these experiences unfolded in a kind of logic, adding my own observations; but for the most part I tried to stay out of the way of what these writers had to say. In some ways this is a combination of many different audio clips, and you could regard it as a radio script put to print.

This "audio documentary" is a sample of people who write at a major university or close by. It so happened that Welsh national poet Gwyneth Lewis was visiting one year, but I didn't go seeking out poets laureate or best-selling novelists or Oscar-winning screenwriters or scientists published in *The New Yorker* per se. (I did seek out outstanding poet Diane di Prima, elderly and ill, because she was a friend whose experience and art needed to be recognized and shared.) These writers happened to travel in the orbit of a great institution, with some more celebrated than others; and even after so many public conversations, by no means did I run out of participants. Many more writers remained on my list for conversations when the project came to its end. But what this means is that the insights these people share about writing come about as a result of a fairly random process. Still, it's comprehensive enough, the sample population large enough, that all of their voices flow into a stream of observations that make sense, and they reflect off each other to confirm or counter each other's experiences.

The "How I Write" conversations went on for more than thirteen years, and soon after launching the program I began working on this book. I had to wait until I had enough conversations and other material to develop chapters, but I wrote commentaries from the start. I had to arrange for transcriptions of the talks, and then pore over them trying to divine correlations between people's insights and stories. For these writers it was an hour or two of talking, which they soon forgot or remember only vaguely. But I would relive these conversations on tape or in a transcript again and again. I would recall oral historian David Dunaway relating the oral history of an angry Pete Seeger putting his foot through Woody Guthrie's mandolin, Shelley Fisher Fishkin explaining how getting stung on her rump by a toy bullwhip on the banks of the Mississippi radically changed the direction of one of her books on Mark Twain, Adam Johnson sharing how he learned storytelling from rifling through his neighbors' garbage cans and listening while working on construction jobs to the tales of Vietnam vets and ex-cons.

With such scenes rattling around in my head, I compiled compendiums of excerpts on specific themes, such as what happens when someone gets stuck or how a writer gets ideas. I was able to fish through many transcripts and create very thick albums of these excerpts, and then I read through them, trying to understand each topic more deeply. The next step was to sift through one topic and place selected voices in new arrangements to unfold ideas from my own understanding. I wasn't going to throw in everything; I wasn't going to vacuum up every word. Some people received more attention than others, many terrific stories and comments were sadly left on the editing room floor, and some participants were hardly represented at all. All the while, I held new "How I Write" conversations—new voices with beautiful stories and exciting ideas—and again and again each compendium had to loosen its belt to let more in. Unfortunately, during some conversations, the recording system failed and I only had unreliable memory to rely on. For those who participated or who attended, please forgive the uneven representation of these conversations.

The chapters of this book follow the major line of topics that came up in the conversations: Chapter One, the different ways people learned how to write; Chapter Two, their attitudes and feelings toward writing and what motivates them; Chapter Three, what happens when a writer gets blocked; Chapter Four, the different ways people work—their physical environment and how they handle time, relationships, and more; Chapter Five, how writers get ideas and how they launch into a project; Chapter Six, the ways writers fashion arguments or create ideas, images, and stories; Chapter Seven, how style is driven by field or genre; Chapter Eight, how research connects to style; Chapter Nine, the different approaches writers employ to revise their work; and Chapter Ten, a final reflection.

How We Write: The Varieties of Writing Experience is not a textbook or a handbook on how to become a writer. If anyone reading this reflects upon their own writing, and if they pick up one or two insights that can apply to them, that would be splendid. But it's primarily a conversation, a medley of voices celebrating a craft that delights and dismays each of us, and a conversation the reader is invited to join.

Naturally, events intruded during the dozen or more years working on this book—family obligations, job demands, wars, illness, my own publication of other books, and other excitements—and many times I had to put the book away to take it up again later. It was hard recalling where I was in the story, and I would have to reread (and then rewrite) the whole book each time. Interruptions hindered me from being able to maintain concentration, but these breaks did allow me to reenter these conversations at an even deeper level, and with additional material from more recent dialogues.

Most of the writers I invited were glad to participate. A few of the writers declined: they wanted to write rather than talk about it. However, the late biographer Diane Middlebrook was exceptionally eager; she was the only one who sought me out and requested that we have a conversation as soon as possible. Not long after our conversation, she was diagnosed with the cancer that ended her life, so perhaps she had a premonition that her time was short; perhaps she felt an urgency to tell the story, before it was too late, of how she did the work that was so important to her.

During our talk, Diane Middlebrook contemplated the whole purpose of writing—that desire to have something to say and the hope that someone will read it. She was working on a biography of Ovid when she passed away, and she adopted a version of the classical writer's thoughts as a kind of motto:

> Even though we have to die, occasionally some people leave something behind that makes other people feel they have been addressed in a continual stream of intelligence—that someone has joined the stream of literature and passed it on to you, with all of the artifacts that could be built into it in the historical moments in which it is made, and delivered it to a future so that we could all share it.

Many writers want to join that stream of intelligence; they too want to pass their crafted words on to the future. (Her family and colleagues completed her biography of the young Ovid posthumously.)

I enjoyed the company of the people who engaged in these conversations.

Since the project began, a few have moved to other universities and some have retired. Others have passed away: Diane Middlebrook, George Fredrickson, and Richard Rorty. I hope that all of their remarks, along with their crafted words, are delivered to the future.

- Most of the "How I Write" conversations can be found as video or audio recordings at Stanford on iTunes at https://itunes.apple.com/WebObjects/MZStore.woa/wa/viewPodcast?id=385404247

- The conversation with Clarence B. Jones can be found on C-SPAN at http://www.c-span.org/video/?312251-1/conversation-clarence-jones

- An excerpt of the conversation with Scott Saul on researching Richard Pryor is at https://www.youtube.com/watch?v=c2JGYtvi790

- Transcripts for a limited number of conversations can be found at https://undergrad.stanford.edu/tutoring-support/hume-center/about-hume-center/annual-events/how-i-write-series/how-i-write-archive/how-i-write-transcripts

I invite you to join the conversation.

■ ■ ■

In addition to the participants, my great appreciation goes out to all who helped in the "How I Write" project, named and unnamed. Cosponsors of the project include Susie Brubaker-Cole for Undergraduate Research Programs; Charles Junkerman for the Stanford Program in Continuing Studies; and Julia Bleakney, Clyde Moneyhun, Wendy Goldberg, Jerry White, and the late John Tinker for the Hume Center for Writing and Speaking; Julie Lythcott-Haims for Undergraduate Advising and Research. Additional support came from Andrea Lunsford and Marvin Diogenes for the Program in Writing and Rhetoric, John Bravman and Harry Elam for the Office of Undergraduate Education, and Jonah Willihnganz and Natacha Ruck for the Stanford Storytelling Project. Great appreciation goes to Azin Massoudi Richa and Rebecca Siegel for help producing each event; Lina Yamaguchi for her assistance preparing flyers and for recording many of the conversations; Stanford Events for their audio and video work; and Brent Izutsu, Aaron Kehoe, and Katy Ferron for posting the recordings on "Stanford on iTunes." Thanks also go to

Tigerfish and Paul Garton transcription services, Gabrielle LeMay for her excellent copy editing, Mary Renaud and Marjorie Ford for additional editing, Stephen Vincent and Elizabeth Wales for their editorial support, and Dennis Gallagher for his professional book production guidance. Because this was a research project, I followed guidelines for permissions from the Institutional Review Board for Human Subjects, and I thank the members of the IRB for their care and flexibility.

As always, my deepest gratitude goes to my family for their patience and support.

To Diane Middlebrook, who was consistently ebullient and warm, always encouraging and brilliant, I dedicate *How We Write: The Varieties of Writing Experience*.

Terry Castle

CHAPTER ONE

. . .

Love, Work, and Baboons: Learning to Write

WHEN RENATO ROSALDO emerged from his stroke, poems suddenly came to him in English and Spanish—a remarkable, happy inspiration. But he also had to learn to write again, in a new way, returning to both languages of his childhood. He didn't have to start with his ABC's; thankfully, the stroke wasn't that debilitating. But he did have to rethink what he did— how to give particular words to feelings and ideas in two languages, how to shape phrases and sentences. His experience learning to write poetry was dramatic, and it underscored the ways writing is a complicated neurological and physical act for each individual. At the same time, the act of writing is a social process, despite how we work all alone in the privacy of our own heads. Even when we sit by ourselves with paper and pen or keyboard and monitor, we're constantly in communion with imagined readers; even if it's just a single word on a page, that word is crowded with a lot of people and their experiences.

Little kids who learn their ABC's and middle-aged anthropologists who suddenly begin to write poetry for the first time—even in two languages simultaneously—are both involved in similar processes. Everyone who writes must *learn* how to write. That's obvious—the skill doesn't just sprout up like a wildflower, and it doesn't seem to come as a result of natural growth the way understanding and speaking a language come, from infancy on. There are sophisticated tools involved: alphabets, pencils, keyboards, vocabularies, grammars. Even skillful writers have to start with their ABC's, moving on to words, sentences, paragraphs, essays, arguments, styles, genres, and more. Mostly, we remember very little of how we learned the basics, our first scribbles, at a very early age—unless someone else remembers for us. Literary critic and biographer Arnold Rampersad grew up in the West Indies, and his sister remembers how he learned his ABC's by means of a Victorian teaching technique: he would trace letters in the air with his finger.

Often, the earliest writing experience most people remember is scrawling their name on walls or other forbidden places with crayons. "I've asked people for twenty years about their early memories of writing," said Andrea Lunsford, who studies these sorts of things. "The most frequent memory of writing people have is of writing their name." She can't remember that moment in her own life, but she's interviewed thousands of people "who can remember the moment when they could put their mark on the world, make letters that were both them and not them." She described that important moment as one of "differentiation, where you see yourself from a new perspective. You're taking on the beginnings of a self that is separate from your family, your mother—and that's a really important moment."

As kids grow a little older, they are often prodded by a kind of desire that pushes them in the direction of words, and that motivating force can be dramatic enough that it gets chiseled into memory. Harry Elam, a stage director and scholar of August Wilson and other African-American playwrights, was drawn to the theater when he wrote a play in the third grade "to get a girl to kiss me." It was a Christmas play, and he wrote it so he would be the lead playing opposite her. Shrewdly, he crafted one scene so that she had to kiss him. He realized that he could actually mold reality to his wishes by scripting it, and he got the kiss. The possibilities of writing for the theater opened up from there.

Young love is definitely a motivator. I wrote a poem for a girl I pined for in seventh grade. I drew a picture of her, bought a bouquet, and handed her several pages of a terrible poem—"Your lips are like cherries, your eyes are bright stars. ..." She showed it to her friends; they all giggled; I was humiliated. Most of all, it didn't work. However, the other seventh-grade boys were impressed, once they stopped snickering; they liked the idea of wooing with words, and I would hire myself out to write love letters at 25 cents a crack: "Your legs are like sidewalks to the moon." If you can't get love, at least you can get money, and that little bit of incentive pushed me to keep writing. I read Edmond Rostand's *Cyrano de Bergerac* some time later, and it confirmed that putting words in other people's mouths could be a powerful act, even if it led to my own heartbreak.

Fred Turner is a communication professor who, before becoming an academic, was a journalist; before that, he too wrote poems. Here, also, love had its role to play, but bloomed at a different stage in life—and with more success:

> I started writing poems very, very early, like in grammar school. And I wrote them all the way through college. My senior thesis in college was actually a collection of poems, which I dug up out of my wife's files today because I hadn't seen it in twenty years. I gave it to her when she was my girlfriend, and now we're married—which is wild in its own right.

This is encouraging news for all those handing over their verses to their heart's desire.

Sometimes there's an inexplicable attraction to writing itself. "When I was about ten," recalled anthropologist Paulla Ebron, "there were these little ads in magazines [saying] that you could be an artist or you could be a writer for some money. I guess it was a correspondence course." For some reason, the ad did its job, and she sent in her coupon. "But they told me I needed to be a little older, or have my parents sign at the end, or something." Literary critic and biographer Diane Middlebrook couldn't remember a time when she *didn't* write. "I just always did." And she was even able, at a very early age, to get critical acclaim and a lot of encouragement as a result: "I had a poem in the *Spokane Daily Chronicle* on the cartoon page when I was eight years old," she said. "It stays in my mind as a very thrilling experience." She had written a great many books by the time we spoke, but she still glowed with pride at her earliest childhood triumph.

For playwright David Henry Hwang, family history drew him at the age of ten to his very first writing project. "My grandmother fell ill and we all thought she was going to pass away," he explained. "She was the one who kept all of the family history. So I remember thinking, if she died, it would be doubly tragic—because we would lose my grandmother, of course; but we would also lose all this history." He was born and raised in Los Angeles, and his grandparents were living at that time in the Philippines. So he asked his mother if he could spend the summer with them, and his parents agreed. That summer he did "what we would now call oral histories," getting his grandmother to tell the family stories and recording them all on tape. "Then when I returned to the states, I compiled them into a 90-page nonfiction novel, which got Xeroxed and distributed to my relatives." And, he laughed, "It got very good reviews."

Hwang only began writing plays when he was an undergraduate at Stanford, and from the time he wrote his very first play, *FOB* ("Fresh Off the Boat," a term for recent immigrants), he began to explore the complexities of human identities—Asian, American, Asian-American, male, female, immigrant, and so forth—all of which resonate in his plays, such as *M. Butterfly*, and in *Yellow Face*, the play he was developing at Stanford at the time we had our conversation. Looking back, he realized that "the one time I did engage the medium of writing, it was to try and understand my own identity in some larger context—to understand where I'd come from, and to begin to put my existence here in this country in a kind of historical frame."

As a kid, novelist Adam Johnson also sought to dig out his own identity, but he did this with a little help from his neighbors. His parents had split up, and he moved to another state with his mom, who was a doctor and was busy with her practice. "I was a latchkey kid," he explained. "And all the time I would go down in the alleys, I would open the trash cans behind people's houses and try to figure out the families inside by the garbage they threw away." His neighbors complained about his snooping, and his mom tried to talk him out of doing it, but he didn't really understand. He was "trying to figure out what a family was, who people were, by what they threw away—walking around and spending lots of days doing that." In this way, he learned that lives could be pieced together through shards of evidence to make stories.

After high school, Johnson worked as a construction worker for several years, and he learned yet another way to relate to the world through stories. "At that time, Vietnam vets were young, vital men in their late thirties who were still alive and telling stories, [and] ex-cons could get jobs. Now they're all drug tested and fingerprinted and they have different lives, but I did work with storytellers a great deal." When he finally went to college he didn't do very well, and his friends kept steering him to courses that were easy A's—History of Music, Family Studies, Jazz Appreciation. Finally, a friend said, "Creative writing, Adam. It's the easiest A in town."

> I think epiphanies happen in retrospect. You look back and you see that was the turning point. Looking back, that was probably my one epiphany: taking a fiction class. Ron Carlson, a wonderful fiction writer, was new there and had a lot to give. And suddenly all the flaws I had been told I had in my life—that I was a day-dreamer, a liar, a rubbernecker, and an exaggerator (which is the

worst one because you don't get anything for it and you can still get caught)—they came together to make a story that was suddenly valuable and that was worth something. I had never had that feeling before, and all I wanted to do was just keep writing stories from then on, and [work at] figuring out why and what they mean.

Reading, of course, is a key path to writing, often because reading becomes the avenue to experiencing new realities and to exploring (or escaping) identities. Ramón Saldivar, literary and cultural critic, grew up bilingual in Brownsville, Texas. The whole city was a Mexican barrio, as he described it, and his family lived in the middle of that barrio. One day, when he was eight years old, he came home from school to see a strange sight: "There in the middle of the living room was a pile of beautiful white-bound gilt-edged books, and I was astonished. Where did these come from? What were they doing in my house?" His parents did not buy books. "As far as I can remember up to that moment, there were only two books in the house. One was the Bible—but you don't read the Bible in Mexican Catholic homes (it's just there as a showpiece)—and the other was a textbook on how to be a plumber. And my father was not a plumber." Professor Saldivar speculates that his father must have come across the book at some point and considered learning to become a plumber, but he never did. "I didn't read either of those books. And I've often regretted it," Professor Saldivar joked. "My life would have been richer if I knew something about the Bible and something about plumbing."

But then, sitting in the middle of the combined living-room-den-dining-TV-room of his four-room barrio home were "these beautiful books that, certainly, from the look of them, were much more expensive than we could afford; they must have amounted to two or three months' worth of our grocery bill, at least." It turned out that the pile in the middle of the room was a set of the 1958 *World Book* encyclopedia. That was his entry into reading and the larger universe beyond Brownsville. "From that moment, I had the sense that words come together in these complicated and interesting ways. In this set of books the words are arranged alphabetically from A to Z. And you can pick the B words and do lots of readings about brontosaurus and bronchial tubes and anything else having to do with B. The idea of the palpability of words," Professor Saldivar explained, "organized in a certain way." He marveled at the pleasure of such palpability: "I read the whole thing that summer from A to Z."

That pile of encyclopedias allowed him to exult in language and knowledge. "Books are not part of our daily life, and to have access to that was a huge and important step," he said. It was "the foundation for a shorter step, which would be trying out language in written form." Reading allowed him to imagine that "I could have a role in the construction of that entity," the written word, the book.

To Ramón Saldivar, there is an "exciting universality" communicated by the way the encyclopedia packages knowledge between the covers of a single book or set of books. "That's why it was that enlightenment breakthrough. It gave us the impression that one can encapsulate and possess universal knowledge. That is the allure."

The encyclopedia stood out as a gift, as well. He never asked his mother how the encyclopedia set arrived, but he did imagine what had happened. The salesman was "probably an overly tired, exasperated, poor man. It had to be a man, since in 1958 walking in the Mexican barrio in South Texas— a woman couldn't do that." He contemplated the vision of this tired and frustrated man walking up to his house to "convince my mother that of all things in the world she needed to buy a set of encyclopedias. I value those books for that reason," he explained. "Having it at home and having my mother bring them to me was important on a deep emotional level. She knew what I wanted. That's how I felt at that moment and [have] felt ever since. All those things come together." It was the combination of the rare book and deep, abiding maternal love. They provided the path to reading, and then to learning how to write.

Leonard Susskind really *was* a plumber. And that fact leads to a different story of how someone learns to write.

Professor Susskind grew up in the South Bronx, and in 1961 he was a student "with a somewhat unorthodox academic record" at CCNY who also worked as a plumber. He is an acclaimed physicist today.

During our "How I Write" conversation, Professor Susskind read a passage from his book *The Black Hole War: My Battle with Stephen Hawking to Make the World Safe for Quantum Mechanics,* which would appear two years later. The excerpt described his turning point in college when he met John Wheeler, the famous Princeton professor who worked on the quantum theory of gravity in the 1960s and '70s. One of his professors, Harry Soodak, "a cigar-chomping, cussing [CCNY] professor from the same Jewish … working-class background that I came from … took me down to Princeton to meet him. The hope was that Wheeler would be impressed and that I would be admitted as a graduate student, despite my lack of an undergraduate degree."

His mother thought he should dress properly for the meeting—meaning that he should "show solidarity" with his working-class roots and dress in his work clothes. "These days, my plumber in Palo Alto dresses about the same way that I do when I lecture at Stanford." But in 1961, plumbing in the South Bronx was a much rougher profession. "My plumbing costume was the same as my father's and that of all his [roughneck] plumber buddies—Li'l Abner bib overalls, a blue flannel work shirt, and heavy steel-toed work shoes. [And in my case,] I also sported a watch cap to keep the dirt and grime out of my hair."

The cigar-chomping professor picked him up early to drive to Princeton, but when he saw the plumber in his outfit, "he did a double take":

> The big cigar fell from his mouth, and he told me to go back upstairs and change. He said that John Wheeler was not that kind of guy.
>
> When I walked into the great professor's office, I saw what Harry meant. The only way I can describe the man who greeted me is to say that he looked Republican. What the hell was I doing in this Wasp's nest of a university?
>
> Two hours later, I was completely enthralled. John was enthusiastically describing his vision of how space and time would become a wild, jittery, foamy world of quantum fluctuations when viewed through a tremendously powerful microscope. He told me that the most profound and exciting problem of physics was to unify Einstein's two great theories—General Relativity and Quantum Mechanics. He explained that only at the Planck distance would elementary particles reveal their true nature, and it would be all about geometry—quantum geometry. To a young aspiring physicist, the stuffy businessman exterior had morphed into [the appearance of] an idealistic visionary. I wanted more than anything to follow this man into battle.

Susskind never did become Wheeler's student, but the encounter did change his life, and he became a physicist. The whole story is startling, and he writes the tale with flair.

Today Leonard Susskind is a leading scientist in a very specialized field. He's also written many books and articles to make physics accessible to the educated public, becoming a gifted illuminator of highly abstract concepts. But as a young student, the plumber-turned-physicist couldn't write well. He came "from a neighborhood and a background where people spoke a very funny kind of English. It was called 'Bronx English.'" What's more, not everybody in his working-class family knew how to read and write. "But my father and mother knew how to read and write," he recalled. "I don't know why I was so challenged and unable to write." He goes on to tell his story of failure:

> I always considered myself a seriously writing-challenged person who had zero ability to be able to communicate with the written word. I was so bad at it, or other people thought I was so bad at it, that it was a disaster in school, and throughout school I was constantly in remedial English classes. I don't really know why. I could spell, my grammar was okay, my punctuation was okay— although I really have had a lifelong war with the semicolon. But other than the semicolon, I was okay. I didn't know what was wrong with my writing. All I knew was that I couldn't get a decent grade in English. English teachers continuously considered me seriously challenged, and put me in remedial classes.

This didn't seem to make sense to him, even back then. He knew he was a very good storyteller. He could tell jokes and was always good with words. He was a capable spontaneous speaker. "I don't know why I didn't bridge the gap."

Like Ramón Saldivar, reading brought him to writing—although no one brought him a pile of encyclopedias. First he had to find the books, or they had to find him. He read his first book, Kenneth Grahame's *The Wind in the Willows*, when he was twelve years old. "I was blown away."

> My aunt bought me *The Wind in the Willows,* and I read it, and I just thought, "This is magic. This is something magical." By the time I was fifteen, somebody else gave me another book called *Huckleberry Finn,* and I read that. Again, I loved it. Here I was, a kid in the South Bronx, mostly playing basketball, stickball, all these things that kids did in the South Bronx. My friends, believe it or not, were not readers, and I don't know that anybody read. But again, when I was sixteen, somebody gave me a copy of, of, all things, *Washington Square.* This is not the sort of thing that a sixteen-year-old kid in the South Bronx was reading. I mean,

I didn't know there was a character called Henry James, didn't know who he was—and I read it, and I loved it.

Finally, before going to college, he read Franz Kafka. "Kafka just caught my imagination, and I've been reading Kafka ever since. I read Kafka over and over and over again, and I don't know why." Susskind called upon James, Twain, and Kafka to be his teachers, and he learned from his masters. He no longer needs to worry about being sent to remedial writing class. He has honed his writing skills in a tough field, making the cosmic implications of physics understandable to ordinary people with such books as *The Cosmic Landscape: String Theory and the Illusion of Intelligent Design* and *The Black Hole War: My Battle with Stephen Hawking to Make the World Safe for Quantum Physics.*

The discovery of books in a world without books is a central part of Saldivar's and Susskind's learning stories, as it is with essayist and cultural critic Rebecca Solnit's. She was in love with stories long before she even learned to read, and when she did, she learned quickly and well. For her, books were boxes, "and suddenly I could open all the boxes and unpack the treasures inside, and it was incredibly rich and magical for a kid." When her family life got "stranger and stranger," she "piled up a castle of books around me and lived in it." In first grade, she wanted to become a librarian because "they got to live with these books all day." And then she realized she could have an even better relationship with books, "which is to write them."

Steven Zipperstein, a historian of Eastern European Jews, also came to writing because of books—not a castle, but more a mountain of them. "I grew up in a bookish home," he said. His father was a CPA and a book collector who had amassed over 30,000 volumes by the time he suffered a devastating stroke at the age of seventy-eight a few years before our conversation. Instead of just the Bible and a book on plumbing, Professor Zipperstein grew up with so many books that they "filled every bit of the house." His father had so many volumes that he constructed a special building in the backyard of their home in North Hollywood to house his library. Here, too, love played a big role, but in a different mode.

Professor Zipperstein also read out loud from notes he had written before our conversation. His father was "a seemingly conventional Orthodox Jew." But his obsession with books was considerably more than conventional. At the same time, the father's library pushed the son in unorthodox directions. The boy read Spinoza at fourteen, "and a year or two later, I spent a singularly depressing but also oddly useful summer devouring all of Eugene O'Neill's bleak family dramas." He would crawl into corners of his house, behind old couches and in crevices, hugging the walls, going to these private spaces to search for knowledge and rationality in books. He sought, "quite simply, a source of peace. Elsewhere, Nietzsche, Spinoza wreaked havoc. In the house in which I was raised, they protected, they shielded. They dispensed not only wisdom, but no less importantly, they [also] sent in shafts of light amidst an emotional whirlwind I'd only then begun to understand."

But all around his father, encircling the entire family, "was chaos." His father constructed the library "to shield him," but the library itself was "a study in chaos, with books helter-skelter, bought often by the pound." The library was a "mountain of erudition and schlock"—treasures alongside trash. His father would scoop up books, "sometimes hundreds at a time, buying often seven, eight, or more copies of the same book that he placed side by side. Books instructing women how to achieve orgasm sat next to popular Judaica." He constructed shelves of fine wood, filling them with five or six columns of books "with little obvious order. The library soon took on the wild aura of a Lower East Side electronics shop. Soon the room became too crowded to work in, and my father spent most of his time before his stroke writing on a card table in my old bedroom."

Professor Zipperstein explained that there was a lot of emotional turmoil in his household, with little talk. Talk was regarded as "a furious, almost ever-present affront to the senses." Talk was like a challenge "to sanity itself. My father used books as his moat, as his imperfect barrier against the terrible noise that surrounded us. ..." Books became the vehicle for getting close to his father. "By my late teens, my father and I could enjoy peace of mind together side by side only in bookstores. ... As fiercely as both of us loved books, it wasn't books that were, if we were to admit it, truly central to our quest, but just the silence." Books provided peace, not just a shared solitude. Professor Zipperstein took what would seem to be a natural step, and he climbed from reading to writing. Surrounded by so many books, the next step was to write them.

Of course, school is where most people learn to write—sometimes with pain. Andrea Lunsford's family moved when she was in second grade, and when she went to her new school, she discovered that they were doing cursive writing, but she could only print. "My teacher made me sit by myself that day, and she said, 'You know, I'll show you this some other time, but you just sit over there and read.' I went home that night just sobbing. I just threw myself on my mother and father and said, 'I'm never going back there until I can do this weird thing that they're doing.'" Her parents were kind and attentive, and they immediately started to work with her on how to shape those curvy lines into letters. Shelley Fisher Fishkin, also an English professor, was such a smart kid that she actually skipped the grade when they taught cursive. She never did learn that skill well—she says that even she can't read her own handwriting. She continued to print, and as soon as she could she switched to a keyboard—a typewriter and then a computer.

Often, a teacher in high school or college made a difference, or an educational program actually worked. Mary Lou Roberts was educated at a French Catholic school by nuns who were, according to her, "very into writing." She was "a very badly behaved kid, always getting kicked out of class." But what saved her from getting kicked out of school altogether was that she was able to write. One day her teacher gave her class an assignment. She gave the students a picture of two ducks falling, and then asked them to write in response. "Instead of writing about two ducks falling," Professor Roberts recalled, "I tried to write from the ducks' perspective. It was really exciting to do that." Writing meant imagination, inviting her to see the world from different perspectives. "In some ways writing was the secret side of myself; I kept it hidden because I loved to do it. But I had appearances to keep up, a gang to run—so the sisters knew I was a writer but didn't tell anybody."

The order of nuns would sponsor national writing contests every few months, and this made a big impression on her when she was in the eighth grade. Everyone in the school would write on the same topic, as would students in other schools around the country run by that order. The contests would have strange rules or topics. For example, she was instructed once to "take three unrelated words and create a story." Students would get the morning off from classes and would write from nine until noon. If you wrote a good essay, it was passed on to the national competition. Her essays were always sent forward to the national, and she really loved that. Writing at this point had all the qualities of a game—a source of delight and rewards, and not drudgery.

David Kennedy, a Pulitzer Prize-winning historian, experienced a different kind of Catholic influence on his writing—one that was more boot camp than game. He began learning how to write at a Jesuit high school in Seattle in the 1950s.

> The Jesuits at that time—and I suppose for all their 500-year history—have paid great attention to all the rhetorical arts; not just writing, but speech, as well—various forms of writing and speaking: debate, extemporaneous speaking, persuasive writing, expository writing, narrative writing, you name it. And the school that I went to was very, very emphatic about the necessity of learning those rhetorical arts.

As part of this emphasis, he would write 1,000 to 1,500 words a week during all four years. He would also go through drills for six-week periods:

> You could not write anything using the verb "to be." For the next six-week period you could write nothing using a preposition. For the following period, you could never use the passive voice. In the next period, you couldn't use an adverb. ... Of course, nobody writes like that for real; but what it did, for me, was to make me extremely sensitive to the English language. ... Those exercises gave me a tremendous sense for both the limitations and the excellencies and possibilities of the English language.

David Abernethy, a political scientist, described the influence of his tenth-grade teacher. He would give out assignments to read over the weekend for an essay. "Come Monday morning we had fifty minutes in class with no notes to write an essay," Professor Abernethy explained. "He would set the essay; we'd write it. Your job was to come in there having organized stuff in your head, but then answer the question he posed. I think it was a marvelous experience, a tremendous amount of work. The adrenaline was flowing throughout that process of fifty minutes, but I felt that it improved my writing quite a bit."

The influence of teachers extends throughout all levels of education. David Kennedy, for example, learned to write well—specifically, how to write history—from his mentors in graduate school. He sat at the feet of his dissertation advisors—John Morton Blum and C. Vann Woodward, the great historian of the American South. Both Blum and Woodward considered themselves to be very self-conscious stylists, and they took care to convey that same attention to style to all of their students. The two teachers believed that, for a historian, "one of the greatest sins you could commit was to lapse into a kind of jargon that could only be understood by other specialists." Martin Luther King, Jr. described Woodward's *The Strange Career of Jim Crow* "as the Bible of the civil rights movement." Kennedy explained what he thought Dr. King meant: Woodward's book "historicized the regime of segregation, and therefore made it imaginable that the thing, which a lot of people assumed had been around forever, could be dismantled, because it had a specific historical origin and specific model." What an accomplishment for a historian—to write for a very broad, educated audience, trying to reach beyond the realm of specialists, and actually making people realize that social systems get built, which means they can also get dismantled. "He thought that's what all of us should be learning to do under his hand," Kennedy explained. "And I took that lesson very dearly to heart."

Not everyone learned as protégés of esteemed professors, or even in school at all. When I asked how Rebecca Solnit learned to write, she replied, "I never went to high school, and that was very helpful." The audience laughed, and she explained: "It was the '70s, and nobody was providing a lot of adult supervision." Eventually she got her GED and went to community college and beyond; but by not having the influence of formal teaching, by instead reading incessantly, her style grew individually and without constraint at the same time that she became an independent thinker.

It's hard to imagine a more independent writer than poet Diane di Prima. She emerged as part of the beatnik scene at a very early age in the 1950s, although the beatniks never called themselves that until somebody else came up with the term. Once she decided that she was going to be a poet at the age of fourteen, "it wasn't really a happy moment, because I knew immediately what *wasn't* going to happen." As she put it, she was forgoing "matched dishes, a washing machine, a regular consensus lifestyle of any sort" in exchange for the freedom to create any way she chose. That first night, she was sad, but "got it out of my system." She had been caught writing when she was in summer school, and the teacher made her read a poem out loud: "It was all downhill from then," she joked.

Once di Prima decided to be a poet, she also made sure to write every day. She had a lined composition book that had the slogan "No Day Without a Line" in Latin on the front, and she maintained that practice throughout her life. She went to Hunter College High School in Manhattan, where she read the romantics, but her school was so intellectual that "reading and loving the romantics was a no-no. You would rather be caught reading a comic book than Thomas Wolfe's novels. I would lie and say, 'Well, oh no, I'm reading *Archie*.'" But she met with a like-minded group of girls before class, including the future poet Audre Lorde, and they would read their poems to each other. That was her first "workshop."

She dropped out of college after her first year, and was largely self-taught, initially through a combination of three influences: "I studied with Keats and Pound," she said. "Keats's letters told me everything I needed to know until I found [Ezra Pound's] *ABC of Reading*." She needed to learn a bit more, such as mastering "the building blocks of poetry—the image, the dance of the language, and the music of words." Those three elements—Keats, Pound, and the building blocks—constituted her initial education, along with her sessions with Ezra Pound himself.

At that time, Pound was confined as a patient at St. Elizabeths mental hospital in Washington, D.C. rather than face a trial as a traitor for making radio broadcasts in support of Mussolini during the war. Despite being very shy, di Prima decided to go visit the poet: "I'm not going to lose the opportunity to look this man in the eye and talk to him." She had sent him some poems in advance, and he wrote back: "They seem to me to be well written. But—*no one ever much use as critic of younger generation*." She took this as encouragement, but this was an important lesson that gave her direction for how to teach later in life: "Keep my hands off younger people's work. Try to grasp what they're after, and if I can figure that out by hanging out with them, then I could nudge them in that direction." She could suggest books to read, but she kept to that idea: *Not much use as critic of the younger generation*. Di Prima went to St. Elizabeths with a friend and stayed at the house of Pound's lover, Sheri Martinelli, visiting with the poet every day for four or five days. The hospital staff knew she couldn't be there for long, so they let her in frequently.

After she dropped out of college she spent half the day writing and half studying. "I took the agenda, more or less, that Pound proposed, and taught myself some Homeric Greek so I could sound out the poems." She also studied classical Greek grammar and Latin. "I'd study usually at home, and then I'd take my notebook and go out and write, run around the city and write. And then the typing and revising happened at home in the evening. We needed very little, so $70 a month covered the rent. The house was $33, the apartment—four of us lived in it. It was a cold-water flat. No heat. Bathroom in the hall." Her bohemian lifestyle flowed from her commitment to her art—not the other way around.

Philosopher Richard Rorty, another independent thinker, also learned to write outside of school, by working for his family business. "My parents were both freelance writers, so everybody in the house was always pecking away at a typewriter. It seemed the natural thing to do." Rorty learned how to touch-type at an early age, so he was pretty fast. He worked on editing his school newspaper as well as his parents' articles. "When my parents needed a manuscript retyped I would sometimes retype it for them—and quietly edit it."

"Were they good edits?" I asked.

"Oh, yeah! Occasionally my parents would give me drafts to read to get a reader's reaction to what they were producing. And I would have views, so from pretty early on I was caught up in the process of revising and editing."

With so much journalism in his house, didn't Rorty become interested in becoming a journalist himself? Not at all, since that would have meant competing with his father. But there was another reason: his father would complain that "academics were lazy slobs that took the money out of the mouths of honest, hardworking journalists like him. The professors didn't need the money because they were on academic salaries. They shouldn't be selling articles to middlebrow magazines, because people like him should be getting the money." But the more his father talked about "what a soft racket the academic life was, the more I wanted to be an academic rather than a journalist." After all, it's a better racket.

"Yeah, it turned out that you could get a salary and also make good money on the side," he explained. It was refreshing to hear the high-minded philosopher talk about intellectual work in the university as a racket, at least as a deadpan joke, and he definitely avoided competing with his dad. But it was all that pounding of the typewriter keys as part of his parents' journalistic production outfit that taught him how to write. In a similar fashion, Mark Twain learned his craft by setting acres of type for newspapers and books when he was a printer's apprentice; and by setting both good and terrible prose for the press, he learned a thing or two about how to manufacture a sentence.

Philip Taubman was a working journalist and editor at *The New York Times* for decades before retiring to write a book about nuclear disarmament as a professor in security and arms control at Stanford. He didn't have to hammer out his own father's articles on a typewriter as a kid, but his father, a renowned music and drama critic, did precede him at *The New York Times*. Between father and son they put in about eighty years at the paper. It was his father's example that inspired him to become a newspaperman himself, and one particular incident did it.

In 1958, when he was ten years old, he went with his father to the World's Fair in Brussels. The big exposition turned out to be a confrontation between the Soviet Union and the U.S. over cultural dominance. "Each country was determined to send its most distinguished cultural institutions to perform." Taubman had the extraordinary experience of going to see the Bolshoi, the New York Philharmonic, and more—"a fabulous cultural experience. But in the middle of it a prima ballerina of the Bolshoi was arrested at a department store in Brussels and accused of shoplifting." At the height of the Cold War, this was a huge scandal, and his father switched from his mode as a critic to being a reporter, spending the whole day racing around trying to learn what was happening.

"The epiphany of this—I was on my way to go to sleep early, as a ten-year-old would, and he was on the phone dictating his story to the dictation room in New York—this was like a technology of the Jurassic period, but he had to get on the telephone and dictate it word for word to people in New York who were taking it down on typewriters." At that time there were no fiber optics, and if you were talking across the Atlantic, the voice was not that clear—so each of the reporters had their own way of dictating. When Taubman's father would get to a name, he would spell it out; this was especially important for complicated Russian names, and Taubman listened to his father intently. More than a half-century later, he remembered the military code words his father used, reciting them: A for Albert, B for Bravo, C for Charlie, and so forth.

> For me, this was an incredible, romantic notion that he was on the telephone in this hotel room in Brussels and there was someone sitting in New York taking this down, and next day on the front page of *The New York Times* his words would appear. That just caught my fancy, and I literally never turned back from that moment on.

So the romance of it, the intoxication of speaking across the globe to have your words appear on the page—the ego of it, as Taubman acknowledged—made him want to join the same profession that Richard Rorty rejected.

Because of his father's work, he was able to get lessons in writing in other ways. Since his father was the drama critic, he was able to go to a lot of theater, and from age twelve to eighteen, he probably saw forty to fifty productions of Shakespeare's plays at Stratford-upon-Avon, the Old Vic, the American Shakespeare Theatre in Stratford, Connecticut, and other Shakespeare venues. "I fell in love with Shakespeare. I'd like to think that somehow that influenced my writing." He really can't point to anything that meant that he wrote with anywhere close to Shakespeare's artistry, but watching all those plays "certainly inspired me about the English language."

Not everyone had a positive experience with parents who wrote. Estelle Freedman, a feminist historian, related the pain she felt when her mother closed the door to do her work:

> She wrote freelance poetry for magazines, nonfiction articles, some short stories. And writing was a traumatic event in our house. My sister and I still share the stories of growing up with my mother locked in her room writing. And [us] pounding on the door: "We're hungry! Come out!" And her saying, "No, no, I'm writing." So we learned how to pick a lock to get in and get her out of there.

Writing became associated with trauma.

Nancy Packer, who writes short stories, also had to find the time to write with a family around. When she found her two-and-a-half-year-old daughter pulling the ribbon out of her typewriter, she knew she had to do something, so she began to write with the door open to her study. Sometimes her children would climb on her lap—and sometimes her dog would—while she typed away. Both of her children, who became writers themselves, were saved from the particular trauma of locked doors.

Estelle Freedman had even more to deal with. She started writing at an early age, and her mother was always highly critical of her work. Her mother had never graduated from college, yet she took what Professor Freedman called a "professorial line" about her daughter's work. With that type of scrutiny, she often felt bad about her writing. "I was always *trying* to be a writer, rather than writing from what I felt or what I thought. There was a transition only quite late, in graduate school." She moved from being overly self-conscious—*I'm trying to be a writer, I'm trying to write*—to knowing that writing happens in a completely different way for her: "I need to know what I feel, I need to know what I want to say, and then I will put that in words, and the product of that is called writing."

As a feminist scholar, Professor Freedman was "always acutely aware of the connection[s]" between the private and the public, the personal and the political; and of the history of how difficult it has been for women to find the time and space to write, much less be recognized. She learned to be as protective of her work as her mother, while she also grew to understand how difficult was her mother's uphill climb and how not to repeat her mother's ordeal.

Susan Krieger, also a feminist scholar, felt a different tension while growing up, because her father was the writer in the house and his "attitude toward writing was affected by the fact that he was a man." He would write with the door to his study ajar. Noise didn't bother him. For years he wrote "in the city room of a newspaper and in the headquarters of a union." When he wrote at home, getting interrupted by a child wanting attention or by a doorbell ringing "was not jarring for him. I often felt that my father welcomed household interruptions. They did not last long. They were a relief from the pounding out of words he normally engaged in. They were an opportunity for company." He did not feel the need to barricade himself in his office, as Estelle's mother did:

> Because he was a man, my father did not have to fight for room for his writing. He did not have to worry about whether doing his work meant he was holding out on his children, or to consider it competitive with other obligations he ought to fulfill. Writing was his central obligation. It was the way he earned his living. It threatened to overwhelm other things, not the other way around.

Susan Krieger's father regarded writing as "disciplined factory work," a labor like building a house or digging ditches; and she too approached writing as a trade.

In order to learn a trade, you need to practice it. As simple as that sounds, that's the bottom line. Welsh poet Gwyneth Lewis remarked about MFA programs in creative writing: "They taught you how to revise, the technical thing; but they didn't teach you about the whole life thing. For example, the need for discipline." She emphasized that "it's always worth-while presenting yourself at a regular time, whether you feel inspired or not." Despite many of the assumptions about poetry, she offered that "in fact, writing has very little to do with feeling—it has to do with regularity." You need to permit your subconscious to act, but you need to do this on some kind of work schedule. "The muse isn't a person at all," she observed. "It's an aspect of language." The only way to make that muse come to life is through the practice of language itself, although that practice can come about in many different ways. This is especially true for the muse assigned to fiction and poetry.

Nancy Packer started writing fiction after graduate school at the age of twenty-five. "I realized you didn't have to be a genius; not all writers were Faulkner." She had always been a reader, so she wasn't closed to the idea of becoming a writer. And, as she explained, "I had nothing better to do, anyway." When she moved to Stanford after her husband got a position at the university, she had the good fortune to be admitted to Wallace Stegner's writing workshop. She realized that showing her work to friends was a big mistake—they can ruin a writer by wrongheaded criticism or abject praise. She learned from someone who knew something about writing, and she advised anyone who wanted to write to do the same. Professor Packer received back a short story from Stegner with the comment: "This baby is a long time learning to walk." Suddenly she understood, and from that time on she would jump into her stories: "Now my stories start in the first paragraph because Wally said that." He wasn't exactly the muse, but Stegner was the experienced, inspiring teacher like the elementary and high school teachers other writers mentioned, except at a higher level.

Many writers hunt for MFA and other writing programs, seeking peers, models, constant feedback, new techniques, and more, as did Abraham Verghese. Now a bestselling novelist and memoirist, Dr. Verghese is above all a physician, so it took guts or foolish determination to sell his house, call a moratorium on his medical career, and at the age of thirty-five become a student again at the University of Iowa's celebrated writing workshop. Yet it was well worth the risk in the end, and he called his experience at the workshop "a magical time." For two or so hours a week, he explained, the workshop members would critique each other's writing. There was never any talk about book agents or publishing, only what he considered great "respect for the word"—and that led to exciting work. For many of the other writers at Iowa, the discipline of the work was something they had to learn on their own. A lot of his fellow students were too young, many attending soon after college, and they didn't (or couldn't) take advantage of the time, preferring to hang out—often at the bar with the head of the program, Frank Conroy. In Dr. Verghese's eyes, it was a missed opportunity. For him, Iowa was a great open expanse of time that allowed him to take himself seriously as a writer.

Other writers also spoke about getting that expanse of time for intense work, although sometimes that was found far away from any formal writing workshop. Robert Sapolsky is a neuroscientist who writes articles for *The New Yorker* as well as for scientific journals. He did well enough in college when it came to writing. "It was something that I was okay at, but nothing I took any great pleasure in." He never took a literature class in college, or any English course. "I was not particularly into writing," he confessed, until he spent a year and a half with baboons.

A week after he graduated from college, he went off to Africa to get his fieldwork started, working with primates. He did fieldwork at that fairly isolated site for twenty-five years, getting to know baboon society, doing blood work and other tests to understand stress and other neurological functions in our primate cousins. But for the first year, the isolation was hard. He would be alone for hours at a time, going eight to ten hours a day without speaking to anyone. No one to hang out with like those young students at Iowa; no electricity, no radio; and he would get a mail drop about once every two weeks or so. "I suddenly got unbelievably, frantically dependent on mail. As a result, you wind up sending letters to every human that you have known in your life in hopes that they would write back to you." All he could afford at the time were one-page aerogram letters that you would fold so the letter would become its own envelope. He would get them in big stacks, peeling off one extra-thin sheet at a time. Observing baboons, he would notice something interesting every couple of days or so, and he would write on the thin sheet to a friend about it, and then he would write to the next person about the same news, "and you would realize that before the end of the day, you had just written twenty-five versions of it, each of which was a page and a half long."

He kept himself attached to the world through his aerograms, with a drawn-out time delay between sending his missives and receiving a reply. And it eased the loneliness: "If you sent enough letters to people, they would feel guilty and eventually write back to you." He didn't write identical letters about each incident—a spat between the alpha baboon and his rival, for example—over and over again in exactly the same words. "I would get incredibly bored with the damn thing and would thus start editing and make it more concise, and you could see it shrinking until it was half an aerogram, and then I would have to come up with something else to say. So, I think, just sort of in passing, it kind of forced me to start editing." From the 1970s to the '90s he spent about four months each year out in the field, "making the most of the time by myself." Writing became "extremely critical" for both his emotional and intellectual lives. Perhaps he would have approached his writing differently today: with satellite-phone Internet hookup, he could just blog or social-network his way through the months of isolation. Still, he would have ended up doing plenty of writing, although the electronic journal writing would be somewhat different. He wrote by hand, producing volumes of journals while in the field, writing articles for *Discovery* and other popular science magazines. But when he returned to the university, to the hubbub of students and classes and labs and meetings, he could hardly be so productive.

Isolation, necessity, and lots of free time—plus the love and pity of his friends—allowed Robert Sapolsky to learn how to write. Of course, a few years in prison may be able to do the same, and it has for some people—although doing time in the joint is just not as much fun as living with baboons. No matter where you do it, writing can give you both delight and despair. "I have to say that writing is one of the most exhilarating experiences I ever have and one of the most terrifying," said Shelley Fisher Fishkin, a Mark Twain scholar, literary critic, and cultural historian. "And it's always both. It just depends on the stage of the process you're at. Until I've figured out what I'm trying to do and where I'm going, it's just really, really scary, because I wonder if I ever will. And then, once it comes together, it is totally exhilarating. It's a high."

Arnold Rampersad

CHAPTER TWO

. . .

Purpose and Power, Pain and Pleasure

SCOTTY MCLENNAN WAS Dean of Religious Life and the minister at Stanford's Memorial Church. He went to college with Gary Trudeau, the creator of the Doonesbury comic strip. "He took his roommates—I was one—and put them into a cartoon strip. Charlie Pillsbury, one of our roommates, whose nickname was 'The Dune,' gets his nickname into the title of the strip," he explained. And Scotty—everyone calls Dean McLennan "Scotty"—inspired the cartoonist to create the character of Reverend Scott. "It's been a great privilege, since I love the strip. Gary is a great friend and an effective artist and commentator."

Scotty had found it amusing and fortuitous to share the world with a cartoon character—although "it is sometimes problematic to be a walking joke"—and like the cartoon, he's thin and lanky and wears a wispy beard. This Scotty writes sermons, a genre unto itself—and is the author of books on religious quests and ethics in business. His friendship with Gary Trudeau provided him with a model:

> I think, in terms of writing—the whole process—Gary is just inspirational. He is someone who has an uncanny ability to see what is happening in the culture. It seems like he is often ahead of it. So this Reverend Scott character is often doing things, and I think, "I should be doing that!" He had a web page up long before I did; he was involved in a sanctuary movement for Central American refugees in the early '80s, and also in the divestment movement....

Scotty was involved in the same activities, but the fact that Trudeau got out ahead of him was "inspirational and helpful." Again, he draws the same conclusion: "It's been a privilege."

Scotty finds motivation in other ways, too. He told me that when he writes he puts up a sheet of paper "with little inspirational personal quips" in his workspace, along with a picture of a "gorgeous Himalayan mountain." He was astonished at "how the writing takes over once you get the engine turning over," and how "it flows in ways that are quite unexpected." Yet, to set the words flowing and to make sure the current moves in the right direction, Scotty would get stoked with the cultural acuity of Doonesbury, his sense of writing being connected to life—and then he would turn to a few maxims to stay on track.

His maxims are heady, intense, filled with great exuberance, evoking the kind of feeling you might get once you reach the top of that mountain in the Himalayas. Each has powerful implications. I'm intrigued by three that he mentioned: "Live and breathe my passion," "Sing God's glory," and "Write from the top of my head and the bottom of my heart." Of course Scotty is a minister, so God is liable to slip in; but anyone can substitute their own goddess, or whatever oceanic feeling that moves you, to get that powerful sense of purpose, delight, and even ecstatic transcendence. Scotty can dive into his passion while he exults in the beauties of creation, employing his brain vigorously and delving deep into his soul at the same time. With his chart of attitudes, Scotty kicks himself into gear.

These three maxims speak to feelings associated with writing, the goals that animate the work, and the Grand Purpose. But how do people get to the bottoms of their hearts? And what exactly do they find at the tops of their heads? And how do they get there? What motivates writers? What about anger and fear? What about decrying the horrors of devilish humans along with singing God's glory? Does writing conjure joy or pleasure along with pain? Does anyone actually like to write? I suspect that even computer scientists and chemists, along with ministers and novelists, entertain these questions.

Rebecca Solnit writes cultural meditations and histories across all sorts of genre boundaries—books such as *A Paradise Built in Hell: The Extraordinary Communities that Arise in Disaster* and *A Field Guide to Getting Lost*—and she is motivated by a sense of connection and power, that same directness to action that Scotty felt about Doonesbury. "Writers shape beliefs," Solnit observed. "Writing is always very directed to people's sense of who they are, and what's possible, and how to relate to each other." Writing determines "what constitutes pleasure and meaning, what it means to be human.... We are cultural animals, and if you make culture you get to make consciousness." This means that she writes with a keen sense of the consequences of her words, and Solnit constantly explores what she calls "epiphanies and engagements"—the ways awareness connects to purpose and action.

Gwyneth Lewis, who was the Welsh national poet at the time, was asked to find words to put on the Wales Millennium Centre, a new performance place to house the Welsh National Opera and other theatrical and cultural companies. This was a monumental opportunity for a writer to create consciousness on—literally—a monumental structure. "It was a last-minute commission," she explained. "They had been trying to come up with the words for some time but they hadn't managed to. The chief executive said, 'Would you have a go at it, Gwyneth? We've got a weekend to do it.'" She had to describe the great ambitions of a new public building, a new theater, and a sense of Wales in just a few words. "I figured there was nothing to lose, and came up with something everyone liked." The words are carved into the building in six-foot letters: IN THESE STONES HORIZONS SING is in English, and alongside these English words are the Welsh words (as translated) CREATING TRUTH LIKE GLASS FROM INSPIRA-TION'S FURNACE. These English and Welsh passages are arranged so that they run into each other, making additional meanings as the languages collide (such as IN THESE STONES / CREATING TRUTH), so that a bilingual speaker can slide from one language to the other with ease, neither language dominating.

How stunning to capture so much in a pair of lines—the building, the opera, the aspirations—with two languages dancing together. "It's almost become a symbol for Cardiff, almost for Wales," she said with satisfaction. "The building is seen on the TV news as an image for Cardiff. People say, 'Meet me under the Words.'" Clearly, she produced pleasure and meaning on a grand scale, rising to the public occasion—which is, after all, one of the roles of a national poet.

Abraham Verghese is first a physician, but is also a writer; as he said, he "looks at the world through the eyes of a physician, and [does] it with a great sense of privilege and humility." He, too, calls upon epiphanies, and he sees them in the meaningful parallels between writing and medicine: "Physicians are continuously embedded in narrative," he explained.

> Sometimes we are the catalyst for the story or we walk in *in medias res*, so to speak, with the action already unfolding.... As physicians, we are often involved in trying to find the epiphany

of a story. James Joyce used that term to describe that moment in a short story, the "aha! moment," when the subconscious kicks through and everything is sorted out. It's rare that my role is to make a diagnosis as a senior physician—that's already been pretty well made—but my role is to help the hospital staff and the patient to come to that epiphany, which might be as simple as saying, this is the end of what we can do medically *and* the beginning of what we can do medically, by which I mean, we can no longer cure but we can heal.

This seeming paradox is not so mysterious: As he says in his novel *Cutting for Stone*, a physician can at least offer "words of comfort," no matter how despairing the prognosis. Dr. Verghese's sense of words and action flow back and forth, and his literary consciousness allows him to bring the importance of narrative to medicine and to reassert the physician's need for empathy and contact (rather than being thoroughly distracted by what he calls the "iPatient" just looking at the medical data on the computer screen, and never even touching the actual patient). He has a deep sense of purpose that informs both pursuits, and all of his books, his fiction as well as his memoirs, are part of that journey of the physician becoming more human. He connects mind and feeling, describing medical procedures with great eloquence while deepening his understanding of the human heart. It's not surprising that another doctor, Anton Chekhov, is one of his models.

Although historian Estelle Freedman had associated writing with trauma—her mother was the writer who locked her office door to keep the kids out—and had a hard time right through her dissertation, she came to believe that "writing can actually be extremely pleasurable. It doesn't have to be painful. And for me, the more I delay, the more I put it off, the more I resist, the more painful it is and less pleasurable. So the biggest favor I can do for myself is to stop delaying, stop postponing."

Others also have a hard time getting going, such as Debra Satz, a philosopher and ethicist, who says she likes to be writing—but she compares the process to jogging. She hates starting to run (or write), "but once I am doing it I really like it. Of course, after I've done it I feel really great. The starting of it is very hard." Professor Freedman finds her own ways to start, like putting together an outline or doing other exercises to get rid of anxiety and to get into writing. "This can be a pleasurable experience," she tells herself. "Get into it. Don't resist it." She confessed she would not have written a second book if she had not discovered the possibilities for pleasure and the need to force out something, anything, no matter what, in order to get the ball rolling.

For many, Scotty's maxim "Live and breathe my passion" is crucial. Paula Moya, literary critic and Chicana cultural theorist, used related terms: "The key ingredient in writing is focus. And by focus I really mean an absolute and intense engagement with a thought or an idea." Everything she does is geared to getting her into that deep frame of mind. And after struggling to get that focus, she reaches the point when she gets "into the zone," which she described as "a place where, in a way, the world recedes." Even her sense of self recedes, "and there's nothing except that idea. Or that thought that I'm formulating. And that is just such a wonderful feeling when you get there."

Ramón Saldívar described that "zone" as "a closing out of the world, almost like when the lights go down in a movie theater and you know you're supposed to concentrate on the screen in front of you." Professor Saldívar explained the experience as "phenomenological reduction," of concentrating "the realm of your being to a very limited frame of exploration that goes in a mental, spiritual direction rather than in a spatial, temporal one." Victor Wooten, bass guitarist virtuoso who wrote a fictional account of learning to play the bass, describes that kind of focus in musical terms. As he explained, he plays *music,* not an *instrument:* "A kid playing air guitar plays music; there's no technique in the way, there's no instrument in the way, because he has no instrument." In that way, the air guitarist gets completely into the groove—that zone of singing God's glory, so to speak—and the kid does not get stuck on technique or theory, just the joy of make-believe. It really is something akin to the intense concentration of a kid at play completely absorbed in the fantasy world of his own creation. The ultimate point, according to Paula Moya, is to get "that sense of being taken over by something else." Some people may find that unnerving—scary, even—to be absorbed into the gut of a Big Idea or Story or Image; but for many, getting lost is just the prelude to finding themselves.

This process of reduction or focus can even get very involved with the actual instrument and not just the "air" version. As I described in the introductory chapter, literary critic Terry Castle held up a photocopy of a legal-sized sheet of paper with miniscule marks on it, and revealed that when she was a graduate student in the late 1970s she wrote "in this imponderably tiny handwriting." When I asked her what this incredible, odd scrawl meant, she joked, "Pathological is the word that comes to mind." But she went on to explain that she "came up with this minuteness" because she was "worried that I wouldn't have enough to say." Each of these sheets of microscopic scrawls would end up becoming more than twenty-two typed pages. But first she had to get that extreme concentration in order to abandon herself to her ideas. The draft of Professor Castle's dissertation ended up taking just seven of these sheets. *Seven!* But why did she embark on this strange mode of inscription? She didn't really have an explanation, except to say it was some kind of psychological state. She thought she came up with this "minuteness" because she wanted her work "to turn into something bigger than it appears to be," that it would "exfoliate, take up more room, like an atomic bomb, explode into something dramatic." When Stanford distributed computers to all professors in 1982–83, she left her microscopic script behind. She still considers her writing to be a "neurotic process," but she no longer needs to get into that very tiny world of concentration. However, she did receive a bit of recognition for her strange feat when someone curated an exhibition for small works of art, "and he submitted one of the pages of my dissertation. I'm perversely proud of these documents at this point."

Getting pissed off could also help get you into that zone of extreme focus, even if the size of the words remains regular. Professor Moya, the author of *Learning from Experience: Minority Identities, Multicultural Struggles* and other critical studies, engages in a theoretical as well as pedagogical argument with those who she believes crudely misrepresent ideas of minority identities as being narrow expressions of "identity politics." She certainly writes with passion, and I mentioned to her that in a variety of small ways—a comment in a footnote, a phrase here and there—I could pick up that she was really angry, even though her prose was properly restrained and the overall tone of her book was judicious. "My emotions about what I am writing have everything to do with what I'm writing about," she said. "And it's interesting that you picked up on the anger part of it. Because I think that, for me, anger is a tremendous motivator."

When angry, many just sputter into incoherence; but Paula Moya is just the opposite, becoming lucid and deliberate. How did she reach such a calm state? Many, she said, believe that she masks her rage with amiability. But she reveals how she actually achieved her equilibrium, how she "managed to treat or work through a lot of these emotions that motivate the project." Perhaps it's what you would expect from an intellectual: she draws from the work of black feminist poet Audre Lorde on the uses of anger to develop "a theorized way" to deal with her rage:

> I see anger as a kind of symptom. I think of it as like a fever. You know, a fever signals that something is wrong, but it's not itself the problem. So there are things that make me angry. The point is not to stay at that anger as the be-all and end-all of the situation. And it's not just to celebrate it or to feel it. But it's to use it as an indicator of what is causing this anger.

She uses anger as "an intellectual catalyst." It triggers her to investigate why she feels that way, and to work it through until "it's pointing outwards to the world."

For Professor Moya, the causes of her anger arise "from affective conditions in the world. I'm angry at situations, structures." Once she analyzes the social structures and situations, she can figure them out and then "work positively and creatively for social change." Consequently, she doesn't remain angry, although she can bring it back in a flash. As she explained, "I don't walk around simmering." The "theorized way" of dealing with rage "allows me to be amiable." All of this sounds reasonable: she cultivates the kind of intellectual backbone to deal with issues dispassionately—after she's first been triggered into passion by anger. This is a technique—anger turned to composed, measured argument—that many writers have employed. But Professor Moya added that she had additional training in self-control: before turning to academia, she had been the wife of a politician. That meant putting up with campaigns and fundraisers as well as surviving nasty attacks in the press. In the political arena, she learned "to manage situations that I didn't like." She gained a lot of experience "being able to put things diplomatically when I was really ticked off."

Joel Beinin, a historian of the Middle East, tackles a lot of controversial questions from positions that diverge from the typical pro-Israel consensus. He employs the usual techniques of a historian to present his ideas—documentation and argumentation—critiquing positions he finds unsupported or biased. His "natural tendency," particularly when addressing broader audiences—such as in the speech he gave when he was president of the Middle East Studies Association—"is to just let it rip," and go at his intellectual enemies "hammer and tong, and be sarcastic, with all these parenthetical expressions." But after two or three drafts, all those remarks would mostly be deleted. "I give it to my wife, and she takes it all out," Professor Beinin explained. This technique was also used regularly by Mark Twain, who relied on his wife as a sounding board for intelligent popular opinion; if she were offended, he knew he had crossed the line. But because Beinin "internalized this process," learning to sense when he was just venting, he could also edit himself: he would know that he should delete a certain passage "because it has to come out. It's not going to do anybody any good." He might be writing about people "who I think are just outrageous, awful people, completely without integrity," and what they say has "no intellectual value." But "it doesn't do you any good to write that. It's not going to convince anybody. It makes you feel good the first time you write it: Okay, so I wrote it, and I thought it was good; and now it has to come out." He too exercises (or exorcises) his anger (along with his passion for the subject), at least during early drafts, in order to put words down on the page—but then he returns with a cooler, more professional head.

Anger, dispute, controversy—all may provoke a sense of purpose and drive the work forward. "This is the life of the spirit we are talking about here," Scotty admonished himself in one of his maxims; that is, he was writing about ultimate questions, and he had a mission to reach people. Linguist John Rickford has studied Black vernacular, popularly known as Ebonics, for years; and he, too, has a deep sense of purpose—the life of a people's language. When Ebonics was proposed as a tool for teaching Standard English several years ago, there was a huge uproar, much of it based on misunderstandings or, in some instances, willful distortions. Rickford decided to write a book (with his son, a journalist) to make linguistic knowledge available to the broader public. "I was very motivated because there was so much that was totally uninformed. People made this common mistake that if you said anything good about the nonstandard African variety [of English] that you would bring down the English language," and using Black vernacular might "prevent students from learning the kinds of writing that they would need for public presentations, jobs, whatever. So you would get this antagonism, usually based on ignorance, about what would happen." He wanted to explain this and "tell an interesting and exciting story"—and that, he said, "spurred me on." *Spoken Soul: The Story of Black English* by John and Russell Rickford was not only judicious; it was also written in a popular, accessible style in order to reach readers beyond academic circles.

Arnold Rampersad has written a number of biographies, referring to biography as "the higher journalism." Or, as he quips, the genre can also be called "the higher gossip, or lower history," through which he gets the chance "to read other people's letters." Joking aside, he is motivated by the profoundly serious mission to document the lives of extraordinary African-Americans. From the beginning of his career, his books have been "driven by a sense of purpose. What drives me is the sense of how inadequately African-American life has been represented in this country, by blacks and by whites alike. Although, you know, I would say one side would bear the better part of the burden of blame...." He became involved in biography for what he calls "the best of all possible reasons: I thought a book really needed to be written."

When Rampersad first arrived in the United States from the Caribbean where he grew up, he read *The Souls of Black Folk* by W.E.B. Du Bois, published in 1903. "I was overwhelmed by it. It overwhelmed, you know, a couple of generations of black academics and intellectuals and poets.... And then I read what the historians had to say," and he was deeply dissatisfied. "I don't think it was because they were white; I think it's because they were historians with a particular take on Du Bois's life." As a result, he thought that what they had to say was inadequate. Much of Du Bois's work involves sociology and history; and he was of course a civil rights leader, so it was appropriate that historians would approach his work with that focus. "But when they began to write about him in this way, I said, 'You don't understand the man. The person you are describing, this civil rights activist, could not have written *The Souls of Black Folk*. The man is, at heart, an artist.' So that's why I said, 'Well, I'll have to write my own book.'"

Each of Professor Rampersad's books generated its own sense of purpose that pushed him to work. When he began to write the biography of Langston Hughes, he knew that "virtually no one outside of the black community knew who Langston Hughes was. And virtually all of my friends *within* the black academic community despised Langston Hughes—and most of them still do. They regard him as shallow, and so on." But then people would "sidle up to me in all kinds of places" to say, "We need that book." He felt a sense of obligation, almost a calling. He worked with that sense of mission pushing him forward to write the lives of Jackie Robinson, Arthur Ashe, Ralph Ellison—all biographies of accomplishment.

Anne Firth Murray had her mission long before she started teaching at Stanford. She founded the Global Fund for Women and directed it for years. She had derived great pleasure from writing long letters to friends, keeping her journal, and composing poems. They were all pleasures. She also enjoyed writing business plans, grant proposals, and other communications necessary for running a huge foundation with projects around the world: "I liked it, I was good at it, I did it quickly." But when she decided after more than a decade to retire from the foundation that eventually gave away about $40 million a year, she felt she had to tell the story of how the Fund came about. "It's been told in various places by various journalists and others, but *I* should tell it." In the international women's movement, they'd never had time to explain and record what happened—"how it was done, why we did it, how we did it, the struggle, the exhaustion of activism." People came to her and implored her: "Anne, please write this stuff. Publish it. Get it out." That was another obligation, and that kind of writing was a lot tougher than poems or grant proposals.

Then she was invited to teach at Stanford about international women's health issues; and inspired by her lectures, she began to write a book for use in colleges. She discovered that very little actual research had been done on women's health, trafficking of girls, sex tourism, and other miseries. She had plenty of stories—lots of firsthand experience, her own work in the field, and material from activists around the world in touch with the Global Fund for Women. But Anne Firth Murray had the uneasy task of combining her activist impulses with the constraints of academic research and writing: she had to support what she already knew from experience and testimony with statistics, documents, vetted questionnaires, and the like. A difficult job—but here, too, she was propelled by a sense of mission, even though she found little pleasure in the process. When she would learn of children born of rape in conflicts—"the children of bad memories," as they are called in Africa—she would withdraw to her bed to write a poem to express her grief. But now she had the additional responsibility to produce "proof," which was limited or nonexistent, to buttress the accumulation of anecdotal evidence. In this and in other instances, she had to navigate between grief and whatever could be found of evidence. (I know how she felt: when I wrote an oral history of my aunt's survival of the Holocaust, publishers thought it was an incredible story—so incredible they wanted proof. But how do you prove personal experience? In the end, a scholar who had also survived the Warsaw Ghetto authenticated my aunt's story.)

Writing about violence and horror adds considerable pressure to the whole scholarly, writing enterprise. Liisa Malkki is an anthropologist who studies people who live in refugee camps, particularly the camps in Tanzania filled with Hutu people who had fled the massacres in Rwanda (and earlier in Burundi) over decades. Her goal is to learn "what happens when people live for a long time in a refugee camp—what happens to their historical consciousness, the way they remember things." These are places where people are "spatially concentrated and bounded," and can't leave without a pass; and those who seek to visit are restricted from entering. Being confined in this way "intensifies historical remembering," intensifies how refugees remember the violence that originally forced them to flee, whether they are Hutus or Palestinians or Sudanese.

Professor Malkki had additional issues to deal with, such as preserving confidentiality and anonymity; plus, she had to convince people that she wasn't a Tutsi spy. In the course of her work she discovered that the whole process of knowing the world was becoming very complicated: There were "things I wanted to know but didn't want to know, or came to know that I couldn't write about, because it would be too damaging to people, too soul-destroying to think about." She came to realize that "the Enlightenment adage of knowledge for the sake of knowledge is rather toothless" when it comes to the harsh truth that "to know things is to get damaged in the process." She made progress in her work when she came to the realization "that there are things that you don't want to know, or you know and you can't write about, or you know and you don't *want* to write about." Nothing could be a simple "reflection" or "representation" of truth, and she was challenged to understand that her research and writing was an ethical and political practice. She had to make decisions: not just on what would work in a paragraph or on how to structure her argument, but also on whether or not someone could die as a result of what she wrote.

Liisa Malkki struggled with the usual writing problems about "finding my voice," yet she was also involved in yet another ethical problem: how to get rid of her own ego, "not in the sense that I sacrifice myself," but to have a sense of humility to understand how fortunate she was "to be able to produce knowledge, make understanding," despite her limitations. At the time of the Rwanda genocide, she was distraught and reached out to a Rwandan friend who was living in exile, and asked what she could do "to make things better." Her friend "had the courage and the friendship" to give her a tough answer: "You're not the Red Cross. What hubris: to think that anything you do will make this genocide better. It won't be better for generations. Would you say such a thing about the Holocaust?" And yet her friend encouraged her at the same time, underscoring that it's an ethical choice being a teacher and a scholar, and that that was her role. Her senses of mission, purpose, anger, fear, and responsibility were all mixed together; as a result, she was driven to write and to question her writing at the same time—a practice of self-reflection more and more familiar to contemporary anthropologists and other cultural observers.

Of course, not all writing is prompted by pain or anger or by the righting of wrongs. Some people write because they love to write, they have something to say, or they need to tell stories, they need to see the world through the eyes of others in fiction. Novelists are also driven by a sense of purpose, but that purpose is the exercise of the imagination itself. For novelist Tom McNeely, for example, writing fiction often takes on an obsessive quality; he feels compelled to tell stories, describe the world, and invent characters. "I think often in writers there's something that's happened in their histories which makes them need to convey a certain position that they have with the world or with their lives or with people." McNeely doesn't want to overstate this; writers are not that different from other people—it's that this compulsion to communicate is a "difference in degree, not in kind. In other words, I think everybody needs to communicate...."

Thomas Kealey, also a novelist, thinks that "the pleasure of writing is not that different than creating anything else in the world."

> It's just like somebody who's walking around with a hammer and a saw and they want to be a carpenter and they want to bring this table into the world. They want to bring this house into the world. Somebody wants to make a garden and grow things. Somebody wants to write computer programs. Somebody wants to knit a sweater. There's a real pleasure of just bringing something into the world. And I get that pleasure; not every time, but a lot of the time when I write.

At the same time, Kealey thinks there are some things that are different from being a carpenter or engaging in some other craft. For one, he likes becoming other people. "I like to get out of my mind and get into somebody else's mind." He considers that writers may share that with actors, who regularly get to portray somebody else. "I don't necessarily live the most exciting life, but I can go and open up my computer and live somebody else's life. Or put myself in another setting. And there's a real pleasure in that. There's a real pleasure with both escaping myself for a while and turning back to myself at the same time." He finds this dynamic of escape and return addictive, something that's very pleasurable; and part of that pleasure is that it's very playful.

Amy Freed writes plays, and she explained that thrill of metamorphosis, of becoming other people. For her, the theater was a form of healing "for a kid who was a recluse and social misfit and totally tormented":

> Acting was my way of joining the world, of offering myself to the world as a sort of normal person. And then, after I got past that immature, emotional, needy, narcissistic connection to theater, I got hooked on the multiplicity of worlds and selves. The escape from your self is a joyful thing. Life goes by very quickly when you can do that.... The adrenaline junkies all love it, because live performance is a form of love and love-seeking.

But she points out the long-lasting effects that writing had on her, how writing for the theater and not just acting became a tool for her whole life:

> You research everything; you touch every era historically; you investigate other minds; you imagine what every kind of person is like. When you get hooked on that end of it, everything else starts for me to seem very pale.... So the writing end has been great, because that's a place you can stay your whole life, as a writer in theater, going from subject to subject, sphere of interest to sphere of interest.

And, as she noted, "you always have these great parties to go to."

Robert Sapolsky, the neuroscientist who learned how to write by cranking out letter after letter as he sat by himself observing baboons in Africa, now writes acclaimed articles explaining science for *The New Yorker* and other magazines. He relishes the pleasure of doing this kind of writing so much that, like Kealey, he too describes it as addictive, and he uses his studies in metabolism to explain why that's so, at least in relation to scientific work:

> Nothing ever works when you're doing science, and when it works, it takes two and a half years to find out that it's worked. It's a very different sort of metabolic rate than writing, where you can find out in the course of an hour if this paragraph pleases you

or not. So if you're spending most of your time in the sciences, where it's this very holding-your-breath process, writing just has much faster reinforcement rates.

With this knowledge, Professor Sapolsky restrains himself. He does his writing on the train commute from San Francisco to campus, about forty-five minutes each way. He likes the ambience, but more importantly it limits his writing; otherwise, he said, that faster reinforcement rate would turn him into an uncontrolled writing junkie. For him, the contained commute is just fine.

John Hennessy is the president of Stanford. He doesn't write novels, biographies, or linguistic studies. But he was (and remains) a computer scientist, and he's coauthor of a textbook on computer science. Writing, he admits, is hard work for him—as hard as programming:

> They are the two hardest things, because they demand the most focus and attention, mentally. And I can't do either one with background music on or anything that really distracts me. You could be playing the *1812 Overture* and I could read my email because it doesn't require that kind of focus.

He enjoys that mental intensity, the same intensity as programming:

> You're juggling a lot of complex relationships in your head at once as you write a program. It's the same thing with writing—I know where I'm going, but when I sit down to write something, I don't exactly know how I'm going to get from point A to point B. But I know that I'll map it out along the way as I go along. But juggling all that—realizing what I've already told the reader, what I haven't told the reader, what the logical order is to put those things in—is very much like the complexity of juggling the programming process.

What John Hennessy especially enjoys is communicating with someone, that basic connection. His textbook has been translated into half a dozen or more languages, and "I can go around the world and people walk up with a version of the textbook in Chinese or Japanese or French or Italian and say, 'Can you autograph this for me?' And you feel like you've touched people all around the world, and I think that's the power that the written word has that maybe nothing else has."

Eric Roberts, like President Hennessy a computer scientist, enjoys how writing extends the reach of his teaching. "I actually think that's in some sense the most important thing I do. I'm a teacher, and that's of course central; but I have to think of myself as a writer, because you have a multiplier effect on getting those ideas out that's far greater than it can be in the classroom." He is deeply committed to writing, and he believes that textbooks have a crucial role to play in the learning process: "When I see people with all sorts of colored tabs along the side of my textbook and enormous amounts of highlighting, I know that there's an advantage of having that physical manifestation of a book."

Richard Zare is a chemist who works on lasers, and he is adamant about that power to touch people: "The results of science are nothing until they are communicated," he stated firmly. To illustrate, he told a little story of three baseball umpires at an umpires' reunion. They were standing around a table drinking beer when the first one said, "I call balls and strikes as I see 'em – and no one can do better than that." The other two umpires nodded and drank some more beer, thinking about what he'd said. Then the second one said, "That's nothing – I calls 'em like they is." That was an even stronger statement, "filled with veracity." The third one, the eldest of them, hadn't spoken; and finally he said, "Some's balls and some's strikes but *they ain't nothin'* till I calls 'em – and that's what they are." For Professor Zare, "This is the ultimate existential statement of baseball, of balls and strikes," and it's the same thing with science: without making the calls, without describing the experiment and the results, the science simply doesn't exist. He tells this little story (actually first told by the legendary umpire Bill Klem) to emphasize that, in order to be successful in science, you must, quite simply, communicate what you do. "The scientific enterprise is a very creative one, much more analogous to what an artist might do," he explained. "If you told an artist that you could paint but you couldn't show your art, that would be very frustrating. I want to share the excitement, the joy of discovery, from my research." And he wants his work to be *real*. That desire to share keeps him focused, motivates his writing; he makes the call and as a result the scientific result exists.

Not everyone likes to write, of course. One cultural historian flatly stated that he hates to write: "I write only because it's part of my job description" (although this scholar does end up writing beautiful prose). But usually most writers, even those who are not writing stories or plays or other works of imagination, reach a point where being able to "sing God's glory" is exciting, generating that kind of deep concentration President Hennessy described. Despite the pain, most end up finding pleasure in crafting words, particularly because they have a purpose, a mission to create knowledge. "I am probably happiest when writing," linguist Penny Eckert explained. "I love writing; even when I am having a hard time and am stuck, I have no trouble getting to it. And I'm not sure why. I'm most happy when crafting the words, when I've gotten the thing down and am trying to make it beautiful." Professor Eckert studies the language of young people and how gender affects speech, and she has always loved to write. In the sixth grade she would write little books and put covers on them and draw pictures on them. When she became an academic, she began to like writing more and more "because I feel more and more that I have something to say. Not that anyone wants to hear it," she laughed. "But I want to say it."

Paula Moya

CHAPTER THREE

Chopping Blocks

"WHAT DO YOU do when you get stuck?" I asked the late philosopher Richard Rorty.

"I read email and play solitaire," he replied in his typical deadpan. Rorty was very unassuming, very modest. And the celebrated thinker responded to all my questions with a blank Buster Keaton face.

"On the computer?"

"Yes. Or I pace the room, or eat something ..."

"Does that generally do the trick?"

"Eventually," he replied.

An awkward pause.

"Have you ever had a serious block for a long period of time?"

He thought for a moment and replied, "The first fifteen years or so after I got my Ph.D., I had a terrible time writing." He hesitated slightly, his face still deadpan. "And then I got divorced and remarried. After that, the prose flowed like water."

I was taken aback. What could I ask as a follow-up question? Why did one marriage produce writing and the other did not? That seemed far too intrusive, crude even. Our conversation veered off to other things.

But Richard Rorty's response, startling as it was, echoed those of many others—at least in the sense that writing often gets blocked because of emotional, psychological, or social causes outside of the act of writing itself. Psychologist David Rasch called writer's block a "garbage can term" because every kind of anxious feeling or impediment no matter the source can get thrown into it. Dr. Rasch would hold counseling groups with junior faculty who were struggling to write their books: for academics, getting their first book published is the key to the door of tenure, and many of them get so anxious they get blocked. The work doesn't get done, and we often claim it's because of "writer's block"—even though the block often has little to do with writing, at least not directly. It's not self-indulgent, but sometimes it's about how you *feel* about your writing or your ideas or your research; it's rarely some kind of pathological phobia or metaphysical paralysis in response to letters on a page or a screen. As poet Gwyneth Lewis said, blocks often occur because "There are various reasons in your life that you're not honoring the craft or the art." Often, a huge boulder appears on the road because of how you feel about something else entirely—like your marriage—and that's what blocks your ability to work.

Many of the junior faculty, as well as students, are stymied by a feeling of being imposters: they feel that they don't really belong at an exalted place like Stanford; there must be some mistake. Thoughts like these undermine your confidence. The "imposter syndrome" is widespread, not limited to elite places like Stanford. No matter where you are, you get that gnawing feeling that you're a fraud, not truly a writer or a scholar; you harbor insecurities that are often propelled by social hierarchies: I'm not rich, I'm not white, not male, not that smart, not ... *What am I doing at a place like this?*

"I was plagued by lack of confidence as a student," linguist Penelope Eckert recounted, "and I know when my own students are plagued by lack of confidence. The thing we learn to do as academics is to cover it up and act really cool—and learning how to make the final product look as if there had been no glitches beforehand, or as if everything had been done perfectly." According to Eckert, all of this posing ends up contributing to other people's insecurity, "and it doesn't help mine, because I know that I have been covering up." For her, this has broader implications: "Life is not just a sequence of perfect moves."

Another linguist, John Rickford, remembered writing his dissertation by "psyching myself up." He too emphasized the importance of maintaining confidence, and how hard it is to pull off. "The real currency at this level is new ways of thinking," he explained. To complete his dissertation he had to create new knowledge, be original, innovate—and the demands were great:

> So here you are, coming along as a young academic; you are only going to be rewarded for new ideas; and yet you have to clear these ideas in the face of people who are thinking in terms of old

ideas. It takes a lot of courage, and a lot of self-confidence, to do this. I would find that sometimes I would have to say, "For this area, on this topic, I know more about this topic than anybody else" to psych myself up.

It may seem that some academics are arrogant, acting "really cool;" but that may flow from the need to be original—to assert new and even seemingly crazy, absurd, far-fetched ideas in the face of old paradigms. Arrogance—or a demeanor of excessive cultivated self-confidence—can overcome aspects of the imposter complex, a kind of strong "offense as defense."

Another way to exorcise these anxieties is through playfulness. I counsel those who get the imposter bug that they *really are imposters*, that they are truly playing a role—*but so are the big shots*. The secret is this: you need to be an *exceptionally good* imposter; you need to recognize the game, concentrate on practicing your con, and don't worry about anyone else who's working their own con. Sometimes it helps to go right into the fire, a kind of homeopathic attitudinal inoculation. Seriously, that sense of being out of place can paralyze, and anything that helps to keep your sense of worth helps—even role-playing and humor.

Paula Moya, the Chicana literary and cultural critic who has been motivated, in part, by outrage about social inequities, related one particularly invidious experience of that "something else" blocking her work—not the imposter syndrome, but one just as debilitating, if not more. As a graduate student, she lived next door to a senior faculty member in a different department, and her neighbor would come over for tea:

> We kind of struck up a friendship over the back fence. So we would talk, and we started passing articles back and forth. And then at one point I gave him something to read, and when he gave it back to me he said, "Your writing is too clear."
>
> And I asked, "What do you mean *too* clear?" This was something I actually strived for—I thought it was a good idea if someone could understand what I was saying.
>
> He just said, "Well, it's too clear for your field." You know, *English*, high theory. And then I asked, "Well, too clear as in too simple?" And he said, "Well, yeah."
>
> If this didn't cause a major crisis of confidence, I don't know what would. The way I reacted to that was to call other people. I

called the man who would later become my dissertation advisor and others, and they were outraged on my behalf, which helped. It really helped to have other people come and say, "No, that's ridiculous."

But the incident still caused a lot of difficulty for her. She gave the encounter some thought, and she recognized that she "felt a little uncomfortable about the interaction." She mentioned to a friend that her neighbor's manner felt a little weird, and her friend replied, "No, no, don't be silly. He just admires you for your intelligence." But then Professor Moya recalled how "he came over one day, and he brought a copy of his book, which he inscribed to me:"

> I sat down and he came and sat down next to me. And so I hopped up and I went and sat down somewhere else. And it was almost like he was chasing me around the damn house, you know. And then when he left, he gave me a kiss. Now, he didn't connect on the lips because I turned my head. It was right then that I knew there was something else going on!
>
> After he left, I called my friend: "You said he was just interested in me for my mind! *I don't think that's what's going on here.*"

She just stopped answering the door when she could see he was outside, and nothing more happened. Her neighbor later made a move on a friend of hers, which further confirmed that his advances were not in her imagination.

But the worm had done its damage. "It made me feel ashamed," Paula Moya recalled. "It made me feel dirty." She observed that his "casting doubt on my intellectual work was to unsettle me and to insert himself as my savior. *I saved myself,* thank you very much." But, still, the incident, his criticism, unnerved her, even though she considers herself "a very strong, very put-together, capable person."

Chalk this up as a classic case of male sexual manipulation: throw a woman overboard and then dive in to her rescue. But her neighbor's creepy romantic advances only heightened the dynamic that often paralyzes people: criticism engenders doubt, especially when there are hierarchies at play. "There are all kinds of reasons why people tell you things," she noted. "If people cast doubt on you, it's okay to check with others. But you also need to [ask], what's in it for them? What investments do they have in questioning?" And the goal of being clear—which is not at all the same as being unsophisticated—made her feel particularly vulnerable.

Terry Root, a biologist and environmental scientist working on birds and global warming, faced yet another, even less subtle form of gender sabotage. She showed her master's thesis produced at another university to her new doctoral advisor at Princeton to ask his opinion on how to turn it into a journal article. "Do you want to know what I think?" He dangled the thesis beside his desk. "This is what I think about it." And he dropped it into his wastepaper basket.

Jeez, how mean can you get? I suspect that this professor would not have been so cruel and insulting if the author of the thesis that he found so atrocious had been a man. Hopefully, ploys to undermine the confidence of women (or people of color or anyone else) entering the sciences (or any field) are things of the past (although I doubt it). Sabotage like this works very well to paralyze your writing, especially if you lack confidence to begin with, and she had plenty of self-doubts even before her encounter with the cruel professor.

In fact, Terry Root always found writing difficult—painfully so. Quite simply, she was told she was stupid. In fact, she took an IQ test as a kid, and her teachers concluded that, indeed, she *was* stupid. Her school wanted to place her in a special education class, but her mother insisted that her daughter was not stupid. Today we wouldn't even use the term, but Professor Root wasn't really "stupid." It's just that it would take her a long time to read and an even longer time to write. Only at the age of forty did she learn that she was dyslexic. Of course, dyslexia, especially if undiagnosed, is definitely a hurdle to overcome, and not to know it for so many years makes the impediment even worse. However, she did manage to produce a dissertation, as well as articles and books, despite her disability and the negative attitudes of some. Chalk that one up to a triumph of determination. Once she learned of her disability, she was able to develop techniques—for example, to write by hand and never lift her hand from the page so the words wouldn't float away—so writing got a little easier.

During our conversation, someone in the audience who knew the relevant brain science explained that dyslexic people may have problems with small patterns like words or numbers, but they often have exceptional ability with large patterns that other people can't handle. Professor Root was delighted to learn this and observed that, while most people do ecological studies of small plots of land, she does the radically different practice of studying the ecology of *whole continents*. Indeed, a case in point.

Cultural historian Paul Robinson told of how too much pressure and a routine that's too rigid can also create a crisis. He worked on a book on gay autobiography, which "required me to sit down every day and write every day. And I didn't do anything else." He wrote the book during a sabbatical, taking an academic year. He would sit down on his couch, start writing, and, he assumed, fifteen months later he would have a book. But as he soldiered on, he realized that he didn't have "the psychological stamina; I wore myself out with this excessive routine, which I will never do again. As I got two thirds of the way through the book, I lost confidence and got completely depressed." He went to see an analyst, and the therapist encouraged him to persevere. "So I forced myself to sit back down and type stuff, make words; and gradually I got out of this rut. That was a very unpleasant experience, but [it was] an exaggerated version of what goes on in any book-length project: it is a very precarious situation; you have all your eggs in one basket, and you are all alone with this idea." Paul Robinson drove himself to exhaustion—and the end result was to lose his confidence, at least for the short run.

When I worked as an instructional designer and commercial writer, I also had to confront feelings of being inadequate and overwhelmed. At the start of each new job, the monumental task would loom up like an iceberg over the Titanic, and I would dive into a panic attack. One time I began working on an interactive-video training program on microwave electronics. Microwave technology is perhaps the strangest type of electronics around, and as I began reading about weird pipe-like devices and Smith Charts and other arcane calculations, my head began to swirl. "How am I ever going to write about this stuff?" I began to feel zaps of terror shoot up my chest. Soon I was overcome by sudden drowsiness, the world began to swirl, and I dropped to the floor. I literally passed out on the rug in my office.

After snoring for ten minutes or so, I picked myself up and got back to the job. I told myself I had engineers to work with—Subject-Matter Experts (or SMEs) in instructional design lingo—and they knew what this alien world is all about. I'd break down what the SMEs knew into logical steps and translate it into understandable scripts. *I'll figure it out step by step—I can do it!* That was a crucial moment, to understand that I could take one step at a time. Besides, if I failed, my family might go hungry. The fear of no money trumped my terror of bizarre science.

But let me be clear: the panic attacks have never gone away. I still get a panic attack at the start of any new project—yet now I consider the panic as part of the process: I experience it, I recognize it—that old familiar terror—but I can ride this horse. I realize that I can take it one step at a time, and this too shall come to pass. The panic recedes, I pick myself up off the floor, and I get back to work.

For some people, writing is a job, and the whole idea of "writer's block" seems strange. Novelist Valerie Miner had a mentor in graduate school, "a no-nonsense sort of guy," who dismissed the whole notion: "Writer's block? Plumbers don't get plumber's block; why should writers get writer's block? It's just self-indulgent." This may seem a bit too harsh, but Valerie Miner comes from a working-class family—"My mother worked until she was seventy-seven in an all-night coffee shop in San Francisco's Tenderloin"—and she thinks her mentor is right. It's a class attitude: work is work, even if it's brainwork; you don't wait for the right moment. It's not as if she doesn't ever get stuck, but when she does get blocked, she goes on to the next thing and then comes back to the problem area later. She keeps working. Psychiatrist and novelist Irvin Yalom does the same: he moves on to something else; there's always something else.

Many people believe that poets are sparked by "inspiration," but Irish poet Eavan Boland counters that with what she also learned from her mother, who was a painter:

> Painters just get up in the morning and focus on how much light they are going to have and how long they are going to have it. And in Ireland that may not be all that long, especially in the darker seasons. So it's a very practical way of working, and I was very drawn to that. I don't like the idea of inspiration; I'm very suspicious of where it came from or what it came from. So it hasn't been any kind of a governing thing in my writing.

Former *New York Times* editor Philip Taubman also had to develop the work-is-work attitude, as any journalist must. He had what he called "a moment of truth." He was the *Times* Moscow bureau chief when Soviet President Gorbachev came to Washington for a summit meeting and to sign a missile treaty. Taubman had been at the paper for almost ten years, and his assignment that day as the Moscow chief was to write a news analysis of what this meant for Gorbachev. In order to do this properly he had to listen to the Soviet leader's press conference. Gorbachev went on TV and, as was his habit, he went on to talk at length, giving long monologues. "I'm watching, and suddenly I have forty-five minutes to go and I had not written a word. I took a deep breath, and I said to myself, 'Phil, okay, you're going to do it'—*and I did.*" He knew if he didn't do the assignment in the next forty-five minutes, whether or not Gorbachev came to the end of his talk, he'd be out of a job, or at least seriously reprimanded. "At a certain point, if you've been through the fire several times, you know you can do it—the writer's block never reappears." In the last ten, fifteen years he reached the point where he can just sit down and he generally knows what to write:

> I just start writing—I can always go back and fix it. You reach a level of self-confidence. I used to agonize over leads [openings], trying to make them perfect, scintillating. I just realized at some point, if you get hung up on that you'll get stuck. Just go ahead; it's all right—and if it's really not good, some editor is going to tell you anyway.

Taubman would allow himself to write freely, wouldn't worry if it's that good, and would easily go back to revising. Those are the attitudes of the working writer.

Not everyone can punch out words with such speed or ease. Gwyneth Lewis goes through her own panics. She would get stymied and she would tell her husband, "I'll never write again." He would reply, "You always say that." She would deny it, but then he would say, "Yes you have." Reminded that she'd been discouraged before, "It's always a sure sign that something's going to happen," that the block would disappear. At other times she would say, "This is too difficult, I can't do it." Again, he would reply, "You always say that," and she would again protest that she'd never said that before. She described herself as having a type of amnesia, forgetting that she had been down the rabbit hole of despair many times before; but being reminded that it's her pattern helped her to move on. "That's part of the process," she explained: despair, surrender, and then production. And her husband there to tell her that she'd been through it all before.

Playwright Amy Freed would experience a different kind of panic—the fear of running out of ideas, of finishing one project and not having anything more to say. Freed found one interesting way to inoculate herself against her fear of the Great Nothing. When she was halfway through writing a play, she would panic about the next play: "I'd be terrified of drying up, because a play, once it's had its year, it's kind of over. In the old days, playwrights used to be expected to write a play a season, so there was all this pressure to do it." To cope with this fear of running on empty, of having no more ideas, Amy cultivated the future in the present: "I tried in the course of a play that I'm writing to plant the seeds of something that I won't have time to develop in that play, so that I can actually start exploring it a little bit, where I plant my own sort of secret code for what the next play will be in the play that's at hand." She plants these seeds so that "I can start thinking, and it makes me not feel so desolate" before the end of the current project. A good way to avoid postpartum depression: always keep yourself at least a little bit pregnant.

Success can stop the flow as much as rejection. In 1953, Nancy Packer had her first two stories published in *Harper's* and *Dude* (a "girlie" magazine). The stories were so good, or at least their acceptance made her feel that way, that she couldn't finish anything more for five years. Then she married, came to Stanford as a faculty wife, and took a fiction writing class with Wallace Stegner. "I had to behave well and hand something in," so she did. Her need to write for the class obligated her to do the work, and that meant to finish each story without thought of her previous success. She developed a regular time to work, inspired or not. "You can't wash the socks or mow the lawn; you have to sit down and do it," Packer explained. "Once that was established, I was okay."

But then there are the critics—not only those editors who may accept your work for some magazine or toss it aside, but critical readers of all sorts. While writing is an inherently social act, involving other people (especially on the receiving end), most people do it in isolation—alone with their idea, as Paul Robinson put it—and many, like him, won't show their work to anyone until they think it's absolutely finished. "The beauty of writing," Gwyneth Lewis observed, "is that you do it in private and you don't have to show anything in public that you don't think is okay." Keeping your writing private saves you from having some kind of callous creep like Paula Moya's neighbor undermine your confidence—although such isolation can create other problems. But we always write for readers, and we often produce for a very particular audience, and when we know that certain people will read what we produce, that too can paralyze, even if they see it only when it's all done.

Paulla Ebron is an anthropologist, a wry African-American woman with a quiet, sly smile and twinkling eyes. Her book *Performing Africa* investigates the *griots* of the Gambia and Senegal regions of Western Africa. These people are storytellers, historians, singers, songwriters, gossips, matchmakers, community leaders.... Without question, they are very powerful, dynamic people—and they are very determined to protect their reputations and power. Consequently, she was worried about their reactions to what she wrote about them. If they didn't like it, they could publicly mock and humiliate her, and that would be the end of her relationship with the people in that part of Africa. She wrote, as she put it, with all of these *griots* in her head, and with their voices constantly in her ears. She felt that she was always being watched—literally like they were looking over her shoulder—which made the writing a very slow, nerve-wracking process.

Writers who feel responsible to communities often have this sensation of being watched, especially when they intend to show their work to the communities they investigate or to other people who have a vital interest in their research or opinions. (This occurs even when the interested party is dead; ghosts can be as demanding as *griots*.) This sensation is on top of the typical anxiety of knowing that your audience—such as experts in your field, or acquisition editors who will decide to publish your work, or the vast public who might read your book, or professors who will judge you worthy of a doctorate or give you a grade—may actually read what you write. There also may be horrific power dynamics involved: I've worked with several students who came from countries where what they say may jeopardize their safety, so they really did need to be circumspect. Fear of official displeasure or even possible jail time can certainly dam up the flow of words.

These "watching" dynamics can arise in all sorts of ways. A Japanese-American student wrote a thesis on political and social conflicts among the internees in the "relocation camps" for Japanese-Americans during World War II. These complicated conflicts, provoked by a desperate situation, went far beyond simple black-or-white questions of loyalty to America or to Japan. Disagreements became conflicts that erupted into violence, even murder. In the course of her research, this student made a shocking discovery: one of her own relatives was one of the murder victims. Suddenly she had to write her historical account with even more discretion than she had first realized. She knew she would have to write so that survivors and their families would not feel undue shame; but now she also had to write so that her own family would not be hurt by any revelations. That surprising personal connection made the project an especially touchy proposition—and it made the writing even more difficult, at times paralyzing.

Another student did an interview-based empirical study of how police in a local city treated battered women, interviewing the police as well as the staff at the women's shelter—and all of them wanted to see her results. Her conclusions ended up being very critical of the way the police handled domestic abuse; and it made it very hard to write, knowing that she was being "watched" by the men in blue. In the end, she dropped off a copy of her thesis with the police a day or two before graduation, and then ran off without waiting for a response. They wouldn't have arrested her, of course; but she hadn't realized at the start how much her project could involve the possibility of official displeasure.

Many times, it's a question of resolve—like the way Philip Taubman had to bear down to meet his deadlines, or how I had to tame panic attacks to write scripts about microwave electronics. Trying to get something down on paper can become an epic battle of wills, even for very experienced writers. English professors Andrea Lunsford and Diane Middlebrook each had at least one experience of forcing themselves to stay at the job for hours at a time, wrestling with their demons until they overcame their blocks. Professor Lunsford remembered that, early in her career, she wanted to write a review of a book she admired greatly but didn't "want it just to be all adulatory." She had a hard time getting started, and she told herself, "Okay, Andrea, you cannot get up until you have written at least ten pages." She ended up being there for a very long time, forbidding herself to get up before she produced. "I just said, 'I'm bigger than this,' but it was awful." Other than taking trips to the bathroom, she wrote all night until the job was done.

Clinical psychologist David Rasch tells the story of one graduate student who installed a seatbelt from an old car on his writing chair: he would buckle up and lurch through his work for hours, the seatbelt keeping him from falling off the chair and running away from his work. Hazel Markus does research on the differences between cultures, and she describes how the Japanese have a term for stubborn persistence: *face-the-desk*—and you have to *face-the-desk* every day. When she would get stuck she would tell herself: "Okay, this is my *face-the-desk* time. I just can't get up. If I stay here, something will happen." And then she would force herself to write something, *anything.*

Many writers can't simply buckle up; they need a break from face-the-desk time to get unstuck, and distractions can help. Take a shower, wash the dishes, go ahead and relieve your brain with some other activity. Like Richard Rorty, play solitaire or go for a walk. Melena Watrous writes fiction, and she would take a break with "other repetitive activities like running or knitting, something that's using my body or my hands that's not writing." Anthropologist Paulla Ebron would take that other activity in a musical direction. When she would get stuck writing, she practiced her cello. She was just learning, so it was much harder than writing. After hacking at the strings for a while, writing seemed so much easier.

Rebecca Solnit noted that when she pushes herself, sometimes "I'm trying to go faster than the writing can go." Sometimes she needs to get away and let the well fill up again, as Mark Twain described his own process. She too had the experience of being a working journalist meeting deadlines, but "I have had periods where things weren't working." And she observed another, more critical aspect of the work-is-work attitude: "Our model for production we have in this culture is Fordist; it's the assembly line; we want a steady pace grinding out product eight hours a day if not twenty-four hours a day." When she quit her regular job decades ago to write her first book, she didn't want to be "one of those people you run into who was always working on something that never appears." She had contracted to write her book, and thought writing was simple; it was pretty much typing. "And if writing was typing—and typing at sixty words a minute—I should be able to write a book in three days and so should anybody else who can type." But of course writing is not merely typing; most of the time there's a considerable amount of thinking involved, "which looks a lot like doing nothing." You can mistake worthwhile pauses for being stuck:

> If you're a Fordist assembly line, there's something terribly wrong
> if the Model T's aren't rolling off every day every six minutes. ...
> One of the conundrums of writing is that you'll have to let things
> happen spontaneously and yet you have to work all the time—it's
> not either/or. So occasionally I let myself *not* roll any more Fords
> off the assembly line every six minutes.

One graduate student would stretch out on the floor and think for hours at a time. Friends would walk in and ask what she was doing, and she replied, "I'm working." They were skeptical.

One of the most common ways to stop the assembly line is simply to go away. "Getting away and not being so inside the problem," as novelist Tom McNeely described that distance. "And oftentimes, if you step away from it long enough, it doesn't seem like such an insurmountable problem anymore." Yet, as literary critic Alex Woloch put it, "One question is how long you put it away." For some people it can be years, but most of the time it's a day or two or a week. "I might look at it the next day," Professor Woloch explained. Other than psychological interference coming from the rest of life, he figured that "there's going to be a logical reason for the block" that has something to do with his argument:

> On some level you have figured it out somewhere, and it is a question of unpacking all the strands that you know are there. So it is about having some confidence that the argument does exist. It is a matter of giving some scrutiny to the argument and trying to activate the argument—that's when you do the internal outline, see what is the point at which it breaks down, what is the point you are trying to make there, where is the weakness of the problem, why is it so hard to make that point? Is it because it is leading somewhere else, or because you are thinking of a different thing, or that you are thinking of a new issue and need a different framework? Maybe there really is something that is missing.

Some people are at a loss for words or they feel they don't have any ideas, but for him, "getting stuck is when there is too much that you want to say, and you want to say it all at once but you can't." This is not uncommon. As philosopher Robert Reich said, "I have more ideas to write about than I have time to write." It's like the pipe isn't big enough for the flow; and once you slow down the flow or unclog the pipe, the words can appear.

Troy Jollimore is a unique writer, an analytic philosopher as well as a prize-winning poet, and he identified two versions of writer's block. "One is talking yourself out of even trying," he said. "Not even sitting down to write because you're already convinced it's not going to work out." That's those familiar voices chattering that you can't succeed. The other form is going through "draft after draft after draft and none of it is good." Frustrating as that may be, "going through draft after draft is the only way I know of getting rid of writer's block." According to Jollimore, blocks also come up because writing "is so different from almost every other human activity." In other activities, such as baking a cake, "you have a goal that you're trying to get to." When you bake a cake, "you know what the cake's supposed to be like at the end, right? Nobody talks about *baker's block*. There's no such thing. … You can be bad at it, but at this point there's really not any issue about, 'Do I put the eggs in or not?' You've got a recipe. Either the eggs go in or they don't." Writing, however, presents only a vague sense of an end product. "But you don't know what it's going to be like, because if you knew that, you'd be done. So you're not just trying to solve the problem. *You're trying to figure out what the problem is.*"

Claude Steele is a psychologist who works on issues of discrimination such as "stereotype threat"—how stereotypes can actually create realities because of the way people respond to them. For example, when a teacher tells girls before a test, "Girls aren't good in math," sure enough, girls perform according to the prompt of that stereotype; but if the teacher says, "Girls are exceptionally good at math," the results will be vastly improved because of the power of suggestion. He too suggested getting away from his computer, away from his writing desk, and to sit in his chair "and read somebody I like." At the time of our conversation, he was reading a novel, *The Crazed* by Ha Jin. "He writes really nice sentences. I got the book because I heard him on NPR, and Ha Jin learned English only ten years ago, and he won the National Book Award, and is almost by necessity learning how to write simple sentences. So that seems really irrelevant to the writing block, I know; but you just kind of want to relax and get away from it a little bit." Often, he pulls out from his files a favorite short story by Saul Bellow before starting to write—because it's hilarious and brilliantly written, filled with all sorts of Yiddish idioms—even though he would never write anything like it.

After relaxing, Professor Steele would turn to a process similar to what Alex Woloch described, a kind of unpacking:

> I would probably start writing some notes down, like: Well, what am I thinking about in relation to this problem? I may even start saying: Why do I think I'm having this block? I would just write down anything that was on my mind. I wouldn't be trying necessarily to do the project. I would just start writing: Well, how come I can't think about this? What is it about this problem that makes it so hard for me to get to the next stage?

He starts writing, "like notes to myself, like a journal or something," and he think-writes to get going. He writes anything, doesn't hold anything back, and lets it all flow:

> A singer that I heard interviewed said, "I always have to decide whether I'm just going to surrender to this thing or whether I'm going to try to drive the bus"—meaning, it's much better to surrender to the thing. So you're trying to find that string that's going to let you just be unselfconscious and surrender to thinking about this problem.
>
> What is it you're thinking about? What's the idea? Where is it going? If you just start writing to a person, like talking to your mother about this, that's the thing—talk to somebody who really is familiar with this stuff.

Talking is good, and having a sense of talking while writing can be very helpful. But if you really do want to talk, you need friends who are willing to listen.

I've determined there are two types of friends. One friend listens and argues with you, tears apart your ideas, unravels your story, forces you to explain yourself—and in the course of that give-and-take, you begin to understand what you're talking about. This friend can be a total pain in the butt—and you're glad, because you're wrestling with what you're doing, and that helps. Another friend listens to what you have to say, nods regularly, seems to be attentive, but doesn't have a clue what you're talking about. She just nods, bobbing her head up and down like she's a rubber ducky—and you're glad, too. The critical friend is great because she challenges you; but the rubber ducky is terrific because you are, in effect, talking to yourself—yet your thoughts are reverberating off of real flesh. You could talk to a wall, of course; and that could be useful to a degree. But it wouldn't have the same effect: human flesh promotes brainwork, while walls don't seem to produce the same chemical charge.

I've found that some people try dictating what they want to write. This is like talking it out, as Claude Steele suggests; but you actually record the talk and then transcribe your own words. That way you're not actually writing; you're transcribing—and you can then go on to edit what you have. Or you can get your friends—the critics or the rubber duckies—and have them take dictation as you speak (and you better buy dinner for these friends). Or you can get a voice recognition program so that you can cut out your friends and save money on restaurants. Again, though, any kind of human interaction, even with an amanuensis, tends to promote thought.

David Brady, a professor of public policy and deputy director of the Hoover Institution, employs data analysis at the core of his policy calculations. For Professor Brady, this means that dealing with "writer's block is pretty easy" because he can walk away, so to speak, in a different fashion. The nature of his work allows him to do related tasks that have nothing to do with writing: "I just go look at some data. I mean, when you're at the office you can enter data. You can always enter data." Writing is the only thing he considers to be "work," so data entry really isn't work. "You can still feel good at the end of the day when you can't write. … You can always go to the computer and enter data and run some regressions on statistics and, you know, 'Well, I got something done,' and go home." This can also be a great procrastination device—just go ahead and crunch some numbers and think that you're making progress while you're just stalling for time. But in limited doses, this can be a good way to get relief while still plodding ahead.

Historian David Kennedy also finds recourse in data, or in his case, historical sources, to get over his block. When he's not sure of what he's saying, or if he can't say it "with conviction or authority or authenticity or documentable evidence, that's one of those agonizing moments when you ask yourself, 'Why'd you ever get into this business?'" If the block is rooted in a question of evidence, that's fairly easy to address, for a historian. Kennedy goes "to the archives or the library or whatever and find out the answer. That's the simplest kind of block to overcome." But if he feels, like literary critic Alex Woloch, that he's lost the thread of the argument; or that "the elements don't cohere in a cogent way; or that the evidence is actually pushing me away from a conclusion that I thought I could substantiate, but now it looks like maybe the conclusion's going to be something quite significantly different—those are deeply discomforting moments." David Kennedy can't explain how to deal with them except to "seek your way through them."

One technique for working through blocks is to reach back for another kind of source altogether. Shelley Fisher Fishkin, Mark Twain scholar and literary and cultural critic, found relatively late in her career how useful the autobiographical can be in terms of opening up questions of scholarship:

I'll try starting an essay with something that gives a sense of why I care about it. And sometimes it's just talking to myself and explaining to myself why I'm writing about this. Sometimes that turns out to be the way to begin, remembering what it is that sparked my interest in this topic, or what autobiographical experience has bearing on it in some way. And a few times I found that that's actually been a very fruitful way in.

Like Claude Steele, she needs to write her way out of the block, talking to herself, getting words down on paper or screen. She'll unscramble it all later when she revises.

For Diane Middlebrook, that whole scramble of words, getting that draft down, was the toughest part. "I suffer," she confessed. "I think writing is miserable, miserable, miserable work. Revising is better." Writing the first draft is simply "producing the stuff that is wrong. It just feels that you are making messes"—and that's fine, as others have noted: she can then return to clean up that mess later. And cleaning up messes is what many writers do. I tell students to put up a sign where they write: "CRAP IS GOOD." Accepting the unadulterated crap of the first draft alleviates a lot of pressure for many writers. Annie Dillard popularized the idea of the shitty first draft, freeing a lot of writers from paralysis; but she didn't invent the notion of crap as liberation. I learned this long before on my own, as have many writers, although she's made the dictum famous.

Terry Root once had the opposite drilled into her. When she was a graduate student, a professor noticed red correction marks all over one of her essays on her desk, and he cracked: "If you'd gotten it right the first time, you wouldn't have so much trouble." For a lot of people, that is a completely exasperating notion—getting it right the first time—yet they obsessively strive for it. Most writers almost invariably get it wrong the first time; it's part of the process. They write something, anything—and then they massage it, cut-and-paste it, upside-down it, shake-rattle-and-roll it—and the thing starts taking shape. Such is life.

For most writers, perfectionism is death—or at least a major cause of writer's block. "You have to let it go; you can never have the perfect manuscript. Among many scholars, perfectionism is a terrible enemy," says historian Peter Stansky. Most experienced writers aspire toward excellence but not perfection. Excellence means you need to accept the crappiness of the process and develop what you have into something outstanding. But perfectionism is an unrealistic fantasy of instant genius, a prescription for paralysis. Rarely does something come out just right the first time. The word processor makes this even worse: the words appear so good on the screen, it's as if the work's already published—and how can you write terrible stuff when it already looks like a book? The fonts just look too nice for such bad words. It becomes too hard to go on.

Writers try all sorts of techniques to trick their brains out of the perfectionism syndrome. One student who was writing a brilliant thesis comparing the work of three different choreographers suffered from debilitating perfectionism. It was agony producing anything. Coaxing didn't seem to help—she expected beautiful words to dance on the page, and they came out instead like clumsy oafs stomping on her feet. I suggested all sorts of techniques, but nothing seemed to help—and her project's due date was fast approaching. Finally, after lots of talk, we agreed on how to get her out of her block: she needed a job—and a boss. That is, she needed someone to tell her what to do and a regular schedule.

I became that boss, and I arranged for her to come to work in my office, setting up her laptop on a table near my desk. Her class schedule was pretty flexible, so she would work Mondays, Wednesdays, and Fridays from 10:00 a.m. to noon and 2:00 p.m. to 4:00 p.m. with a generous two-hour lunch break. Perhaps she had suffered from too many overdemanding, overbearing Bolshoi masters, and she had gotten to crave that heavy hand. I would have to fit the bill, play the role. But there was a catch: she had to produce four pages a day—AND THEY HAD TO BE FOUR PAGES OF CRAP! Her boss would not accept the four pages if they were elegant, polished, and lithe. Not at all. Her boss demanded that they be klutzy, crude, and—yes—crappy. Every workday, she came in and pounded at her keyboard. I could hear her moan and curse, and I scolded her dutifully, and told her to get to work: *"More crap, young lady!"* It took her a few workdays, but she did start to produce; and the pages were, as she feared, crappy. "Good," her boss exulted. "This is pure crap!"

Soon her tyrannical dancing master entered her own head: she took over, became her own boss, and tossed me out. She went back to her own dorm room to work, demanding crap from herself. It was still hard, painfully so; but she was able to crank out a few pages at a time. She came to accept crappiness and learned to revise—and we did a jig when she finished.

There are ways of "chopping blocks" short of recruiting your own boss.

One technique I learned from a professor is to turn off the monitor and write directly from brain to fingertips. Of course, you can't do this if you have a lot of statistical data or quotations; but it works well if you're trying to articulate your argument, explain a process or an idea, unfold a story, or work out a scene in a script. Your eyes don't get in the way with all those perfect-looking words glowing on the blank screen. You probably can't go on too long like this—a paragraph or two, and then you can turn the monitor back on and edit what you've done. You can do something similar if you write by hand: throw a towel over your hand or write in the dark. Just make sure your hand goes down the page and you don't end up writing over the same line again and again.

Quite a number of people are sentence-by-sentence perfectionists. Their brains won't allow them to move on to the next sentence until the current sentence is completely polished. This can make for a very slow process, as they labor to craft each sentence before they move on to the next ordeal. That means holding a lot of sense in the brain. Some have told me they have no problem with such slow going—and they like the step-by-step process. One professor described how he puts brackets around words he doesn't like, or small notes or phrases in bold, even a bracketed note for an entire paragraph or section—some kind of visual sign that cries out, "This is awful, Brain. I know it, and you know it, Brain. Now LET ME GO!" That helps him move along a bit faster. You're basically asking permission of your brain to release you from your perfectionist craving so that you can make progress—and you promise your brain that you'll return to fix up the mess later.

I've found faculty and students alike who prefer to write by hand because it does NOT look published the way the words do on the screen. It's unofficial, just a bunch of scribbles, so they feel more at ease producing a rough draft. Some also like it because handwriting slows down the brain, allowing them to keep a steady pace and not race ahead with their fingers chasing their Daytona 500 thoughts. Then there's the opposite: as I mentioned before, Shelley Fisher Fishkin skipped the grade in elementary school when they taught cursive. As a result, she can't read her own handwriting (and she claims no one else can either); and printing by hand is too slow, so she *must* write on a keyboard. (Students today begin learning to keyboard with their first text message, and many schools no longer even teach cursive—so they may have that particular hand-eye coordination skill taken from them.)

A student in Latin-American studies was the first to show me the Dirty Words Cure for writer's block. She would start her day writing on her computer by pouring out a string of obscenities. She would curse out her professors, all of the university, the entire universe, blasting out obscenity after obscenity—*Goddamn Stanford friggin $^%@^#$^&~*—*and then she would seamlessly slide into her subject: "In Guatemala, the different textiles represent each village. ..." Amazing. Block and delete became crucial in this instance, of course. Imagine her professor reading all of those outrageous curses, thinking they were directed at him? (And some were!) But she was able to get the words flowing, and felt an exhilarating sense of liberation—that's what's important.

The Dirty Word Cure is similar to other free-writing techniques that people use to crank themselves up to write, but with a twist. After discovering other students and professors who would also hurl expletives and obscenities to start their stint in front of the computer, I realized it was a case of chemistry in action. My student would get herself revved up, letting that adrenaline flow into her brain, employing her fear and frustration to her advantage and grabbing a thrill to shoot out forbidden nasty words. With all that adrenaline sloshing around, she would then break through to her actual project. She was pumped. *Screw you, Writer's Block!*

Leonard Susskind, the physicist who has been called "the father of string theory" (he actually prefers to be known as the father of his kids), finds, like Paula Moya, that anger can have a salubrious effect and jumpstart writing: "If I get some email that pisses me off, for the next two days I write—oh boy, do I write especially well." He doesn't respond to the email with anger—such rashness could be dangerous—but he directs his energy to the task at hand: "If something gets me upset and angry, I then write very well for a while. It breaks blockages. It's probably just adrenaline. You get your adrenaline up and stuff starts happening."

Psychologist David Rasch knows about getting stuff to start happening— in particular, unleashing the power of fear and anxiety. He did a little exercise during our "How I Write" conversation. He told the audience to close their eyes and "go inside and think about the work that you haven't done yet that you should be doing. Think about all of it, and then feel in your body what that feels like." Then, at the count of three, he invited everyone to make a noise to express that sensation. One, Two, Three: a raucous combination of moans and groans was let loose; even a shriek or two pierced the room. That's it, that's the feeling, that's the nagging doubt, the anguish of feeling too much weight or fear or some other encumbrance that keeps you from doing what you need to do. Do the Dirty Word Cure or find some other way to spit it out.

No one has to like writing. Plenty of students would rather be doing economic regressions or problem sets or playing basketball than write an analytical essay on Schopenhauer or a short story. Diane Middlebrook moaned that writing is "miserable, miserable, miserable"—although she said it with so much gusto that she failed to convince me that she didn't actually enjoy the pain. As I mentioned in an earlier chapter, one professor writes with clarity and great style; yet he said he hates to write, absolutely hates it. He declared that he writes only "because it's part of my job description." This sounded like real misery, but even then I harbored doubts. Historian Paul Robinson and many others don't feel joy doing the actual writing, but they do exult at "having written" (as Dorothy Parker once said)—at handing it in or reading it in print, the delayed gratification after it's all done. So, liking what you do is not a requirement; it's the same as you not needing to like to drive to be a bus driver. You just go out, grit your teeth, and do your job.

But most people do find that cultivating their little patch of words gets to feel good, becomes a real pleasure. "Writing is its own reward," Renato Rosaldo observed. "Just saying it right, getting it right—I find it very hard to separate what I'm feeling or thinking from how I'm saying it," and that's a pleasure. Many of the writers I've spoken with have to remind themselves what they like about writing or why they're doing it in the first place; they need to tell themselves that there's actual pleasure despite all the agonizing. Novelist Malena Watrous reminds herself of this with regularity. She writes in the header and footer that appear on every page of her word processing program: "If you're not having fun, why are you doing this?"

Hazel Markus

CHAPTER FOUR

. . .

Costumes, Cultures, Rituals, Metabolisms, Places

A STANFORD STUDENT told me in a workshop that she wore her high school prom dress whenever she worked on her senior honors thesis.

I thought she was either a charming eccentric or a character from a creepy horror film.

"It makes me feel good when I write," she explained simply.

When she wore that dress during her high school prom, it was a night to remember, and that gown made her feel special—or at least that's what I imagine. When she wrote, she wanted to be transported to another state of mind: to be someone adored, dressed up, elegant. Perhaps the fact that she could still fit into her prom dress after nearly four years of college dorm food—well, I'm sure that could be special, too. No matter what, when she wore that dress, her sense of self would change—she would feel different, out of the ordinary: the dress turned her into an actor of sorts, and the character who would wear that prom dress would write with confidence about anything—including her research on the possible causes of massive die-offs of bees in the United States.

"Part of writing is role-playing," writing instructor and playwright Kevin DiPirro observed. "You have an image of who this person is that's supposed to write." Just as we can have a picture in our heads of who may be reading our work—our audience—we can also have a picture of who may be writing those words. It could be that cartoon character of a scholar with pipe and leather elbow patches—or a prom queen. DiPirro suggests that you can change that image, and experiment by becoming different people—by writing as a woman if you're a man, for example. Some students have told me they do dress up in order to play the writer they imagine themselves to be, even if the role is not as odd as that of a prom queen. Sometimes, clothes such as a prom dress can enhance a writer's self-image, just as a costume can help an actor to create a character in the theater. And if writers don't consciously role-play, their outfits can at least get them into the right frame of mind.

One student in ROTC would put on his uniform whenever he would write: he was "on duty" while hammering away at the keyboard, sitting at attention. In a similar fashion, several students would get dressed up for work—jacket and tie or skirt and blouse—because the notion of being "on the job" helped them to get focused. Historian Robert Caro would do the same: he would get up in the morning, dress in a jacket and tie, have his coffee, then step into his office at home to write. Caro explained that he wears his jacket and tie

> because I'm inherently quite lazy, and my books take so long to do, and my publishers don't bug me, so it's so easy to fool yourself into thinking you're working harder than you really are. So I do everything possible to make myself remember this is a job I'm going to, and I have to produce every day. The tie and the jacket are part of that.[1]

The costumes could get pretty fanciful. One demure girl would always wear a cowboy hat when she wrote, to make herself feel as if she could ride the wild bronco of words, sentences, and paragraphs. A professor would perch a tiara on her head to work—a queen of composition. While writing about a figure during the Revolutionary War in American history, a student would put on a period wig and a shirt with ruffles in order to get into character. An African-American student would tie a kerchief around her hair and make believe she was Toni Morrison: she doubted that *she* could write her essay, but she was certain *Toni Morrison* could—so she became Toni Morrison. Eventually, that sense of being a creative, confident writer like Toni Morrison grew inside her, and she no longer had to convince herself through the make-believe of a kerchief.

Most writers are not terribly concerned about what they wear when they work; but for many, there has to be some kind of outfit that's just right, that helps to get them into the mood. Psychologist Hazel Markus believes that "you have to be comfortable" when you write. She draws a line at writing in a nightgown, however—although Paula Moya does prefer "old pajama kinds of clothing." Poet Gwyneth Lewis rolls out of bed to write, and has "difficulty getting out of my pajamas because I'm writing from first thing in the morning while my dreams are still vivid." Even though students are mostly writing papers and not poems, some students do write in their pajamas or even in their underwear. A few have told me that they even write in the buff. I suspect the nudity is for reasons of comfort, or perhaps to help them feel that they are baring their souls—or at least their butts—to the work at hand (alone in their rooms; not in the library, of course). Hazel Markus thinks that "there should be some distinction between clothes that you would sleep in and work clothes, and you've got to have writing clothes." In fact, she has a favorite sweater: "I've probably had that sweater for ten or fifteen years. And I won't put that on unless I know that I'm going to spend some chunk of time actually trying to write." When she does put on the sweater, it's "my signal to myself that I'm going to actually try to get some serious sentences on the page." If her sweater is hanging on the hook in her office at home for a long time, that's a signal that she hasn't been getting to work.

For all writers, work conditions, attitudes, and methods combine with costumes, necessary habits, and specific preferences to become an individual mode of production—all practices for "getting some serious sentences on the page." All of this makes "a culture of writing," in the phrase used by historian Mary Lou Roberts.

Here are some examples of this mix: One student told me she raised her bed up like a high-riding pickup truck. Then, late at night, she would take her laptop and some snacks, pull her sweatshirt hood up onto her head, throw a blanket over herself, and crawl under her cave-like raised bed in order to write. In that cozy, protected darkness, she would find the bright places in her mind.

Two young women would wear bracelets and rings to get a tactile sense of their hands as they pounded their keyboards; they liked that weight on their wrists and fingers, and they could actually sense the production of words as their jewelry jangled. Then they would drive to San Francisco, about forty miles, to plant themselves in a coffee house to work. After a couple of hours the two friends would move on to another coffee house, spending the day moving from cappuccino to cappuccino. They enjoyed the hubbub of the café, sitting anonymously at work, none of their school buddies around to bother them. Driving such a distance meant that they had made a strong commitment to write; after all, if they didn't produce, they had just wasted their time and their gas money. They were good enough friends that they wouldn't interrupt each other with small talk; they would instead reinforce each other's concentration—and they would be there for each other to relax with during breaks, which meant they wouldn't get distracted by feeling too lonely.

Another student wrote about the symbolic and political meanings of ancient Egyptian obelisks that decorate European capitals (obtained as imperial loot). He always wanted to write with the sun beating down on the back of his head, the heat cooking his thoughts; and he would move around his room, or from desk to desk in the library, or around the quad, taking his laptop wherever he could go to follow the sun. Of course, this would not always be possible, so at night or on overcast days he would wear a wool cap to keep his head warm. It worked—and he ended up winning an award for his thesis. These scenes—the under-the-bed cave, the long-distance café crawl, and the heliotrope pilgrimage—are all dramatic instances of creating "writing cultures" in the personal sense.

"Writing is like a ritual," psychology researcher Claude Steele said, adding yet another dimension. "It needs to be renewed. You need to have these little devices that kind of make you happy to do it." Historian Mary Lou Roberts provided examples of those ritual devices, along with the ambience and style of working that would make her happy. She described having "a nice office and a nice study, but unless the office or the house is neat, I can't write." Sometimes her writing space is so cluttered and messy that she has to clean it up before she can start. "There's a tradition for me of coming to a desk, and sitting down, and feeling this incredible sense of peace" because everything is clean and clear. Hazel Markus rejects such neatness: "Oh, no, I cannot have a clean workspace. That's terrifying. I have to be surrounded with my piles of journal articles and books all around, and then that makes me feel sort of cozy." Clutter made her feel comfortable, and she described her abhorrence of neatness as "the terror of a clean space. I'm not quite sure what that is, but when it's sufficiently messed up, then and only then am I ready to work." Literary historian Carol Shloss described how "I live in a nest of papers." She humorously considered getting a clothesline and hanging all of her notes with clothespins so she could work "surrounded by my thoughts."

Another ritual involves sound. As a college student, Mary Lou Roberts would listen to the same Marvin Gaye tape over and over when she wrote, hearing it so often that she can't listen to it anymore. But now it comes "as a shock to some of my students" that she listens to a radio station that features "really bad soft rock." The fact is that she is no fan of soft rock, but "I can't listen to good music, because I get distracted." She can listen to music she likes when she does something tedious and somewhat mindless, like footnotes; but when writing original material, she needs to be irritated by music that bothers her. "I find that as a writer I am best off when I am a little bit distracted. Because if I get too focused, I get stuck; I am thinking too hard about it. I need to either go away from it and come back, which works really well, or I need to be slightly distracted." So the soft rock station "is perfect because the music is listenable at a certain level, but I'm not totally distracted by it."

I've met many writers who will listen to music they do like, just so long as there aren't any words—at least words in a language they understand—to "totally distract" them. I did meet one student that was a musician writing a thesis in Symbolic Systems (logic, computers, cognition, linguistics, psychology, artificial intelligence, and the like). He told me he couldn't listen to any music when he wrote. "No. I'm a musician, and I'd actually have to pay attention," and that would keep him from being able to concentrate on his writing. "Okay, so you write in silence," I assumed. "No," the musician responded in a matter-of-fact way. "I like white noise, so I listen to talk radio." But isn't talk a distraction? "No, talk radio's just words." That was astonishing, although I could see how it made sense. For most people the rants of Rush Limbaugh or some other radio blowhard would clog their thinking, but he was not a word person; he was a music person, and Rush was just noise to him.

For Diane Middlebrook there was no question, and she was emphatic. She must have "absolute silence." She had arguments, "kind of impolite ones," with her students who said they listened to music as they worked. "I don't think that writers can write when some other art form is in the background," she declared. "Writing demands so much of your attention that anything in the background is an interruption." Perhaps so, at least for her; but clearly, what constitutes the source of distraction or interruption is different for each person: the preferences vary, and there are those who insist on dead silence.

Despite Professor Roberts's confession that she was "a really anal person and hates messiness," she went on to say, "chaos is very important. If you stick with chaos long enough, exciting things will happen. If you don't live with it, if you just tidy things up, you might not find the most important or interesting story to tell," she explained. "So for me, feeling the chaos is really hard; by chaos I mean standing in front of your screen thinking, 'What the hell is this about?' It is all about taking chaos and making it orderly." As part of this dynamic of turning chaos into order, she would take breaks to play a computer game—FreeCell, a kind of digital solitaire. "I'm great at it, so I feel this incredible sense of mastery." She would take these regular game breaks mainly to rest her mind, but also "to satisfy my need for mastery and control. Then I go back and I'm ready." She would actually do a lot of thinking as she played the game. "I spent a year at the Institute for Advanced Study [at Princeton]," she confessed. "And I got everyone there into it—even [eminent anthropologist] Clifford Geertz was playing FreeCell." These rituals or habits, such as bouts of FreeCell (or Angry Birds or more current games), can be shared and can even become contagious among serious thinkers.

How people take breaks is another part of the writing culture, and playing a computer game is only one outlet. "I'm a soap opera watcher," said literary critic Marjorie Perloff. "So if I start at 9:00 in the morning, I think, 'Well, I only have to go until 11:30, and then *The Young and the Restless* is on,' and I'll stop for a while and clear my head. And that's something to look forward to; it's like a reward for having written for a while." Other cultural critics have written extensively on soap operas as part of the culture of housewives, and Professor Perloff, who writes about avant-garde poetry, acknowledges that type of interest:

> But I hate to think about it that way, because I just want to enjoy it. And it's so ridiculous, the things are really so wonderfully ridiculous. In the soaps, nobody ever has to take out the garbage. And if you want to fly to Rome tomorrow, you just call up—even if you don't have any money—and the next thing you know, you're coming from Genoa City and you're in a first-class seat, right? And you're going to Rome and there's nobody in the seat next to you, ever, unless you want there to be some man in the next seat.

Her reward for work is to lose herself in this delightful fantasy world.

Others take breaks or reward themselves in other ways. In drama professor Harry Elam's case, his reward would be to turn on the TV to watch a basketball game. Political scientist Terry Karl would go out to get a latte or reward herself with a gummy bear. Historian David Kennedy described himself as "temperamentally a very peripatetic person. I move a lot. So when I'm writing, I'm on my feet a great deal, pacing around the house or the yard or whatever." When he "can't get the next word or sentence out," he would get up and walk around, take a long run or a long bike ride. At certain times he would take a break by throwing darts at a dartboard. Another professor, somewhat chagrined, confessed that she would take a break and reward herself with a cigarette. Not good for trying to stop smoking, but giving in to the nicotine urge does work well as a reward, too.

Conditions can change from book to book for any writer, as well. Arnold Rampersad worked with Arthur Ashe on his autobiography as the tennis star was dying from AIDS. "And as he was dying, I was writing in his voice. My son was then very young, and he would be watching cartoons—'What's up, Doc?'—and so on. And I'm writing very sad stuff. The challenge was fun. Well, it wasn't fun, exactly; but the job had to be done, and I just was able to sort of block it out." There seemed to be something strangely productive in the incongruity of his son's oblivious joy in Looney Tunes playing in the background while he had to cope right before him with Ashe's quickly approaching demise. Mark Twain had to write humorous sketches for *Roughing It* during the time his infant son died, his wife was gravely ill, and other instances of sickness and death swirled around him. It was no easy task trying to produce laughter, although he would later acknowledge that pain is the source of humor: "There is no laughter in heaven."

When Arnold Rampersad wrote his biography of Jackie Robinson, his writing culture was marked by yet another contradiction. "I would get up in the morning and I would be drawn to listen to an album of Kathleen Battle singing Mozart. It is the most incredible album and piece of singing. It's a wonderful, wonderful album. But I would put it on and this beautiful, limpid voice is out there and I'm writing about, you know, Joe DiMaggio, and other sensitive beings," he said, with a sarcastic laugh. "I thought, something is wrong here, Arnold. You should be listening to blues or jazz or something like that—if you're listening to anything at all …"

Professor Rampersad believes that there may have been two reasons why he was attracted to this ritual of listening every day to Kathleen Battle singing Mozart. First, the recording was beautiful, "and we all have ways of being obsessed by a particular song or symphony, a particular piece of music, and want to hear it again and again and again in a kind of insatiable way." But more deeply, perhaps, he recognized that when Mrs. Robinson specifically requested for him to write her husband's biography, she had told him that she didn't want any sportswriter doing it "because all they're concerned with is sports, but there was a life before baseball and a life after baseball." He told her that he knew exactly what she meant. "I will tell the whole story," he promised. "I'll give equal importance to the before, the middle, and the after, with the baseball in the center."

He thinks that Battle singing Mozart wasn't anything calculated, but it was a reminder to him over and over "as I got up to write, that the story that appeared to be relatively facile and shallow had, in fact, a profound heroic dimension to it." Hearing the music while working on Robinson's life reminded Rampersad of the boys who were poor and less educated than he was that he had known when he was growing up in the West Indies. "And I couldn't help but notice their dignity," how those boys "were like figures, in different senses, out of Homer":

> And I guess maybe listening to that music confidently reaffirmed to me that you have to remember that you're not dealing with some "limited" baseball player; you're dealing with a human being with aspirations, with a desire to be at one with the eternal. I'll never understand why that album drove me so much. And I do not know whether it damaged the book by leading me into cadences and into ways of thinking that were inappropriate. All I know is that I felt, in my gut, that that was the right thing to be doing at that time in order to create.

Mozart arias, soap operas, or computer games—it's apparent that configurations of one kind of art or stimulus can motivate another, as incongruous as that may seem to be—either as relief, as inspiration, as background, or as obstacle to be overcome.

Every writer must also know her "literary metabolism," as novelist Valerie Miner called it; that is, every writer must get in touch with her body, know what time of the day she prefers to write, know what fuel or equipment she may need—to ensure the care and feeding of the writer, so to speak. "This is going to sound corny, but I remember the first day of graduate study at Columbia," historian Estelle Freedman confided. "They called all us new graduates into the lounge, and some guy in a little bow tie got up and said, 'Here's what you need to know as a graduate student. You should always have your pencil sharpened before you start writing, and be sure you've eaten a healthy meal.' And I just thought, oh, please, I can't believe this—this is so kindergarten." But she came to understand that he was absolutely right. "It's like I need my pencil sharpened, I need the pens there, I need the books that I'm going to need, and I need to not be hungry, to know that I have a block of several hours where hopefully there'll be no demands on me or no distractions."

When to get that block of hours is yet another preference, and often a struggle. "Some people work at midnight," novelist Valerie Miner related. "A friend of mine writes at a donut shop in the middle of the night." But those preferences can be all over the map. "I'm a morning writer," Miner explained. "I need a quiet place, my own space, and I need a lot of light." Mary Lou Roberts used to work at night but now writes during the day because "it takes a tremendous amount of energy" to write. "I'm more of a midday writer," she explained. "Get on the computer, do your email, warm up, peak around 2:00 p.m., come down." Then she would go off to teach a class.

Fiction writer Scott Hutchins likes to write in the morning, keeping his time hacking away at the keyboard under control. "I actually don't do nine to five, even when I can," he said, because the quality of his work takes a steep decline. He could continue writing, but then the next day he'd look at what he did, and think, "Wow, I just ruined everything else I've worked on." For Hutchins, "a good three-hour block in the morning is just perfect for me. I'll get what I need to get done. Flannery O'Connor had this great description of her work schedule. She said she spent the mornings writing, and the rest of the day getting over it." That seemed to fit Hutchins, as well.

Scott Saul teaches at Berkeley, but spent a year at the Stanford Humanities Center to work on a book on the early career of Richard Pryor, and he too is a morning person. "I've been getting up before everybody in the world," he said. "I get up about 4:30, and I still live in Berkeley, so I'm here by 5:30, and I find that that is actually a very wonderfully tranquil time, and that it is good for thinking." Stanford President John Hennessy also works very early in the morning, particularly because that's when he can find peace and quiet, with no urgent requests or university business: "There are relatively few people who want to have a meeting with me at 5:30 or 6:30 in the morning, so there always is that time."

Robert Reich, who writes on ethics and social policy, went through various stages of determining and then modifying his literary metabolism. As a student, he would cram work for twenty-four or forty-eight hours before something was due—a typical adrenaline junky—but when he became a professor and then had kids, that was simply not possible. "I had to adjust my writing routine, and I set aside four hours in the morning," Professor

Reich explained. The library has carrels that faculty can claim as their own, and he "would show up at 7:30, when the library opened, three or four days a week; work for three, four, or five hours"—and then he would schedule to do his teaching in the afternoon like Mary Lou Roberts. Now he's "currently experimenting with new writing habits," although he hasn't yet found a new one as productive as his early morning escape to the library. Nonetheless, Professor Reich affirmed the need for some kind of daily routine, no matter what it is, so that:

> I will emerge at the end of that extended time with something done, whatever the time period is going to be; and even if I haven't written a paragraph more than the previous day, if I set myself to concentrating, devote myself to the enterprise to the extent that I make this a near daily habit—even small chunks of time—[I can] get into a rhythm.

David Kennedy also has a morning routine. He would "get up around 6:00 or 6:30, have a bite to eat, go to work and try to work solid from around 7:00 a.m. until noon, even if it's not coming. Just stay there." No matter what, he would keep himself nailed to his writing desk and "try to force something out." He had read that Ernest Hemingway wrote 1,000 words a day, roughly four double-spaced typed pages. And he considered that to be a perfectly legitimate output per day for a professional writer. Kennedy adopted that standard, trying to get out 1,000 words a day. "But the general regime," he emphasized, "is that I try to stay at the writing desk for four or five solid hours," although he would go for breaks and reward himself by taking walks or throwing darts.

Fred Turner, a former journalist who teaches communication, would also cultivate a workplace schedule and environment. He too was "very rigorous about putting the butt in the chair." He too demanded that writing become a routine. "When you get to the state where you're actually writing a book, for me it's literally like taking yourself to jail for a while. You just have to go lock yourself up and put the hours in." So he would arrive at 8:30 in the morning at his jail cell, his office on campus, and he would start off by looking out the window and writing a page on whatever he saw. "Ah, yes," I imagine is how he would start. "There's that student again, locking up his bike and talking with his girlfriend." Warmed up on random observations, he would get into his book and, if he had no meetings or classes to teach, he would work through the afternoon. "I can go eight hours of writing," he said. "My goal in any given day when I'm doing a book is about five pages of text." He would feel he "had a really good day if I get five pages of prose down there at the end of the day."

Playwright Amy Freed would put in a minimum of three hours of work per day, and she'd work four or five days a week, even "if I just stare and sit at a screen, no matter what, if it's ten o'clock at night. And if life is good, I can be effective for about six and a half hours and that's it"—and after that, she loses her sense of judgment. But she clocks in the hours, doing her face-the-desk time, "and it's helped me to start measuring my self-worth by number of hours rather than quality of work, and [to know] that the only way to write is [by] writing." She realized she had to "accept the great amount of crap that I have to write first before I write anything good." Once she understood the principle of *crap is good*, she accepted her output, no matter what. But as far as when to write, she was adamant: "I can't write in the morning. I can't stand hearing writers who talk about being at the computer at 9:00. I can't even think before noon, so that's bad. And I usually chew up great chunks of my day right in the middle, you know: 12:00 to 4:00 is my usual work hours. It's too late to do anything else with the day, so I don't recommend it; but that's what I have to do."

Not everyone can write for days on end, since life intervenes. Abraham Verghese, novelist and physician, has a hectic schedule because of the "day job I love." He may have to do rounds at the Stanford hospital, and he grabs time to write whenever he can, feeling fortunate for those periods that he can get two or three days in a row. "I'm a firm believer in the incremental method," he said. Grabbing small chunks of time, writing bit by bit. One way or another, "Get your ass in the chair and start writing," even if it's only for a couple of hours.

John Rickford, the linguist who coauthored *Spoken Soul*, noticed that he would get very productive during the summer months; but when teaching during the regular academic year, his students naturally became the priority and his writing dropped off. Nevertheless, he defined a time period when he could work: "I always had to begin at home at the beginning of the day, before any other thoughts started: before teaching, shopping, telemarketers." And that meant he began to write even before breakfast. He had also discovered another work method while he was writing his dissertation: rigorous time management. He showed slides of part of his schedule for *Spoken Soul*, which was going to be published by a trade (nonacademic commercial) publisher. He pointed out so many hours in January for one chapter, or to finish another chapter in February, when to write a version and when to revise. Of course, these plans change, but "if you don't have that goal, you can go on forever":

> The thing about trade publishers is that they are not as forgiving as academic publishers. When they say the book is coming out this day, they mean it. So I would have to write something for twelve hours, revise another chapter for three hours, and find six more hours in that week for the project. Then I have to finish Chapter Eleven, finalize the other chapter, and so forth.

Other overhead slides showed details of his schedules—how many pages, how many words, days, hours, minutes. He would always update these schedules, scrawling in new times. "My plans are never realistic," he admitted. "But if my plans were realistic I would never write; I would be so overwhelmed that I would give up the project. If that piece of paper, my guide, gets blown away from my desk, I can't work until it is back on my desk."

But where is his desk? Place is yet another key component in finding a writer's literary metabolism: "I wrote four books literally in a closet," Valerie Miner explained. She once had a Murphy bed in a tiny room, and she would lift her bed up to work; and after she wrote those books, she moved to a place where she could look out on a driveway when she wrote— "and now I have a lovely setting with a big window. When I go to artists' colonies, they ask, 'What are your requirements?' And I say, 'Quiet and light.'" And, as is typical in many artist colonies, she would be assigned a bucolic room in which to work. Marjorie Perloff had no need to seek out a beautiful place away from home, since she actually lives amidst beautiful greenery. She would write in a spacious den with a large window overlooking her yard; and through the glass, she would look beyond her lawn at a bucolic forest: there's actually a park adjacent to her property.

Adam Johnson writes in the library of the University of California, San Francisco Medical Center. It's on the fifth floor on Parnassus Heights overlooking Golden Gate Park and the Golden Gate Bridge—just a jaw-dropping view. Like others with kids, he had to contend with demands of family life. He has a small office next to his garage in his house, and his children would play in the room above it. "I would work even with earplugs in, and they would be upstairs playing, fighting—chaos!—breaking things, laughing. I had to put the test to my work," he explained. "Are these imaginary people more important than the real people I'm spending time away from? And [they're] not. My kids needed me. So I had to get away from that guilt feeling."

That's when Johnson started working in the library. "I don't have Internet access there; I don't have a passcode to get online. That's the single most important thing"—the forced exile from the Internet. "And it's a public library; I'm there with everyone." He employs an Excel spreadsheet to keep track of his work: "I track how many words I write, the time of day I write, where I write, and how many of those words make it onto my project, so I can tell the quality of my writing. Then I have, sometimes, notes that I'll take, like 'not feeling well' or something like that." He started observing that if he wrote at a particular time of day in the library he was producing a certain amount of quality work. "That was the library. And when I'm in the public library, you know, you get your iced tea out and your little lumbar pillow and your cord and your iPod. And to go to the bathroom in the library—honestly, you've got to pack it all up and take a trip." Every time he had to relieve himself he would have to take all his gear, so he would tell himself, "I can make it another half hour." As the result of all these factors he produced a lot—while holding it in. I know I wouldn't be able to write there because it's too beautiful and I would be distracted gazing at the Bay. And I can't control my bladder as well as he does. Yet it works marvelously for Adam Johnson.

Not everyone has such an idyllic writing spot as a high-rise library on a hilltop with a stupendous panoramic view. Amy Freed found her first place to write plays when she worked as a cocktail waitress in a hotel in San Francisco. "I wrote my first play on a legal pad standing at the cash register," she said. "It was a real slow lobby bar, so I could get a lot done on the day shift. Actually, it was really good. I should go back there, because it was nice and quiet," she joked. Now that she is a successful playwright, it is harder for her to write because her attention is constantly divided. "It's like I usually have something in production that requires minding, and that's harder." Freed found that the splitting of focus between the production mind (casting and other practical concerns) and the writing brain "is much more disturbing than the menial jobs I used to do."

It may be hard to imagine scribbling behind a cash register, but journalists and others who write for a living train themselves to write at any time, in any situation, under any circumstances. "It's very nice if you can get back to your desk and write at your computer, or if you can sit down with your laptop in a quiet place," said former *New York Times* journalist Philip Taubman. But that's rarely the case. "You end up writing standing up, on buses, backseats of cars, sitting on the ground." He recalled when he was assigned to Afghanistan back when the Soviet Union was the unlucky great power ensnared in that country. He would be out all day in the midst of war; it was dangerous, but he would return to the safety of his hotel room to write up his report. "Even at the best of times electricity is not always available in Kabul … and I'm frantically trying to write my piece for the *New York Times*, and of course the lights go out and the elevator is out." He went down to the lobby looking for some kind of emergency light to work under. Nothing doing. He ended up spending the night in the lobby with his flashlight tucked under his chin, writing in the dim glow. Of course, he acknowledged that it could have been far worse. Under even more difficult circumstances he would have to dictate his story over a phone, as his father once did in Brussels when he was a boy, "and pray that it looks okay the next day."

I remember writing an article in a notebook in an apartment in Beirut after an interview with Yasser Arafat in 1981. The massive Israeli invasion loomed just months ahead, while the Lebanese civil war still raged intermittently. Artillery boomed just blocks away, but my host told me not to worry: two or three blocks were like miles in Beirut; the war was far away—so I went on scribbling amongst the thuds. A few weeks later, that street was destroyed by a car bomb. Afterward, it sunk in that my writing during an artillery barrage and the danger of car bombs may have been my "test under fire." I realized that if I could write under those circumstances I could handle most anything—except, perhaps, writing while seasick.

Nancy Etchemendy endured that particular challenge. She writes children's literature, mainly for middle school kids; and when she was assigned to accompany an expedition to Antarctica on board a scientific research ship and produce a daily blog, she hadn't accounted for seasickness. She couldn't hold any food down; got weaker and weaker; and could barely get out of her bunk to barf, much less write. She ended up taking just enough medicine to keep her retching under control while her mind remained unclouded, although she never did gain her sea legs. Despite persistent nausea, she did her duty for the kids, and bravely took her position at the keyboard to punch out reports and download photos of icebergs, sea life, and all the rest of the news from the bottom of the world. I'm convinced her test under fire was far more trying than mine.

Graduate students often have to put up with unstable writing circumstances, and, like journalists, they need to adjust constantly. Jeremy Sabol recalled his many workplaces when he was writing his French dissertation:

> Six cities, two train systems, eight research libraries, maybe ten apartments. So I didn't get a consistent place in which to work; and that was a problem, definitely a problem—especially in the beginning, when my wife and I were living in New York and I had been commuting back and forth. And when I was working on my first chapter, it was my first time living full time in New York— working in my apartment for the most part, because I didn't want to spend the money to ride the subway down to the library.

Learning to work in new conditions was costly, and slowed his progress considerably. "There was the matter of getting to a place and trying to work there and not having it work out for countless locations—countless time wasted for me." He learned the academic equivalent of writing under the war conditions Philip Taubman described. By the time Jeremy Sabol got to Stanford he found himself able to adapt more easily to a new office, to writing on a new train system, and to working on different computers in each location. But such instability was never much fun, and surely slowed his progress.

Neuroscientist Robert Sapolsky was particularly attached to working on trains, as I pointed out in an earlier chapter. He lives in San Francisco, and would spend two hours of his day commuting to and from Palo Alto. "I can do a lot of writing there; the phone is not going to ring, so that has been helpful for my writing." It also helped him restrict his output: he didn't want to feed his potential addiction to writing for *The New Yorker* and other nonscientific audiences. By limiting his writing time to the two hours of his commute, he also limited the danger that other scientists would ultimately trivialize his scientific work by regarding him as a "mere" popularizer—which is what happened (unfairly) to Carl Sagan, the astronomer who spoke of *"billions and billions* of stars" on public television. Because Sapolsky kept his literary production down by writing only while riding the train, he avoided becoming "Saganized."

Novelist Thomas Kealey would also write during his commute on the train, and the time of the commute also shaped his work. "The train usually takes about an hour; and you can't really go anywhere else when you're on the train, especially when it's moving. It gives me a specific block of time to open up my novel and work on it. I usually think that I can complete maybe two to three pages." This has affected his output and possibly even the form of his fiction. The length of his writing for each train ride is "about that two- to three-page thing. And when I'm going back up to San Francisco—when we hit South San Francisco—I'm like, 'We've got to wrap things up really soon.'" If he gets on a roll on the train, "instead of going home to put my feet up and watching *Lost* or *America's Next [Top] Model*, which is very tempting, I will instead go to a coffee house down Valencia Street and I might put in another hour." He would take the momentum of his writing on the train to the café. "I feel like I can ride that energy out a little bit longer. So I'll go and I'll write for another hour at the coffee house."

On Saturdays, Kealey would go to the UCSF medical school library—that particularly beautiful place with stupendous views of the city and the Golden Gate Bridge where Adam Johnson would also work. "Saturday is my big day. I'll write for three hours in the morning and then two in the afternoon. I'd like to be like all of the famous writers we hear about who write for eight hours a day, but that's really not very realistic." Sometimes he would put in as many as five hours, sometimes as little as fifteen minutes. What matters is that he would make progress. "Every time I open up that file for the novel, I see that I either wrote five pages or I wrote five sentences. It reminds me that I'm running a marathon in the novel, and not a sprint. And as long as I'm making some kind of progress with it, I feel like I can make progress on that specific day as well." Then, when he would begin his commute on the train the next week, he could keep on adding the two or three pages inspired by the music of the rails.

When Meg Worley, a doctoral student in the English department, wrote her dissertation, she combined the train and the coffee house in a dramatic fashion. At a certain stage of writing she bought an unlimited pass on the commuter railroad, took her seat on the upper level of a double-decker, and rode the rails all day. "When I didn't need books—when I was just writing—I would ride until the laptop batteries ran out, and then I would write by hand." She worked while riding up and down the Peninsula between San Francisco and San Jose (about an hour and a half in each direction). But when she reached the next stage of writing—revision and careful editing and documentation—she shifted her location to a coffee house near Stanford and the railroad station. "I moved in there, spent six hours a day there; and when I finished, I gave the owners a present—they were so good to me." She believed this combination worked well, because on the train and in the coffee house "there was some stimulation, but not too much. If I sat in my carrel in the library, not a thing moved, including the neurons." Rocking motion or mild social hubbub kept the words advancing.

There are other modes of transportation that can produce results. Peter Stansky, cowriting a book on George Orwell, realized that his coauthor "had great trouble finishing projects," so he "finally had to take extreme measures." They took a freighter to England, which meant a month of sea breezes and writing. Fortunately, unlike Nancy Etchemendy, seasickness was not a problem. Stansky's coauthor was a very busy publisher and editor, so the only way they could finish was to be cut off from the rest of the world. Others have found writing on airplanes productive as well; squeezed in with others, scribbling or pecking away on a laptop with nowhere else to go, many are able to form a snug bubble—sort of like that student who would crawl under her bed to write.

Most writers like to stay put, avoiding trains, buses, boats, planes, and the like. Given the sedentary nature of writing, the prime real estate is often a professor's office on campus. Historian George Fredrickson would regularly show up at 9:00 in the morning and work a full day, in the same way that Fred Turner would plow ahead at his office on campus. Likewise, philosopher Richard Rorty worked at school and said there wouldn't be any distractions there. I found it a little hard to believe that no one would bother him. Wouldn't students come to speak with him in his office? "They don't come," Rorty replied. "Occasionally they come during office hours, but very rarely does anybody knock on the door outside of office hours." Perhaps students were too intimidated by the reputation of the soft-spoken scholar—or perhaps he radiated such intensity that people stayed clear of his force field.

Most of the academic writers I spoke with say they write at home, not at work. "I don't know people who work in their office," said Hazel Markus. "My office is like a subway stop." People would constantly want her, and she would have to dash off to meetings or to teach—very different from Rorty's quietude. "No, it's not a place for work. It's a place for writing emails or maybe memos, which is another kind of writing.... But for me, when I'm trying to begin a new paper or a new chapter, I think I have to be at home." I heard similar remarks in many other conversations.

An office at home also offers distractions. Social scientist David Brady, for example, can't write at home because "there's stuff to do"—he would get tempted to turn on the TV. He has more than one office—one in the public policy department, another where he is deputy director of the Hoover Institution, and more. He would go to his one office dedicated to writing, and roll all the blinds down. "I have nothing in there, no books, nothing—so that when I'm there, I have to write." In that shuttered retreat he would pull out "a collection of fountain pens. Some of them are expensive—they range anywhere from like $75 to maybe $300." Every article or book he'd ever written was handwritten "on special legal paper that takes fountain ink, and [skips] every other line, and I actually like the feel of the pen and the paper and the ink, and I like doodling. So I've never typed a single page or printed or anything." Once he'd finish in his writing room, he'd hand over the pile of papers for somebody to type up. "It costs me a lot of money to do it," since he would have to pay handsomely to transcribe his handwriting. This could work out because of the excellent penmanship he learned in Catholic grade school: "My handwriting is readable to the typist," he said with some satisfaction. "I don't get very many complaints."

David Brady could be broad-minded in his tastes in locale, though; and at times he would seek out just the opposite of his hidden cave. He would also take his fountain pens to public places, "where there are all these people around and they're yakking and talking." He would lose himself in the white noise of a student center or a coffee shop. "The last paper I wrote was in Mountain View at a pearl milk tea place. I was like forty years older than anyone else, and no one bothered me," although the kids did eye him with curiosity, wondering what this old guy was doing there. "But I wrote for about four hours on one pearl milk tea." Between his secret hidden office and the public places, he would always manage to find his quiet niche of solitude.

Psychologist Claude Steele would also employ two spaces for writing—an office at home for a scientific audience, and other rooms and public places for a popular audience. As he explained: "When you're writing for a scientific audience, you've got these reviewers over your shoulder, and you're worried about every nuance of your argument because it's going to be argued with and reviewed and evaluated against data. So that's a different kind of writing than when you're trying to just focus on the process of evoking some understanding in a general reader." Consequently, since each type of writing is very different, he would find it "helpful to actually write in different rooms when you're writing in two ways, because if you're writing in the room you always write scientific stuff in, everything is going to come out that way." And if you produce scientific writing in the environment marked for the general audience, it will come out with a popular style.

Claude Steele's science room is an office at home with a telephone and email—all of the usual office equipment: "I spend a huge amount of time in that little room!" But when he writes "the popular stuff," he tries "to write that all over the place, like cafés and trains and airplanes." Perhaps because he was writing to a broad audience, he preferred those public places—although he emphasized that both types of writing are demanding, albeit in different ways. "You're much more worried about making sure the sentences are being clear and being understandable to a broad audience in that kind of work than in the scientific stuff," he explained. Scientific writing *should* be clear and coherent, "but the higher issue, there, is going to be the scientific review of the research you're reporting in that article. You know, it's easy to be a scientist and not worry very much about writing." That's because scientists tend to focus more on "the nature of the research and the design and the statistics and those kinds of things." But he always enjoyed writing, so he would insist on paying close attention to his scientific writing, spending a lot of time making sure his prose would be clear and readable.

Troy Jollimore, the intellectual switch-hitter who writes analytic philosophy and poetry, works in a variety of different places. "As far as I can tell, there's very little system to it," he explained. "I would like to say something like, 'I go and sit by the creek when I'm writing poetry, because that's where poetry happens.' That's not the way it works." The way he does work is to write wherever it's convenient; "and wherever I'm not very likely to be interrupted, basically; and wherever I can have the materials handy"—whether for logic or verse. This means his office at home or a coffee shop or other places. He's learned an important lesson, which is "that by changing the setting, you can definitely turn a not very productive day into a better one." But, given his two very different arenas of work, there's still "no particular type of setting that seems to work for poetry or for philosophy."

Although some professors have different chairs for different types of writing, like Professor Steele's two distinct places for scientific and popular writing, for the most part people do *sit* when they work—but not everyone. Playwright David Henry Hwang would start out in bed and make it as far as the couch. "I was always a write-in-bed guy," he explained; and like Gwyneth Lewis, he would "write as close to the dream state as possible." Hwang would write late at night "and put the pad next to the bed and get up in the morning and kind of groggily reach for the pad and start writing again." Like other writers, getting older and having kids forced him to change his work style. Now, he'll start writing at about 10:00 a.m. and work until about 1:00 or 2:00 p.m., "and then I'll start doing business-related things." But he has kept at least one aspect of his bedroom style in this new schedule—in fact, even bringing a bed to his office: "I still tend to prefer writing lying down. So I like to write on yellow legal pads, I like to use a pen, and then I lie on my stomach on the floor or on the bed." After his longhand version, he would eventually transcribe it into his computer, with the transcription process becoming the first edit. "If I'm structuring a story or something, I don't necessarily have to do it longhand; but if there's anything that I need to get into more deeply, it's almost like sometimes just picking up the pen I feel like I go another layer deeper. The word processor doesn't really do it for me, for some reason." So, the combination of lying horizontally and fielding an upright pencil would allow Hwang's imagination to flourish. "It's very bad for your back, to lie on your stomach and prop yourself up on your elbows and write that way; but I—I don't know. I guess I have to sacrifice something," he said, laughing.

Others also write lying down, but it can sometimes be more than a preference. "I'm disabled, and I have a reconstructed spine that's made out of metal," political scientist Terry Karl explained. "And the single most painful thing for me to do is to sit at the computer—period. To this day, I don't know how I write, if you want to know the truth. I mean, I write very, very slowly because I have to get up constantly." This could get very frustrating, making the "psychic pain" of writing, as she described it, even more intense. "There are times when I say I'm never writing another word, or I'm going to find a way to write standing up or lying down or sitting this way or sitting that way or dictating." She had tried many different approaches, such as lying down or standing up by a high table. I know several writers who can't put up with sitting for long stretches, whether because of back problems or simply because they get antsy. Some have set up their laptops on a podium so that they can stand up as they write, a health recommendation in general. "I have tried so many different things," Professor Karl exclaimed, and she continued to seek alternatives to sitting, even though she would persist despite the pain.

Experienced writers come to understand the different ways they work, cultivating their work style at an early age. They comprehend their preferences—how to dress, where to go, what rituals to perform; they take the pulse of their metabolisms, cultivate their rhythms, and come to terms with their quirks. Anthropologist Liisa Malkki created her work zone: writing at home, ritually wearing a 1950s-style apron, putting on the dishwasher, gathering her dogs on her sofa, and turning on CNN to drone on in the background like Muzak. "Somehow, I jump," she said, acknowledging how all of these different quirks get her going. No matter how she discovered that an apron was what allowed her to be creative, she stuck with that uniform.

Meg Worley, talking about her discovery of where she preferred to write, on the train and in the café, summed up the writer's equivalent of the realtor's maxim of "location, location, location": "Find the place where you write best; keep looking, keep wandering the earth, until you find that place—*and then plant yourself there.*" The same advice could also be offered on what time of day to work, how to schedule the different aspects of a complex project, when to take breaks, how to insist on the right music or none at all, whether to put on an apron or a cowboy hat or to make for a neat, clean desk or a holy mess. Find the way you work best, keep experimenting, keep wandering through all the possibilities, until you discover your particular writing culture—and then, once you know, *plant yourself in the midst of all those habits, rituals, quirks, persistent desires.* And for all, even if you're experienced and feel comfortably set in your ways, it's worth checking out different modes of doing things: even if we know we thrive in silence in donut shops at 2:00 a.m., it may be worth trying to write under the high ceilings of a church at noon. Perhaps we will discover new ways to release ideas, new ways to articulate the language of our purposes. I never had a prom dress, but I will write the next chapter of this book with my broad-brimmed hat tilted on my head like Walt Whitman.

---

[1]Robert A. Caro: "Rising Early, With a New Sentence in Mind," in "Sunday Routine," *The New York Times*, May 4, 2012. http://www.nytimes.com/2012/05/06/nyregion/on-sundays-robert-a-caro-writes-always-dressed-up.html?ref=nyregion.

David Henry Hwang

■ ■ ■

CHAPTER FIVE

"Grandma Needs a Mimosa": How Writers Find Ideas

"WRITERS SPEND A lot of time just trolling for ideas," playwright David Henry Hwang observed; and coming up with ideas is a crucial prerequisite for any writing, whether they are topics for empirical research or plots for novels or characters in plays. "Sometimes I think writing is like fishing," Hwang continued. "You kind of toss your line in and sometimes you catch a fish and sometimes you don't. An idea for a show or play or whatever can come from anyplace—someone else can suggest it; it can come from a newspaper article; it can come from your family history; it can come from a personal experience. It's just anything that gets you excited."

Novelists are well known for trolling through reality to find fiction. "Writers are always collecting bits of inspiration, scenes that they're seeing," novelist Tom Kealey said, citing a recent example:

> One day I was on the train and this grandmother got on with her two grandkids and she was dead tired. Obviously, the two grandkids had run her ragged. And when she sat down she let out this big sigh, and one of the grandkids said, "Grandma needs a nap." And Grandma looked at her and said, "Grandma needs a *mimosa*."

"You can't pass that up," Kealey laughed. He immediately wrote the scene down in his ever-present notebook. "All writers to some extent keep a writer's notebook," he added. "Some people keep their specially bound, fifteen-dollar, thirty-dollar notebook. And others of us write ideas on cocktail napkins and on our hand. It's a good day when I'm just writing all over my hand." Once he harvested the scene in his notebook he would come back to it sometime later, and it could be a grand breakthrough.

Other times he would see a note and be baffled: "'Man walks dog in rain and meets grandfather.' And I'll be like, 'What the hell was that?'"

Gavin Jones got an idea in a bar. Some people were talking nearby, but he didn't pay attention as he nursed his drink. Then, amidst the clink of glasses, he heard one voice above the others ask, "Why doesn't anyone talk about poverty anymore?" Jones had an epiphany at that moment. As a scholar of American literature and culture, this remark sprouted into a question related to his area of research: Why is poverty neglected in the overall study of American literature? As a result, he wrote *American Hungers: The Problem of Poverty in U.S. Literature, 1840–1945*. The original question had triggered a series of questions, with Jones stating the problem, the absence he sought to fill: "Scholars have largely overlooked the complexity of poverty as a subject of representation that runs throughout U.S. literature." *American Hungers* addresses that by looking at works by Herman Melville, Theodore Dreiser, Edith Wharton, James Agee, Richard Wright, and others from a new perspective. Clearly, a critical thinker would have to be receptive, the pump primed, for such an offhand remark to mutate into a book. But if Gavin Jones could find the guy on the bar stool who'd asked that question, he would give him a copy of the book, buy him a drink, and thank him for all the trouble he caused.

Robert Sapolsky would get ideas for popular essays about science while overhearing gossip and other cultural conversations and by reading broadly outside of his field. He would particularly appreciate "crappy contemporary-culture-type stuff." He confessed that he is "completely obsessed with *People* magazine; it's the most fabulous source of material for science articles." Wait. Why in the world *People*? "I'm fairly socially disconnected," he explained; as an academic, he would be working on his science all the time, fairly isolated. "So I have no idea of what's going on in most of the world out there." Asked how *People* magazine helps, he responded:

> People magazine allows me to recognize the names of the most important humans on earth for the next ten minutes. It just gives me an anchoring for cultural references. I'll just be reading along and stumble into something or other that's really quirky and bizarre and will spend the next two months obsessing over it.

Sometimes material related to his field, neuroscience, could spark an essay. He wrote an article for *The New Yorker* after he came across a short piece in an academic neurology journal with the question, "Why can't we tickle ourselves?" He found it extremely interesting. "These people had actually done experiments with a tickle machine where they showed what parameters you need to modify so that people can now tickle themselves. And another group picked up on this and discovered a subset of schizophrenics who *could* tickle themselves. This was just irresistible, so I went berserk with this for about two months and wrote up something." At the end, his wife was greatly relieved that his tickle project had come to a halt, and he would finally stop talking about tickling all the time. Professor Sapolsky explained that, once he exhausted his obsession, he would get the idea out of his system with an essay, and he wouldn't think about it again; he would "just stumble into the next weird, quirky thing."

Some writers combine a number of different suggestions to cook up an idea and keep cooking as they go along. Dr. Abraham Verghese began work on his novel *Cutting for Stone* when he attended the writer's workshop at the University of Iowa. He knew he wanted to write a book that would celebrate his love of medicine; that the plot would be set in Ethiopia, where he is from, but would end up in America; and that he would focus on a young Christian Indian boy like himself who was very precocious in learning medicine at his age. "I knew I wanted a mission hospital," he said, remembering the work of missionaries in Africa—and he wanted a nun. Nuns fascinated him, and he had in mind the image of a beautiful nun he had met in medical school in India—Virgin Mary Kumar—who, he recalled, didn't remain a virgin very long, and ended up marrying one of the other students; she became the inspiration for the novel's character Sister Mary Joseph Praise. With this constellation of items Dr. Verghese began to think through the plot and develop the characters, although he began to write without a plan, without knowing how it would end. The novelist John Irving scolded him, "Abraham, if you're just making it up as you go along, you're not a writer, you're an ordinary liar." Typically, a scientific experiment needs to be designed before it's begun, with at least an expectation of a hypothesis; but, liar or not, Dr. Verghese had enough of a concept to begin writing a novel—a different kind of experiment—even though he didn't have everything (such as a plot) worked out. This happens a lot in fiction writing.

Irvin Yalom, a psychiatrist, wrote his novel *When Nietzsche Wept* as a type of thought experiment—the "What if?" that philosophers love to entertain. He had long been interested in philosophy because "there's so much more wisdom there" than in much of psychological theory. He thought it would be "a good teaching vehicle for students to learn about psychotherapy if I could take the students back to when psychotherapy began, to just the beginnings of it, let's say 1895"—when Sigmund Freud and Josef Breuer published their first case study of hysteria—"and see how the field actually emerged." But he also had a second idea: "Wouldn't it be interesting if we could imagine our field if it had not been invented by someone from the medical scientific tradition but by a philosopher? By Nietzsche?" He continued:

> Imagine what might have happened if Nietzsche—who was a man who lived in great despair in his own life—could have been placed in a certain moment in history where he would've been enabled to invent a psychotherapy from his own published writings that could have been used to cure himself. That's the thought experiment that was somewhere unconsciously in my mind.

What if Nietzsche, obsessed with a woman, met Josef Breuer, Freud's early collaborator, who was also obsessed with a woman they called Anna O, who was the focus of their case study of hysteria; and what if, using Nietzsche's philosophy and Breuer's insights, they were both able to cure each other of their despair? From this, psychotherapy could be born.

Dr. Yalom uses other sources from the history of psychotherapy as well as from philosophy for his fiction. He also gets ideas from his clinical practice. Patients describe strange or poignant situations or describe their dreams in therapy sessions. He used as an example one man's dream:

> The dream had something to do with a man and a woman meeting, and they were having a reunion. They were lovers when they were young, and now it's fifty years later and they had arranged to meet at a certain spot. The man shows up, and finally after a half hour the woman shows up. They hardly recognize one another. And they begin to have a conversation.
>
> The man says, "I've been waiting for you all these years," with the expectation that now they were going to have a reunion and get married and spend the remainder of their short times together.
>
> The woman doesn't remember that she ever promised such a thing.

Or he would take a situation such as the patient who lied through years of group therapy that he was highly successful in life. However, after this man suffered a terrible injury, Dr. Yalom went to the hospital, met the man's family, and discovered that his patient had been lying the whole time. He had been covering up years of failure and misery. This left the psychoanalyst with a dilemma: should he tell the other men in the group, or should he keep the man's secret? Several plot ideas could arise from this revelation and from the dangerous consequences of telling the truth. No matter what, whether an actual situation such as this or someone's dream, "I feel it's incumbent on me to get the patient's permission. I will go back to the patient. They probably will have forgotten this. It's a minor little thing." But he insists on getting permission, since it involves the confidential doctor-patient relationship. Tom Kealey can overhear Grandma saying she needs a *mimosa*, but he doesn't have to consider ethical responsibilities, doesn't need to get her consent.

For fiction writers who teach, the classroom can also incubate ideas, whether from students (like Dr. Yalom's patients) or the creative mix of reading materials. Adam Johnson received the Pulitzer Prize for *The Orphan Master's Son*, a fiction told from the mindset of North Koreans. In 2004, he taught a class on novels at Stanford. "I usually like to throw in one memoir and look at how real people in nonfiction write about their real lives versus the conventions of how writers falsify people's lives. Especially if you look at the development of the novel—they were falsified memoirs, or the roots, I believe, of the novel," Johnson explained. For his class he chose to discuss *The Aquariums of Pyongyang* by Kang Chol-hwan and Pierre Rigoulot. "It was about Kang's nine years in Camp 15, which is Yodok in the D.P.R.K. [Democratic People's Republic of Korea]. I was really pretty surprised that as an informed person in California—where we compost and recycle and are aware of the world—I didn't know there was a gulag system up and running in the world." Johnson continued:

> Yodok is the big family prison. Camp 14, 18 and Camp 15 are the family prisons. They each have fifty thousand people in them. On the other side of the world they're just waking up right now to go to work. These two camps are Kwan-li-so camps or irredeemable camps for the most part. You don't get sentences or trials and you work forever, pretty much. You go in with your entire family if someone in your family commits an infraction. It's called

the "weed by the roots" or the three-generations rule that Kim Il-sung put in place in the early seventies: to take the infection from around the corrupted citizen, all the people surrounding him go away as well. And that's the terror that the state uses to make families start to police one another.

He began teaching the memoir, and "it just led me down the wormhole." Adam Johnson didn't explain why that particular memoir grabbed him as an example for a class on fiction, but the book's revelations stunned him, provoking the creation of his novel.

Emotional responses to other people's work can also trigger fresh writing. Richard Rorty, the late philosopher, found it easy to decide on a topic to write about "if there's something I have recently read that I very much like or strongly dislike. It's probably easiest for me to write if my reaction to somebody else's piece is: *Boy, is this guy absolutely wrong about that!* Then I produce hypotheses about what stupid assumption he has made that made him say this wrong thing. That gets me going. It puts me in a position to write a sustained polemic." The source text could have been so completely wrong-headed that he would have needed an essay's worth of analysis to set everything straight. Conversely, Professor Rorty also found it easy to react "if somebody says something that strikes me as absolutely right." He could then "wax eloquent about how wonderful this guy is—how wonderfully he differs from others who have written on the same topic." In either case, there's a visceral response that ignites the fuel. For Rorty, writing is easier "if you either hate something or love something. You can use that emotion as a springboard."

Richard Rorty was a philosopher, not a chemist or a novelist. There are lots of differences between the ways an idea grows into a philosophical essay or into an entire scientific project or a novel (even if the novel jumps off of Nietzsche's or some other philosopher's ideas), just as there are differences between the ways expository prose and poetry are generated. Even so, the creative process crosses all boundaries—it transcends all disciplines, all modes of producing knowledge or art. Biologist Terry Root noted how her scientific writing process was analogous to those of many "creative" writers. "How do you come up with ideas that you're going to be tackling?" she mused. "It's more like that you stumble into them." In fact, it seems she even stumbled into biology. "My life has been serendipitous," she explained. She started off in college as a math and statistics major, yet she ended up being a biologist. Her method is to let her interest take her in any direction: "I love birds: that's how I got into biology. I'm concerned about global warming. I put the two together, and I just meander around and look at what other people are doing, get excited, and go from there. I'm not on a straight and narrow trajectory at all."

Coming up with research projects on a set agenda is too rigid for Terry Root: "If I try to force something, I don't do as well." She knew that she had the good fortune to be allowed to study birds, and she could apply that to her concerns about the changes in global climate. Her research ideas would grow from crisscrossing those interests, while her playfulness was powered by a strong ethical sense of her mission. "It's a real privilege to do what I'm able to do," she said. "I feel an obligation to pay back a bit of that to the world, to work on things that are real world problems." Her fun with birds can actually help save the planet.

Professor Root described her search for ideas as "meandering," which makes it seem aimless, even frivolous; but she was very serious about how important intellectual wanderlust was, along with its consequences: "I'm not afraid wherever it's going to take me," she declared, identifying with the way a writer or an artist persists in following a creative impulse.

Once a scientist formulates her research question, she goes down that road no matter where it takes her. The logic of one experiment or investigation, its results or what it reveals, speaks to ones in the past and generates more for the future—a chain of ideas or questions. Linguist Penelope Eckert engaged in that telescoping process of research, and declared that her work traveled "a completely logical trajectory." For Professor Eckert, the questions unfold step by step: "Everything I do raises a new question, and then I explore that question next. This may be just a really wonderful fiction that I've created, but I don't think so."

Poetry critic Marjorie Perloff finds her subjects in a similarly serendipitous or meandering fashion. She was asked to write an "omnibus review" of a hundred books of poetry, but she veered off when she discovered the work of one poet, Frank O'Hara, in an anthology. She was completely enthralled, and was compelled to write one of the earliest critical books about O'Hara's work. "You're going to write about something that speaks to you," Perloff explained. "It does not mean it's the greatest work; it just speaks to you. Nobody could be more different from me than Frank O'Hara, an Irish-American, gay, Catholic, male poet." But she loved his work, his sense of humor; and she knew she liked the kinds of irony that O'Hara employs—so this became her project. Perloff explained that she has had to understand her own taste, "knowing what you like and don't like," and consequently her subject becomes a very personal choice, one that grows from that self-knowledge. "There are going to be certain things I never do like, that are, for me, sentimental," and O'Hara was not one of those.

But it's not only taste; it's what she can offer to the conversation. Poets would often ask Marjorie Perloff why she hadn't written about them or why she hadn't written about some other writer. "It doesn't mean you don't like them," she explained; but she may not have anything particular to say that hasn't been said already. "There are a lot of people I like that I haven't written about because I don't feel I have anything to say that other people haven't said. But that doesn't mean that I don't find them very interesting; it just means—Let's take somebody like Faulkner, for instance. I adore Faulkner. But I don't have anything to say about Faulkner, particularly."

Marilyn Yalom, feminist cultural historian married to novelist and psychiatrist Irvin Yalom, has a lot to say about gender and culture, and she sought to reach "a larger audience than academics on the subject of women's issues" by publishing in "trade presses" rather than university presses. "I was following the model of my husband, who was moving from writing strictly for academics to writing for a more general audience." When Marilyn Yalom did research on women's autobiographies, she became interested in women who lived through the French Revolution, and *Blood Sisters: The French Revolution in Women's Memory* became her first trade book. "You write very well," her literary agent said. "Now, why don't you *write something I can sell?*"

As she'd delved into women's memories of the French Revolution, Marilyn Yalom had come across the social movement to promote breast-feeding as a natural practice for mothers (instead of handing infants over to wet nurses), so the idea for her next book seemed like a very natural next step. "I proposed to [my agent] *A History of the Breast*—and she was able to sell that very nicely," she laughed. A book about breasts was a dream come true for the marketing department, and the book became a bestseller. The little-known reality of the breastfeeding movement, an interesting side story in her initial research, became the jumping-off point for a much broader examination of breastfeeding from a woman's perspective, and *A History of the Breast* did reach the wider audience Marilyn Yalom had sought.

But just getting an idea is not enough. How do you know if it's the right idea, an idea worth the effort? "I think the best analogy is falling in love," David Henry Hwang explained with a laugh:

> You know how you fall in love with somebody, and you begin to be sort of obsessed with them; you get that weird chemical brain-fry, and you can't stop thinking about them, you always want to be with them? It's kind of like that. The good thing about writing is that most of the time you're only working on this project for about two to three years, so you don't have to actually sustain that love, as in real life.

Whatever gets you excited to grab the computer or pad or whatever you write on, "that's what you should be writing." Even if it doesn't work out, even if it's a failure, that idea must be pursued: he always liked that the biography of filmmaker Preston Sturges was called *Between Flops*, "because I think that that's the reality of the experience." But you have to fall in love with your idea to begin with; that's the key—and after that you need to be ready to fail again and again.

David Henry Hwang related how the idea for his hit play *M. Butterfly* took shape as a drama. It's worth following him through the process, since it's a terrific example of how a random nub can grow into a sophisticated production—how a vague notion evolves into a complex, structured creation.

Hwang often worked by being sparked by an idea first, and then he would create a story line: "I think that you can start with an idea, start with a question, start with a theme," he explained, "and you can devise a story." In that process, he would formulate a question—"something that's bugging me, some issue, and I don't know what the answer is. I write the play to find out how it is that I really feel about it." In this case, he heard the news account first—a true story about a French diplomat who had a twenty-year affair with a Chinese actress. She turned out to be a spy and, even more shocking, a man in drag. Like so many who heard this bizarre tale, Hwang was bugged by questions: "How could the diplomat not have known the true gender of his lover? What does this all imply about gender dynamics and playing gender and race?" He had the story of the affair as a starting point, but he continued to ruminate about it for months, musing on how to turn his questions into good theater. Then it clicked:

I was living in Los Angeles at the time, and I was driving down Santa Monica Boulevard, and I asked myself, "Well, what did this diplomat think that he'd found?" And the answer came to me: "He probably thought he'd found some version of *Madame Butterfly*." And at that point, the notion of dovetailing the events of the spy story and the plot of Puccini's opera, *Madame Butterfly*, seemed to me to be a really interesting way to tell the story.

After that flash of insight, the idea needed more of a structure. He compared the way he would develop a play's structure to his approach in developing characters: "Just to kind of get yourself going, you may base a character on somebody you know. It just sort of jump-starts the process. And if the writing's going well, and if you're really engaged with the work, very soon the character that you're writing [about] is no longer the person that you based it on." The characters take on their own qualities, and they become their own persons. Structural development can also be drawn from models: "I tend to structurally base plays on other plays," Hwang said; and he explained how his use of existing plays as models for new ones helped his work evolve into something new, and how Peter Shaffer provided the model for *M. Butterfly*. "For each of my plays, I can tell you what play I was imitating":

> *M. Butterfly* really borrows this sort of Peter Shaffer structure, which you see in plays like *Equus* and *Amadeus*, where you have a protagonist who comes out, who directly addresses the audience, who's at a relatively late point in his life, and who is in some sort of difficult point in his life. And he then goes back over the events of his life as the narrator, and you see these scenes come to life. That is how *Equus* works, that's how *Amadeus* works, and that's how *M. Butterfly* works.

But because of the way Hwang understands human nature, *M. Butterfly* veered away from the previous Shaffer models in one important way. He questioned the idea of someone being able to keep control of his own story. He was skeptical "about whether or not it's possible for an individual to hold on to the narrative of their whole life. I feel that at some point in our lives we tend to lose hold of our own narrative; we feel like we don't have control over it anymore." Someone else steps in to seize command, so to speak; and they tell the story instead of you, with their intentions instead of yours.

M. Butterfly diverges radically from the Shaffer structure by changing who is the master of the narrative. At the beginning of the play, Hwang explained, the character that steps forward and begins to address the audience is, in this case, René Gallimard, the French diplomat in China: "He has control over the narrative. But he begins, over the course of the story, to have an affair with a Chinese actress, whose name is Song Liling. So then in Act Two of the play, the two of them struggle for control of the narrative. And in the third act, the other character, Song Liling, has control over the narrative." Hwang switched the point of view in the last act, completely reversing the power dynamics, radically modifying the Shaffer structure.

Then he moved on to the next problem in shaping this idea as a theatrical work. He needed a beginning and an end, and for that he drew upon the original Puccini opera:

> At the beginning of the play, the diplomat fantasizes that he's Pinkerton, the American lieutenant from the opera *Madame Butterfly*, and that he found his Butterfly. And then by the end of the play, the Frenchman realizes that it's actually he who's the Butterfly and that it's he who was deceived by love. And the Chinese spy who perpetrated that deceit is therefore the real Pinkerton. Once I knew that, it was relatively easy to write the play.

There's a lot more to writing a play, of course—such as creating compelling characters that speak in believable dialogue—so it's not quite *that* easy. But now that he had the idea fully articulated, he could move on to all the other elements. In the end, a small anecdote grew into a full-blown dramatic concept through a dialogue with source texts and structural models.

Cultural reference points and previous creations, but also memory, experience, and history, are all source texts for imaginative work. "A lot of the stories are inspired by my family history, notably my relatives' involvement in the Communist Party," explained Molly Antopol about her acclaimed short-story collection *The UnAmericans*. "With the early stories, I was really interested in just trying to understand what it might have been like psychologically to live under that level of surveillance, with tapped lines and nightly visits from the FBI and all that." Trying to plumb the depths of that extreme experience took her ten years, and throughout that decade what obsessed her kept changing. She spent years living and working in Israel for a Palestinian/Israeli human rights group and also for an immigration absorption center for immigrants coming from war-torn Chechnya in Russia, and those experiences ripened her idea: "I started really thinking about what it might be like to have to reinvent your political identity in a country that really isn't your own and will never really see you as a citizen." After Antopol finished the stories and put together the collection, she realized how *The UnAmericans* had grown even more complex with the collapse of the Soviet Union:

> What happens to you once the things that you've devoted your entire life to become irrelevant in the course of world events? What do you then do with yourself, when you're fighting for this thing that no longer needs fighting for? In the case of a lot of my characters it's the Communist Party. For some other ones it's Israelis dealing with the really complicated and symbiotic relationship that Israelis have with America.

Molly Antopol also sought to understand the consequences of commitment. "What are the really complicated and sometimes devastating effects that one person's quest to improve the world can have on the people closest to them?" This is something she felt personally: You believe what you are doing is the right thing and you feel that you're an agent of good—but in the end you may be hurting the people you love. "I don't know where it comes from, but these questions pop up for me and I always want to write from the vantage of whoever is in the most complicated place fictionally in the story." It took her a long time to write the book because she wanted to get the voices right, creating characters that could act out the emotional ideas. "I just wanted to make sure that I could really see writing as a form of method acting and really try to figure out what it would be like to live in these people's skins," she explained. She referred to a quotation by Grace Paley: Antopol's "idea" for the book was to inhabit what she didn't know about the known—about her family and others close to her—moving beyond autobiographical ruminations to imagine the interior lives of people in positions of isolation, exile, disappointment, and dismay.

David Henry Hwang had dramatic structures to draw from, and Molly Antopol drew from the structures of feelings of her family along with her "field work" in Israel. Whether writing drama or fiction, they had to discover their ideas or even their questions as they wrote. Antopol had the shocks of history and its effects on her family, while Hwang had reference points in the original news reports and Puccini's opera as well as Shaffer's structural framework. Both of them discovered their underlying themes through a kind of journey, and only at the end did they get a sense of the map.

Such searches or wanderings take place in scientific and other academic research as well; scholars swim in the flood of all the work that's been done in their arena before them. When Terry Root said she meandered around to "look at what other people are doing," she described much of what's involved in scholarly writing of any sort—not only in coming up with an idea for a project in the first place, but also in making sure that the project is actually worthwhile. People writing novels, poems, and plays swim in the same tide as scholars do; although the process may seem different, creative writers also sort out the influence of past texts, the imaginations of others. Anyone who writes a novel about a vengeful ship captain driven mad as a result of an injury inflicted by an unusually colored whale, for example, would need to be aware of at least one other book written before they write theirs.

Nancy Etchemendy writes horror fiction for young adults, an exciting type of genre writing; and she put this process of becoming aware of previous work in terms of her own type of output: "I tend to look at any situation in a sort of frightened way," she said, and added:

> Maybe I'm just a frightened person; the world is a scary place to me. For most of us, the world is a scary place and we overcome it; and the older we get, ideally the less scary it gets. … For children, the world is a naturally scary place because they don't have much control over their lives. …

Does this mean that she flips through a library of frightening memories to seek out ideas? "There are certain things that we all find scary," she explained. "If you read a lot of horror you learn what these tropes are, and then your big task is to just not write clichés. When you're working in a genre it's sort of easy to read a few items from a genre and think, okay, now I can write this." But Etchemendy pointed out the real danger—"that you'll write something that's already been written without knowing it." She listed a series of tropes in horror stories, such as ghosts, werewolves, vampires, and zombies. "It's amazing the number of stories written about all of those things, and you may think you're writing something very original, and you find out that's been written by Saki or Edgar Allan Poe." You need to read extensively in the genre, she advised, to make sure that you don't tread down old trails.

For scholarly work, the need to search the literature is perhaps even more crucial. "Do I have any value to add here? Am I just re-plowing the old furrow?" David Kennedy posed the questions historians ask of any article or book idea. "Am I actually going to say something new about it? Do I have new evidence? Do I have new perspective, new context, whatever it might be?" Kennedy spoke of "the drill"—the approach to history that professionally trained historians apply to their work—"which is to know the territory, know the literature, know the field, know what has been said, how it's been said, from what point of view, in what context it was written, what factors influenced the saying of it in that way." Literary critic Marjorie Perloff put it more bluntly: "You can't attempt to write anything until you've read all the scholarship on the question and know what everyone else has said."

It's hard to get a grip on *all* the scholarship in a field, and learning how to do that is what goes on in graduate school. Students work "to achieve some level of mastery over this rather vast territory," according to David Kennedy. "What have those who've come before said? What are the lines of argument and conversation, disagreement? How has the topic been construed, configured, put together? Why does it have this shape, and so on? Why is the dialogue this and not that?" The research work can be prodigious, so students learn how to tell which book or article is accurate, which author is reliable, what approach is important and what not: they learn how to evaluate. Given the large and growing body of work in many areas, this surveillance can be exhausting, even debilitating. One graduate student, working on a study of Shakespeare plays, insisted that it was imperative to read every piece of criticism about Shakespeare before he could write anything. With so many centuries of criticism and so many more articles and books produced each year—he couldn't possibly keep up. He needed to discriminate, not just accumulate. What he thought was a virtue was actually a prescription for failure. He never did finish his dissertation.

The formal section of a research paper called "Literature Review," or something similar, can actually become a small gem. The literature review provides the meaningful context of any project within the universe of already existing research; in natural and social sciences a section of any research article is often called a "literature review." "Meaningful context" can elevate scholarly research from disconnected observations, from empty number crunching, or from simplistic chronologies, to a higher level of significance in the field. In many respects, the literature review presents the justification—the *raison d'être*—for a natural or social scientist's work, and there's a great deal of beauty in that. Often, on a more mundane level, the lit review plays a key role in getting grants to do the work in the first place. A lot of students regard the literature review as tedious busywork—but it can also be an elegantly argued survey of a particular corner of the cosmos.

■ ■ ■

But you still need to cultivate ideas. Getting the big idea for a book or an article or an experiment is a major achievement. But even as you go along, working that big idea, you're cooking up more thoughts, branching out, elaborating, or twisting back on your original concept. David Abernathy, almost done with his massive analysis of European colonialism around the world, felt that something was missing—some assertion of ethics at the very end—and he described how that idea arrived: "I went through my final chapter, on the moral evaluation of colonialism, and literally about a few hours before I was supposed to send that chapter off, I was having a shower—I do a lot of thinking in the shower—and it suddenly occurred to me I hadn't really said what drove the thesis, what drives the book." Then, what ended up being the penultimate paragraph came to him while in the shower. It was a statement of moral complexity:

> The imperial project consumed the lives of millions of human beings and blighted the lives of millions more. Its worst aspects—the transatlantic slave trade, plantation slavery, forced labor, sexual exploitation—should not be forgotten or excused. . . . Things fell apart for non-Europeans—many things, under the assault. But colonialism was not just the sum total of its worst-case scenarios. New crops, medicines, and occupations extended the lifespan and enhanced the welfare of millions of subject peoples. New ideas and beliefs were not only comforting and enlightening, but also empowering.

A shower here produced a way to express the strange ironies and puzzles of history—the good that is brought about despite the horror. Think about it: a *shpritz* of hot water.

Perhaps it's the relaxation or the heat on the back of the head or the fact of being comfortably nude and alone, but a lot of people report getting ideas in the shower. One professor gets so many ideas that she put up a waterproof grease-pencil whiteboard in her shower and writes out her ideas or phrases under the spray. Some students have told me that they bring portable whiteboards to the shower. It's a good suggestion for those who thrive while being irrigated, but I suspect that the first several times you bring in the grease-pencil board your brain will go on strike. After a while, your brain may get accustomed to your new habit, not notice the board, and go back to its usual distracted-yet-attentive state while being lulled by hot water. One student uses the shower regularly to come up with ideas on how to move forward in her essays; every time she reaches an impasse or a difficult place, she jumps into the shower, sometimes taking three or four a day. No whiteboard in her hands, but at the end of each shower she comes out refreshed and ready to write.

Taking multiple showers a day may be excessive—and probably bad for your skin as well as your water bill. But it's one way to cultivate thoughts. People who write are often on the hunt for techniques—places to go, figuratively and materially—to find them. You may be writing a book and need to keep thinking about the project for months or even years, so cooking up ideas is not a one-shot deal. Writers take great care in growing new ideas, molding them, allowing them to transmute—and I learned of a variety of techniques. Taking showers is very popular, but so is washing dishes. Gwyneth Lewis explained that, "part of the skill of writing over a long period of time is trusting your subconscious to come up with a solution.... It's a question of taking your mind off the intention to do anything. It's a paradox—you fulfill your intention by not aiming for it."

Gwyneth Lewis swims a lot and gets a lot of ideas in the pool, as do many people. Fertile thoughts during swimmer's high are very possible, but what's especially tough is *remembering* an idea while doing laps in the pool. Some swimmers tell me that they get one good idea then repeat a key word of the idea over and over in a mantra until they reach the locker room. "You have to park them somewhere," Lewis advised. "I park them *there*," she said, pointing at her abdomen. "It's a spatial thing. I remember asking some poets in Wales where their muse was in relation to their bodies. Everybody had a different answer—*there* or *there* or *there*. When things are going well, it's a physical sensation. ..." Swimming is similar, and the physicality of the exercise can promote creation of a mental space to park an idea in—*and* the ability to remember where that space is. "You have to lock it up in some form," she said; and she would rely on mnemonic devices, usually using the first letter of the thought. If the idea were "peppermint," she would repeat the letter P until she was done. That pretty much means one idea per swim, for most people—but many would be grateful to find and hoard that lone nugget. Some joggers do the same, remembering one idea their whole route, repeating it to themselves. Remembering while running has become easier now that people can run with their lightweight smart phones and can quickly record thoughts while jogging in place at a stoplight or even in stride.

Walking for ideas is also very common. Most "think walks" seem to be at random times, with no particular or regular itinerary, but not all walks go that route. Computer scientist Eric Roberts walks from his home to his office on campus, about a mile and a half every day—and that walk, back and forth, is reserved for thinking. Some professors have adapted a technique introduced by the Roman orator Cicero to memorize speeches. They would create an *idea landscape*, identifying every part of the topography with one or another aspect of their project—an outline of their work writ large in buildings, fountains, and groves: Hoover Tower means this, Memorial Church means that, Rodin's bronze *Thinker* represents something else. Then they would move through the topography of their idea, literally walking from one point to another in their project, reviewing and elaborating their thoughts as each landmark appeared.

Driving is another wonderful distracted-attentive practice. One professor would get so many ideas as she drove down the palm-lined road out of the campus that she would have to pull over repeatedly to jot them down in her notebook. Another has a long commute to Sonoma and would scribble notes while driving. My immediate reaction when she told me was to ask her to let it be known when she drove so I would make sure I was off the road at that time. Not safe at all. Both of these writers—and everyone else driving and walking—have benefited from new technology: they now record their ideas on their hands-free digital devices.

Along with showers, sleep is big on people's lists of idea factories. Simply, "sleeping on it" is not just a common phrase; it works. Sleep is acknowledged as being one of the main techniques for refreshing our mental screens, no matter what we do, although it can be problematic in terms of self-consciously cooking up ideas. "These days, I'm inclined to sit in my computer chair and just look out the window," physicist Leonard Susskind said while describing the evolution of his techniques. "In an earlier time, when I was younger, I would go out for a ten-mile run or something—which I can't do anymore, and I don't. I think a lot before I go to sleep, and I always worry: an idea that I get—am I going to forget it by morning?" His solution to this worry is to write it down:

> I finish writing, often, around nine o'clock. Then I go to bed and I read, and when I'm finished reading, stuff goes around in my head. I start thinking of ideas. How to fix things, and how to make them better; new ideas, new explanations—and I'm always afraid I'm going to forget them by morning. If I don't write them down, I do forget them in the morning. So I keep a pad by my bed. Once or twice, I have woken up in the middle of the night and thought a little bit, had an idea, and did it in the middle of the night. Mostly, it's the hour or so before I go to sleep. Stuff pops into my head, sort of free association.

Many allow that semi-sleep free-association state to flourish, and it's probably been a standard practice for centuries.

Several professors told me of employing a modified lucid-dreaming technique to stimulate their work. One professor explained that he would lie in bed, roll his project around in his mind before falling asleep—he would *not* agonize over his work; that would be self-defeating—and upon waking up, he would reconsider the seed of the idea he had planted the night before. He said that roughly 80 percent of the time a new thought would blossom, or at least some revision of an old one, and he would make progress on what he was working on and still wake up well rested. The idea is that you prompt yourself and, as you sleep, one part of your brain putters around with that suggestion while the rest of your brain takes the usual nocturnal break. Those who practice this technique say that lucid dreaming really aids their work, but I'm not sure everyone can be productive in that way. I know I have a hard enough time trying to calm the circus in my mind, and planting a thought might stampede the elephants.

Writers also use the in-between state of waking up to cultivate ideas. Some favor the "morning pages" technique, scribbling something out on a pad first thing in the morning, no matter what it is. Nancy Etchemendy would also make a habit of writing in the morning "before I wake up," which she found to be very useful, especially for horror. "I have nightmares, as you might imagine someone writing horror would have," she said with a broad, wry smile. "A lot of my best ideas are from dreams, and I tend not to remember them unless I jot them down." I wonder if Edgar Allan Poe did the same.

▪ ▪ ▪

Once you dream up an idea, now what? An idea starts to grow, often in surprising ways, once it reaches the light of day. George Fredrickson narrated his experience of enlightenment as a historian:

> Once you have an idea, you begin reviewing the secondary sources and even your primary historical sources, then questions come up, things that you think need to be further explored—you might develop a tentative feel of what you are likely to find. So you have this sort of framework—and then your research gives you material to either confirm or contradict the hypothesis you have, or give you the sense of an entirely new dimension on the issue that you hadn't heard of. And that's really exciting, because the other historians haven't even thought about this, and you suddenly see something developing from your research that is not in the literature. Then, oh boy, then you can really take off.

Professor Fredrickson's joy was evident: What a thrill to discover some hitherto unknown area of knowledge or interpretation.

George Fredrickson spoke about making a hypothesis, and some kind of hypothesis is essential in a lot of research, especially science: you set up the experiment or survey with a well-informed expectation of what's supposed to happen—and whether the hypothesis pans out or not, you learn something. In this regard, even failure is success: the researcher finds out that this particular hypothesis-path drops off a cliff, which means that the next experiment will turn in a different direction. But in other types of research, it's more an "educated hunch" than a hypothesis. Professor Fredrickson spoke about how, once a historian begins to dig into his material, that hunch is liable to change because of what he discovers. For historians and others, it means descending into the bowels of archives, gathering compendiums of many sorts—collections of manuscripts and documents in libraries or online—or watching people, observing cultures, interviewing, considering theories. Once you enter that realm, anything is liable to happen: what's important is to remain open to those different possibilities when they hit you.

Linguist Penelope Eckert explained the origins of one of her books: "I wanted to know the relation between the use of certain vowels that are in the process of changing in the Detroit area, and adolescent social practice." Sounds reasonable (in a linguistics sort of way). To do that, she had to dive into an ethnographic study of Detroit adolescents in order to understand their high school social structure, "and then correlate their use of vowels with where they were in that social structure." She spent a lot of time at a high school over two years, getting to know a lot of young people, recording their speech. In the course of this ethnography, however, she read "everything that had been written about adolescent social categories. And I was shocked to discover that very little had been written … and a lot of what was written was not very good."

Professor Eckert's dismay about the research on teenagers got her moving, but her sense of the inadequacy of the research was then sparked by an already held opinion: "I am sort of passionate about research on adolescents, because I think that the world has made a fortune out of adolescence; there is a whole adolescence industry. And I think that people pathologize adolescents; they clinicalize adolescents." She began to regard her ethnography in a new light, and she became especially curious about a certain segment of the high school population: "the burnouts—these are the kids who are disaffected from school. They don't like school, and they feel they have no voice—and I felt that I had to write a book. So, in the middle of doing my linguistic analysis, I sat down and wrote this book about jocks and burnouts." *Jocks and Burnouts* was not her intended project when she began writing, but as she worked, she discovered something entirely different from her original idea that captured her interest—and because she felt passionately about the people she was observing, she took her project in a radically new direction. People, archives, books, and lab results often tell us that our idea must be changed—or at least put on hold. After writing that book, she then returned to her original goal, and ended up basing her linguistics book on the same ethnography.

One critic of popular culture told me that when she goes out into the field—hanging out at clubs or street corners or malls—the people and the culture she's investigating end up telling her what she should look for; she throws out her assumptions, and her questions change. This may not always be the case, but it happens often enough: you leave your house with one idea, and you come back home with a completely different one.

Anthropologist Jackie Armijo related a similar dynamic. She had spent five years in China researching her dissertation on the early history of Islam there. When she was done, she decided to begin a new project on the lives of Muslims in China today, and what their biggest challenges were: "Instead of deciding what *I* thought was their biggest challenge, I went back out into the field and interviewed a range of people in different Muslim villages and asked them what *they* thought their community's biggest challenge was." To Professor Armijo's surprise, the people told her that their biggest concern was lack of education. She found this startling: "In that part of China they are on average even more educated than the dominant group, the Han Chinese." But something to note for all scholars: she took their concern seriously, and spent years researching education, both religious and secular, among Chinese Muslims. She traveled to Syria and Egypt to interview Chinese Muslims who were continuing their Islamic education overseas, and also interviewed students who had studied in Saudi Arabia, Iran, Malaysia, and Pakistan, with the aim of documenting "the long-term impact of their overseas education on their home communities when they returned to China." Go out and ask people what they want, and they're liable to tell you something very different from what you may expect. The surprising answer to her question continues to fuel her work and push her in new directions. She also takes great pains to translate all of her work into Chinese—a way of making her research accessible to that community, and another indication of her sense of responsibility to the people she studies.

Fred Turner, working on his book *From Counterculture to Cyberculture: Stewart Brand, the Whole Earth Network, and the Rise of Digital Utopianism*, was also surprised, but in a different way:

> There were some things I couldn't believe to be true as I was writing the book. I inherited the standard story about the American counterculture, that it was sex, drugs, and anti-Vietnam protests. What I hadn't really grokked was how much a large portion of the counterculture had fallen in love with Cold War military worlds and cybernetics.

By way of example, he showed a poster from the celebrated 1966 Trips Festival in San Francisco, a massive party with plenty of LSD passing around, "where people danced and felt themselves to be fused with one another in a sort of proto-communal way." Professor Turner pointed out the psychedelic swirls in the poster, but then drew attention to the fact that right in the middle of the poster was an unexpected image, an oscilloscope with a wave pattern. "Folks involved in the new communalism with the counterculture were entirely smitten by electronic technology, electric stuff," he explained. "This is the moment where electricity and energy and information all kind of fused in a new cultural practice. And seeing that, for me, was like—it was so contradictory to what I'd been told that I couldn't believe it. And I couldn't deal with it. I just sort of kept thinking: No, I must be wrong, I must be wrong."

But facts can be stubborn things. "When you feel like you must be wrong, you just keep digging," he said. But the deeper Fred Turner dug the more he realized that a whole section of the counterculture had been neglected in all the writings so far, a trend that involved what he called the "new communalism." Huge numbers of communes were established between 1966 and 1973, more than in any other time in American history. "We don't even talk about that with regard to the sixties anymore. We talk about the Vietnam stuff, the drug use, the sexuality—we don't talk about this huge movement to change how we live together." But he was surprised even more to discover that Stewart Brand of *Whole Earth Catalog* fame and others involved in that movement "embraced Cold War research culture, and that ultimately shaped how we think about the Internet as a space for virtual communities." The Cold War was entangled with a part of the counterculture? And that entwining would lead to the Internet? It was completely unexpected—not the typical hippie, love-peace-love stereotype. He really couldn't believe it, and Professor Turner felt compelled to research more and more, trying to contradict what he had learned, but to no avail. The deeper he got, the more this was confirmed. The counterculture, he realized, was not inherently or entirely a creature of the left, and his book took a decidedly new direction.

Shelley Fisher Fishkin, writing about Mark Twain, experienced a similar radical revision of her original idea, a change that completely altered the nature of the book she was writing. Although she would sometimes get an idea while walking or in the shower like others, she would also get a new idea "from just sitting down and forcing myself to write, and then reading what I've written and finding something that just speaks to me more than anything else." One of her books was "completely derailed" when she was rereading a draft of what she had written and was struck by one paragraph that "was so much more interesting than anything else I'd written." She decided that if that paragraph weren't absolutely central to the book, the book would have to change to make it so. She reorganized the entire project because of the insight she found in that paragraph. Professor Fishkin turned to *Lighting Out for the Territory: Reflections on Mark Twain and American Culture* to read out loud the passage about her visit to the town Mark Twain made famous—Hannibal, Missouri—which today capitalizes on all things Twain:

> Passing through the Mark Twain Riverboat air-conditioned ticket office, I felt the sting of a wasp on my behind. My involuntary "ouch" seemed to frighten the five-year-old boy with bangs who stood three feet behind me, wearing what struck me as an oddly worried expression. He must have accidentally bumped into me, I remember thinking, although I couldn't for the life of me figure out how he could have caused the short, sharp sting.
>
> "Did you hit her?" his mother demanded. The little boy started to bawl.
>
> "Don't worry. It's okay. I'm fine," I reassured them. Then I saw what was in his hand.
>
> The boy held a miniature version of the bullwhip that was the best-selling souvenir among schoolchildren at the Mark Twain Book & Gift Shop. If a child could create that sting with a miniature whip when he wasn't trying, I shuddered to think what a full-grown man could do with a full-sized whip when he was trying.
>
> I turned to the mother of my five-year-old assailant. "Actually, it's not okay," I sputtered. "That's a bullwhip, and he should be taught not to use it on people." She turned bright red, apologized, snatched the whip out of the little boy's hands.
>
> I had come to Hannibal to touch history, and history eluded me at every turn. Until now. I had just been bullwhipped on the banks of the Mississippi. [pg. 65]

When she originally wrote that passage, she thought, "My God, this isn't the book." That's when she realized she was, in fact, writing the wrong book. "It reads more like a novel or a travelogue than a piece of literary criticism, which is what I was going to do."

Professor Fishkin thought she was writing a book about Twain's place in popular culture. But when she read what she wrote about that incident in her draft, her book turned around: "I began to see the ways in which everything that mattered most about him was being erased and whitewashed in the city, because the economy was based on Twain tourism. I realized that the book was really about the country's *erasure* of what made him a powerful writer." Everything clicked.

She had seen the miniature bullwhips for sale in a local souvenir shop, and had seen adolescent boys playing with them on the street in front of the shop; but the larger resonances of what she had seen had not coalesced and their significance hadn't hit home. In the riverboat office, feeling the sharp little sting of the toy bullwhip startled her into recognizing that the brutal violence of slavery and all it entailed was what was missing from the town's commemoration of its most famous native son; it reminded her that Hannibal's saccharine celebration of Tom Sawyer and Huck Finn erased aspects of Twain that mattered deeply – such as his critique of the slaveholding world of his childhood and the racism that persisted long after slavery ended, and his opposition to America's turn toward overseas empire in the Philippines.

She hadn't realized that *Lighting Out for the Territory*, which turned out to be very popular, "was going to be a book much more akin to the kind of books that Mark Twain wrote than the kind of books that I've written." She came to understand that Mark Twain had really been her writing teacher, "and that reading him had somehow gotten under my skin. And I realized his strategy of using travel as a vehicle for social commentary was, in fact, exactly what I needed to do." She also realized that she could use what was "really more of a fiction writer's sense, that you can use details that are in your environment as you're researching something that's scholarly and find epiphanies that illuminate the larger scholarly questions, even though that's not scholarly." She injected that fiction writer's sense of detail—experiential, visual, sensory, the kind of writing Mark Twain would have done—into the typical literary critical methodology, and that sense of detail yanked her approach around. She was astonished: "Whatever it is, this is the first time I had that experience."

■ ■ ■

Even more dramatic than a bullwhip on the banks of the Mississippi was the way an epiphany flowed from a bank vault. Clarence B. Jones, now scholar-in-residence at the Martin Luther King, Jr. Research and Education Institute at Stanford, had been a speechwriter and main legal counsel for the civil rights leader. He told the story of how one difficult experience sparked an image in King's celebrated "I Have a Dream" speech. As the 50th anniversary of the March on Washington approached, Jones explained the process of drafting King's speech. He met with all the leaders of the march in the hotel before the demonstration, each with their favorite idea for the speech, and Jones wrote a summary of what they discussed on sheets of a yellow legal pad in language "that could possibly be used as spoken in a speech."

One part of that famous speech did not come from the leadership meeting but from Clarence Jones's own experience: the extended metaphor that the march had come to Washington "to cash a check"—the "promissory note [of equal rights] to which every American was to fall heir"—although "It is obvious today that America has defaulted on this promissory note insofar as her citizens of color are concerned." King's speech spins out the story of cashing a check:

> Instead of honoring this sacred obligation, America has given the Negro people a bad check, a check which has come back marked "insufficient funds." But we refuse to believe that the bank of justice is bankrupt. We refuse to believe that there are insufficient funds in the great vaults of opportunity of this nation. So we have come to cash this check—a check that will give us upon demand the riches of freedom and the security of justice.

The source of that image goes back a few months before the march, to the bitter campaign to fight segregation in Birmingham, Alabama. Demonstrators, including many children and young people, encouraged by Dr. King, faced the violence of Sheriff Bull Connor's high-pressure water hoses and vicious police dogs. King was jailed, along with large numbers of elementary, high school and college students: "One of the great problems that almost derailed the success of our movement in Birmingham," Jones recalled, "was the fact that we didn't have enough bail money to bail out these thousand or more children who had followed him into jail, children between the ages of twelve and seventeen."

Their parents were putting enormous pressure on the organizers to get their children out, and critics were denouncing King for promoting a "children's crusade" with vulnerable youth. Jones went to see Dr. King in his jail cell to get some advice on how to raise bail money. But the civil rights leader "virtually dismissed me. It's like he wasn't paying attention. I said, 'Martin, do you understand that we have a real problem?'" The issue was increasingly urgent, but King told Jones to work it out with singer and activist Harry Belafonte.

Then King showed Jones a full-page ad in the *Birmingham News* signed by the most prominent white clergymen in Birmingham, who opposed King and his nonviolent tactics. In response to that ad, King had written on "every blank sheet of paper that was available to him; he was answering, scribbling out on the blank pieces of old newspaper, on paper towels, anything that was blank." He was composing what became one of the great documents of the Civil Rights Movement. King gave Jones the paper he scribbled on, telling him to get it typed up. And when Jones returned to the jail the next time, "I put some yellow sheets of paper under my shirt and would bring it into the jail. And he would write. This was done over the course of four days. That's how *Letter from a Birmingham Jail* was written. And I smuggled it out." The Letter, in addition to being filled with cogent arguments, was also peppered with quotes from Scripture and literature—all from memory, and all of it written under difficult conditions. It turned out that the clergymen's wrongheadedness had prompted Reverend King to write one of his most eloquent clarion calls for justice and nonviolence.

But the demand to bail out the "children's crusade" only grew, and parents were frantically pressuring Jones and others. Soon he got an urgent message to call Harry Belafonte, who told Jones to get to New York as soon as possible. New York Governor Nelson Rockefeller wanted to help with bail money.

Belafonte gave him a phone number to call when he arrived, no matter what time it was. He arrived after midnight and phoned Rockefeller's representative, who told him that the governor did want to help, and that Jones should meet him at the headquarters of Chase Manhattan Bank at 47th Street and Sixth Avenue the next morning. It was Saturday and no banks were open, but Jones did exactly what he was told; someone met him and took him into the bank and into the vault:

> I had never at that time seen the inside of a vault except in movies. There's this big wheel, like they opened a door and the door

is about that thick, you know, and they swing the door back. And I look inside and I said, "Oh my lord." There is, from floor to ceiling, nothing but dollar bills, wrapped—most of it wrapped in cellophane and some of it in canvas bags. Rockefeller walks in, takes out $100,000 in cash. Gives me the $100,000 and he says, "This should be a help." I said thank you and I'm trying to get ready to go, because I figured I've got to get back to Birmingham. He says hold on just a moment. There's a gentleman sitting at the typewriter over there. And I go over to the typewriter and he says, "Your name is Clarence B. Jones, right?"

The man was typing out a note, and he said, "There are bank regulations. We have to have something that indicates that we've given you this money." He was typing out a "demand promissory note." In commercial transactions, a promissory note declares that you pay "a certain sum of money at a place on a specific date and time, but a *demand* promissory note is different. A demand promissory note is payable on demand. And normally in state statutes they give you three business days, *but it's payable on demand.* That's a lot of money for one man to be responsible for repayment." Dr. Jones gasped, "Oh my gosh, $100,000? That's a lot, you know. I better not tell my wife I did this. This is crazy."

But Jones signed the note "because I've got to get back on the plane again. And I run to the first payphone" to call Harry Belafonte: "Harry, you didn't tell me that I was going to have to sign a demand promissory note for $100,000!"

Harry said, "Better you than me."

And I said, "But you can afford it. I can't!"

Clarence Jones went back down to Birmingham and gave the money to the bail bond fund. Then he returned to his law office in New York, and a day or two later a messenger from Chase Manhattan Bank arrived. The messenger asked for his ID, then handed him an envelope. "I take this envelope and I sit down in the conference room and I open it and there's the demand promissory note that I had signed. And I turn it over and look." On the back of the note was written, "Paid in Full." The Rockefellers had redeemed the debt.

That experience was so powerful that Dr. Jones included the metaphor of the promissory note in the draft of the speech. "We have come here today," he recalled the suggested words:

... to redeem a promissory note to which all heirs of our republic have a responsibility for. And we are coming to redeem this promissory note because we've received—we've gotten notes before that have been marked unpaid, insufficient funds. We can't believe that there are not sufficient funds in the vault of justice to redeem our promise for full equality.

Martin Luther King took his draft, incorporated the metaphor of the promissory note along with the other paragraphs Jones had developed from the meeting with leaders, revised this, and added his own material. As it turned out, one of the nation's wealthiest families made sure that the fund of America's promise was sufficient. The bank vault where Clarence Jones went to pick up Birmingham's bail money became the source of one of the enduring metaphors in that historic speech.

Terry Karl

CHAPTER SIX

Arguing with the
Death Squad

TERRY KARL HAS written about Latin America, particularly Central America, for years, and she played a key role in the negotiations to end the civil war in El Salvador. For her, the argument she develops in an essay or a policy paper can be "matters of life and death for a lot of people." So to make sure she moves in the right direction, she has developed a technique of entertaining "rival hypotheses." Basically, she asks herself, "What's wrong with my position?" It may seem obvious to question yourself—certainly, no one wants to be oblivious to other possibilities—but it isn't easy in practice. During our conversation, she told a story of how she came to invent her technique of "rival hypotheses" from her experience of the war in El Salvador.

She described being in the country in the early eighties when "a horrible process of state terror degenerated into a civil war." El Salvador was a terrible place to be at that time, and she recalled that, her very first day there, she stepped outside and immediately came across a corpse. "I was heading over to McDonald's next to the hotel and there was a body in the parking lot." It only got worse from that point on.

As a political scientist, she needed to get a grasp on the dynamic leading to such horror in Salvadoran society. Many American academics and the Reagan administration described the conflict fundamentally in Cold War terms—a bloody confrontation between Soviet and Western surrogates—although she and most academic observers outside of the U.S. regarded what was taking place differently: for them, it was a landlord-peasant class war. "Essentially, rich landlords were hiring armies to kill poor peasants in uprisings around land questions," she explained. "So the peasants were all dying. They were on the left and the landlords were on the right. That's the way I saw it when I first went there."

But then she interviewed Roberto d'Aubuisson, the founder and head of the death squads in El Salvador. D'Aubuisson was "an ultra-rightist and a fascist," she explained, noting that calling him a fascist was not an exaggeration or an epithet: he really was a fascist, according to the definition of the term. "He was as far on the right as you can get. He was actually one of the authors of the murder of Archbishop Romero," who was assassinated by a sniper while conducting mass. It was a peasant-landlord war, she told him with some certainty; but in the middle of the interview, d'Aubuisson, who was running for president, challenged her, declaring, "I have more support [from peasants] than you think."

"Why would a peasant support you?" Professor Karl retorted, provocatively. She recalled afterward that having this argument "was one of the stupidest things I'd ever done." You don't argue with the head of the death squads; you mollify the beast and get the hell out as fast as you can. But she foolishly did get into this debate. He didn't have her killed, fortunately; he presented her with a surprising invitation instead: "He challenged me to go into the countryside with him and see his base." She took him up on the offer and "actually traveled on his presidential campaign for several weeks." To her surprise, she discovered that his rallies would always draw contingents of peasants who were not coerced or paid off to attend, and she found other evidence that shook her assumptions to their foundations: "I came out of that saying *The man has a base among the peasantry*. This isn't a landlord-peasant war in the way that I originally understood it, but it really is something else." It wasn't the Soviet-West confrontation the U.S. government thought, either; it was a social dynamic entirely out of the bounds of these conventional paradigms:

> I was lucky enough to realize how intractable this war was going to be because of the way it penetrated communities and divided them—that it wasn't so simple as just a class war. It was a much more complicated story. And I learned that by watching, listening, and saying to myself: What if he is right and I am wrong. If he's right: What would the evidence look like? If I'm right: What would the evidence look like? And I actually made a little list: What would be the indicators?

She discovered that the story didn't fit her description or any other; it was far more complicated. "Now, what if I had such blinders on that I couldn't see that?"

From this dramatic and dangerous experience she devised her approach to fashioning an argument: proposing to herself what she calls "rival hypotheses." For example, since her work in El Salvador, she has written on underdeveloped oil exporting countries, and has drawn the conclusion that, for any country unfortunate enough to have found important resources of oil, there would be an "oil curse": unequal distribution of income, dictatorship, increased misery—not development, as the people would have hoped for. She was pretty certain that the discovery of oil would mess up any underdeveloped country—but what if there was an exception? "In Chad, they're saying they're going to do it right," she explained. "So, just because no historical example exists in modern times of an oil exporting country making it development-wise.... What if I'm wrong? What if they *are* making it?" If Chad were to succeed, "What would be the signposts? What would they look like?"

This method means being open to being wrong, "to be willing to find truth that you may find uncomfortable." Nevertheless, you have to be proactive, you need to go out and look for truth—because if you don't, your own blinders will allow you to see only the truth that you want to see, "and we all have blinders." Biologist Craig Heller, on a panel discussing methodologies across the disciplines, insisted that the goal of all his experiments is to prove that his hypothesis is wrong: he takes whatever steps he can to overturn his expectations. Professor Heller's task is not to prove that he's right, but to show that he's *not wrong*. It's similar to Terry Karl's "rival hypotheses": the idea is to avoid getting too complacent with what seems obvious or "common sense," and challenge your thinking.

In biology you can attack your hypothesis in a number of different, concrete ways; but in the humanities and a lot of social sciences, there are no formal hypotheses; but there are arguments based on evidence. It's hard to shape a compelling, incisive argument, and a lot of writers in these disciplines develop arguments in a variety of ways. Philosophy professor Rob Reich explained the two different approaches he would take to create an argument. One method would be for a philosopher to start with "first principles" and "work out proper relations amongst the principles—a very clean, logical argument. And once the beautiful abstract edifice is complete, begin to consider what it means for the real world." Professor Reich prefers a second approach—moving in the opposite direction, working from the ground up: "I happen to observe something or experience something or read something that actually exists in the real world, and I end up asking myself, 'What's the story that I could tell myself that could justify the arrangement that gave rise to this particular practice or phenomenon?' I start with a very practical thing and push upward" to principles or philosophical concepts.

Professor Reich gave an example from his own work on the ethical aspects of homeschooling. He discovered that in some regions it's possible "to homeschool your children without any oversight from the state":

> Just write a simple note and announce that, for reasons you don't have to disclose, that you're homeschooling your child. I thought that's a curious way to operate a public policy regime for education, and since it actually exists, I thought to myself, what possible reasons could we give to provide for a justification for homeschooling where there are no regulations that apply to the undertaking? By asking that question, I then began to get into what are progressively higher levels of abstraction. I ask what rights and interests does the child have in an education, what rights and interests do the parents have in providing an education, what rights and interests does the state have in providing a certain sort of education—and then you begin rising up this level of abstraction and think about the nature of the balance of these interests and how to work out some arguments about them.

He reaches those higher levels of abstraction by beginning with the assumption that any relevant political theory about the issue has to address questions "about children, about parenting interests, about what the state needs of its citizens." You could think about education as a consequence of all three of those concerns operating as guiding principles, and then "plow downward" into the reality. But he pushes upward instead. Using this method, he drew the conclusion that homeschooling without oversight is deeply unethical for the child, the parents, and for the society as a whole.

"Philosophy is about argument and reasoning, and so a lot of the attention is on the reasons you give for what you claim," according to Debra Satz, also a philosopher. "It's kind of an art to be able to find your own voice and reasons, and also pay attention to the reasons on the other side." She described her work as being engaged in conversations with many other people, and a big part of writing is "figuring out who you are in conversation with." As a consequence, she does a lot of reading before she writes. "I'm not somebody who just sits down and writes outside of a dialogue. I'm always in a dialogue when I write, which means I'm shaped by the conversation." And in getting clear about one's interlocutor, you also clarify "the question that you're in a dialogue with."

As part of that, Professor Satz believes it's important to her and other academics "that the conversation you're shaped by isn't so narrow and turgid that you lose sense of why you're doing what you're doing. So you want to pick out a conversation that matters," not one that's trivial or a minor internal argument, what people often dismiss as merely "academic." Anthropologist and poet Renato Rosaldo framed his approach with the question: "What's at stake?" Whenever people write, they should be making an argument, he explained, and then they need to give examples to prove their case. But first, he emphasized, they must realize the implications for the whole process. One way to consider arguing for what's at stake would be to imagine yourself as a teenager "trying to convince your parents to let you use the car tonight. And so then one of the first things you need to establish is what's at stake: 'Dad, I'm gonna die if I don't have the car. What am I gonna do tonight? You don't have any idea of what this means to me.'" You would need at least one example "to convince somebody that this really matters."

It's not just that something feels as crucial as getting the car for a date—or that it weighs life or death implications, as Terry Karl describes her policy arguments as doing. Clearly, not all types of writing have such dramatic consequences, even when the argument is vitally important. Professor Reich, for example, explained that he doesn't believe that "the vocation of a philosopher or political theorist [is] trying to offer a public policy blueprint for how the world would be better if the philosopher simply could translate his or her ideas into law." Instead, what a successful piece of philosophy can do within the real world, if you want "to create change on the ground, if that ultimately is what you want to accomplish, is to show people how rethinking the foundational level of certain kinds of arguments leads in the end to a certain set of ideas or assumptions or chains of thought about policy matters." In other words, if people change the way they think, they may be able to change their practice. For Professor Reich, rarely does it mean that he would write anything that relates directly to appealing to Congress to pass a bill or some other action. "I'm trying to do something higher order so that the background of thought shifts."

Anne Firth Murray, Founding President of the Global Fund for Women, had a keen sense of what was at stake when she wrote *Paradigm Found*, her account of the birth and growth of the very successful foundation that has given away about $40 million to support thousands of women's rights initiatives around the world. She felt compelled to present an example for others seeking to create an activist organization like hers. The Global Fund for Women is an unusual organization, she explained, and "the story should be told of how that came about." Others, such as journalists, had told their own versions, but she insisted that she, as one of the founders, be the one to tell their own story. While she was involved in running the foundation, there was never any time to tell that story, to "record what happened, how it was done, why we did it, how we did it, the struggle, the exhaustion of activism." People kept telling her that such a book was needed. The account existed only in bits and pieces, and the lessons needed to be shared so other activists could glean from the experience. "People in the international women's movement don't take the time" to relate the stories of their struggles, she explained; they are "simply too busy. And when they retire from the organizations, they do what I wanted to do, which was walk on beaches, prune my roses, and read books." But she realized that "what's at stake" required her to tell that story, drawing from her own experience and sources to argue how the Global Fund was a uniquely creative act.

Debra Satz also responds to a sense of urgency to fashion her arguments. In her own case, she has written about the ethics of "noxious markets"— the buying and selling of things that greatly disturb people, such as body parts, blood diamonds, and sex. "I find you need *chutzpah*," she explains. "You have to believe you've really got something to say that's really important." She emphasizes that, at the same time, you need to be humble, and remember "I'm just part of a big conversation." There are some people who have only one perspective, and no other voice in their heads telling them to think about other views: "Some people only have the *chutzpah*." But Professor Satz continually reminds herself that there are other people who have worked on the topic, and "after all, you're just making a point."

On the one hand, "it's important to have a kind of courage in writing, to be able to stick your neck out. So you're in conversation with other people, but you are also trying to say something that you think hasn't been said, and it's a risk because it's not what everybody else is saying. Otherwise, why would you write it?" But, on the other hand, Debra Satz does remember to check herself, reaffirming that she has only one perspective and not the last word.

Indeed, she thought that those writers who "only have the chutzpah" may be the most successful writers; after all, they don't have another voice in their heads saying, "Wait a second." But she always does consider the alternative arguments. "You will be vulnerable to criticism yourself," she explains, just like the people you're in conversation with. Yet, if you're too accommodating, if you have too much of that voice that says you don't really belong in this discussion, if you doubt yourself too much, you end up not writing. "So you have to have both: the kind of brash, 'I really believe I have something special to contribute,' and 'I'm one among many, and there are other voices that are part of this conversation.'" Otherwise, you might think that you're so important that nobody or nothing else matters: "Trying to keep multiple perspectives but not lose your own voice in the jumble of all the other perspectives—that's the art of doing philosophy well."

Richard Rorty was a very different type of thinker, but he too wrestled with multiple voices. First, he would need to generate his ideas, which meant some form of rough writing: "I have no idea what I think until I see what I've written," he explained, paraphrasing what E. M. Forster and others say. Professor Rorty would start off with a hunch, and then produce a version that was so rough he knew it could never be published. He would set it aside, then a day or two later he would read the draft over sentence by sentence, "taking out the stupider-sounding sentences and polishing up the others." In the course of this process he would come to understand his argument more clearly, even possibly rejecting it. He would start off writing a paper to prove a certain thesis, but by the time he came to the end, his position may have totally changed:

> I find I have reversed direction. I concoct an argument and realize how weak it is. So I reverse polarities. It's not exactly arguing against myself. It's realizing what a critic would say, getting discouraged, and deciding I'd better change my tack.

Linguist Penelope Eckert goes through a similar rough hunch method: she often "go[es] for the jugular." If she is arguing with precedent, "I'll make some kind of a statement, and usually it's very grandiose and embarrassing, and later I have to get rid of it. But the idea is there," she emphasizes. "I just have to make it a little less self-serving and pompous."

Paying attention to the other voices in the conversation, arguing with precedent, entertaining rival hypotheses, or anticipating what a critic might say—all of these are ways of addressing arguments that oppose yours. Rob Reich feels that it's crucial that he actually writes out counterarguments fully, accurately, and without distortion. Formulating counterarguments is not just "taking a bunch of abstract jabs at the position you're trying to advance." You need to make "the strongest possible counterarguments against your position." Then the writer systematically works through all those objections, showing why in some sense they're insufficient or not explaining what needs to be explained. Professor Reich drew from his experience to underscore the value of elaborating the counterargument:

> The strongest philosophical arguments give as much ground as possible to the opposition before mounting a defense of one's own position. Otherwise you're just dealing with a straw man, and it's quite easy to show that your argument has something to recommend it. But in order to demonstrate your argument is superior to others requires giving full weight to positions that run opposite to yours.

Donald Kennedy, biologist, former president of Stanford, and at the time of our conversation editor of *Science*, put it this way: "If you don't do it, somebody else will. If there is a contrary position that can be raised as an argument, it's very much the best tactic to identify it and dispose of it if you can."

Professor Kennedy also noted that sometimes in the search for contrary positions the writer may even end up with "two opposed points of view on something" and both seem valid. "You wind up making a choice, but you really have respect for the arguments on both sides." He believes that it's good to be really honest about the fact that there seems to be more than one well-reasoned position. "Look. It's a close call," he said, describing what he believes is the honest approach for taking a stand. "Here's where my preference lies, and it's for this reason. But this is going to be an argument that's going to be with us for a while."

There's a temptation, Rob Reich noted, to undertake the search for counterarguments mechanically, "especially if you've taken high school debate." The debate-team approach tends "to view argument-counterargument as a kind of game to play." Let's find some arguments just because they're possible, come up with some idea just because we can, "and then scribble them down on a paper and call that an essay." Playful debate is useful, but to argue a position just because it's possible, "in the end, it's not all that interesting, *and* it also does damage to the ultimate seriousness of the subject matter. We're not playing games with trying to figure out what public policy should be."

Debra Satz does note that it's possible to make "a legitimate contribution to knowledge" by saying "I don't really believe this argument, but I want to give it a run for its money." Perhaps no one is doing this argument justice, and the assertions that others have made to defeat it don't make it, so it's worth giving it a try. She's written essays "where I think, you know, this is a lousy argument, but it doesn't seem like all these other arguments that people have had against it really work. And so I'm going to try to make this argument as strong as I can." Admittedly, she prefers to write by "really trying to figure out what do I really believe about something."

This can get tricky. One student wrote a thesis on an educational policy issue that involved all sorts of statistical equations called regressions that were derived from different sources. She had a good relationship with her advisor, but she completely disagreed with him on the policy issue. She didn't tell him that she disagreed, but decided instead that she would write her thesis *in order to prove that he was right—even though she felt he was wrong and expected that she would not succeed*. She worked up one source of data, cranked out a regression, and ... nothing. And then she worked up another, and then another. Each time, she got similar negative results. Eventually, it was time to finish and graduate. Her results did not actually prove that her professor was wrong—but they didn't prove that he was right, either. Even so, he was confident that, with even more data and more crunching through the statistical machinery, he would be proven right; she was confident he would not, and was pleased that she had undermined his position (a policy position with serious implications in practice). Having a hypothesis that doesn't pan out is no failure for research—in fact, it's a form of success—so she submitted her thesis to great accolades. But she never told her professor that she was indeed very satisfied with that outcome; that for her, failure was a great success.

Middle East historian Joel Beinin also acknowledges all the arguments that are part of the conversation. "Everything is out there," he says; but to him, social reality "is not random.... Society has a structure; you can understand that structure." It's possible to understand the development of twentieth-century Egyptian history, for example; it's not a mystery hidden from human analysis. "There are certain analytical tools to use," Beinin explains. "Not everybody likes the same tools. There is an argument about which are the proper tools. So you put all that out there." Doing so in the framework of an essay or book of his own, he makes a point of giving a nod even to the arguments he finds utterly lacking—but only if he thinks a viewpoint or argument is worthy. He eliminates those that he considers to be absurd or outside the bounds of reason:

> I take seriously the ones that I think deserve to be taken seriously. And that's an intellectual and political judgment. There is an argument out there that God gave the Land of Israel to the Jewish people, and that's why the State of Israel should have all the territory between Jordan and the Mediterranean Sea. I'm not going to address that argument in anything I write. That's, to me, something you believe or you don't. I don't happen to believe it.

While Professor Beinin focuses on arguments that are inside the bounds of reason and not those based on faith, he acknowledges all points of view within those bounds, addressing what he would consider to be serious counterarguments.

Acknowledging disagreement can be very difficult, especially for someone writing biography or engaged in direct personal interactions. At the time of our conversation, Carol Shloss (who had previously written a biography of the daughter of James Joyce) was doing research on Mary de Rachewiltz, the daughter of poet Ezra Pound. She became friendly with her, and moved into her house in Italy. It was the house her poet father had lived in—Brunnenburg Castle, which sits high on a mountaintop and has a turret. Professor Shloss slept in that turret, and it dawned on her that she was sleeping in the room that Pound himself had worked in after World War II. But how would she relate to the fact that Pound was sympathetic to Mussolini, made broadcasts for the fascists during the war, was considered a traitor, and was saved from prison by being declared insane and confined to a hospital? Professor Shloss felt she had to "show the world as she [de Rachewiltz] sees it. I don't have to pass judgment on it, but I have to reveal it"—and in his daughter Mary de Rachewiltz's opinion, Pound was innocent. "Pound spoke on Italian radio—you have to remember that Mary was Italian, she was born there, and Pound didn't want Italy and America at war with each other." Professor Shloss was faced with a delicate dance, having to present her subject's views while noting her own critical understanding of Pound's actions at the same time. She also knew that she would have to investigate the meaning of treason in depth for herself. But the reality behind any of those ideas is that Pound's daughter Mary is a compelling, real person. Ideas come with bodies.

A big part of this practice—of accurately presenting a different argument (or in Ezra Pound's case, loved, lived experience)—speaks to the ethics of writing. Expository writers seriously consider others' ideas or versions of reality in order to be intellectually honest, and also, partly, as a way of strengthening their own case. I would add that this attention to your opposition could also be wonderfully self-serving, even though serving your own cause may sound selfish and not all that ethical. But you enhance your own credibility by regarding contrary views with respect, even as you head them off at the pass. You may be wrong, but at least readers will think you're fair—and perhaps they'll hesitate to toss your book into the recycle bin.

Let me give you an example of self-serving honesty. A student was working on a thesis arguing why Britain should not adopt the euro (this was long before the eurozone debt crisis). She marshaled all her reasoning and data to make her case, but she did not take the arguments on the opposite side seriously, and even sarcastically dismissed the countries that had adopted the euro. I knew very little about the issue, but after I read her manuscript I told her I couldn't accept her argument. So far as I could tell, she presented a reasonable case, but she treated her opposition so poorly, so derisively that, as a reader, I could not trust her judgment.

Interestingly, her faculty advisor, who agreed with her, had no problem with the shabby treatment of her opponents. The apprenticeship relationship between student and faculty guide means the advisor rules, of course; so I told her to go ahead as she was directed. But she wanted to adapt her work for publication to convince people who thought otherwise or were neutral like me, and not just entertain those who already agreed with her. Her allies would appreciate her sarcastic cracks, but what would that accomplish? So she made the revisions, explaining counterarguments clearly, fully, and with respect. Her advisor did not object, since this did not change her basic position against Great Britain adopting the euro, but it did give her far more credibility as she advanced her own views. At least someone that disagreed with her could read her essay without wearing body armor.

When a writer takes counterarguments seriously, she encourages readers to trust her: "There's my point of view," the reader thinks, and nods in recognition. "That's my opinion, and she understands it. That's good. But now she disagrees. Let's see what evidence or logic she uses to knock it down." A very different reaction would be: "There's my point of view, my opinion. But she misunderstands it; she's distorting it. I'm not reading this garbage any more. What's the use? All of her ideas are based on willful misrepresentations, false data, and poor logic." At which point the reader simply chucks the whole thing.

I learned a technique from one social science professor that I've found very useful. At several junctures in his work, he forces himself to write out his argument under the pressure of a five-minute deadline. No explanations, no background material, no rationale for why he is taking up the topic; he just hammers out the essential argument using whatever terminology is appropriate to his field. He does this exercise at the beginning, middle, and end of the project, and he finds that it clears his mind, keeps his work focused, and confirms that he really does have an argument. Sometimes he realizes that his argument has actually shifted, even though he had not been aware of the change; by pushing himself to articulate his argument, he also forces himself to confront his unconscious revision. I've done this with students, offering to put a gun to their heads so that they feel the pressure to spit it out—and I've found that many realize that they had actually changed their minds or vantage points without realizing it, and that by forcing themselves to articulate it, they would discover their actual argument.

A while later I developed another exercise to do some time after the argument-under-pressure one. In the same manner—no explanations, no background material, under the gun of a five-minute deadline—you write out a significant *counter*argument. There actually could be several important counterarguments about what you're trying to advocate—and you can present several, if you wish—but once you do articulate what someone would say to undermine your own position, consider whether or not those counterarguments are right, and why. And if you decide they're wrong, then you're free to formulate intelligent rebuffs in anticipation of those objections—once again heading off your critics at the pass.

Physician and sociologist Don Barr refines this approach of concisely expressing the essence of your argument even further: "If you can't express it to yourself and to your mentors in one or two sentences, it's tough to really get going." Once you have an argument, you can *distill it down to one or two sentences*. (In Dr. Barr's case, he wrote: "What American healthcare needs to do is forget the market and go back to the idea that the most good for the most people is how healthcare should be organized.") Then you can take that single idea and "expand it back up into a paper-length or book-length work." But this process of reaching your argument's essence is crucial for Dr. Barr: "We use the f-word a lot; if you can't *focus* your thinking down to a simple idea, it's really, really tough to get started."

Historian Paul Robinson, on the other hand, finds that squeezing out a brief statement of his argument is too confining, and not the way he operates—and he's not the only one. He thinks through an approximation of what he's going to say before he starts writing. He then writes in parts or sections, so he gets a sense of what the parts are going to be, but:

> I don't try to sit down and work out the argument. I have a sense of what the parts are going to be, and then I go to do the work for a particular chapter. I do the reading for the chapter, and then I write it. And I polish it; I get it into pretty good shape. When I am done with it, it is close to the final form. And then the last thing I do is to write an introduction, and I can shape the architecture of the book. If you start out with an overly elaborate architectural notion of how to proceed, you are asking for disaster. You start writing an introduction, and then the actual text doesn't fit the introduction.

Professor Robinson writes cultural history and not empirical or statistical social science or policy. His approach goes beyond how to develop an argument: it involves shaping an entire piece of writing.

In a similar fashion, literary critic Alex Woloch constructs his argument as he writes—"which is exciting, because you see the intellectual steps that are going into making the argument"—but the full elaboration of that argument only comes at the end. Professor Woloch believes that "in general, I structure my argument around questions—almost riddles—and the answer comes at the end, which in a way is bad. Maybe the answer should come at the beginning?" He did know the answer, somewhat, as he began, however; and he wasn't writing his book as a mystery novel. "You don't want that much suspense; then it is unclear what you are arguing. But there has to be something that isn't revealed until the end; otherwise, why keep reading? I was invested in discovering stuff during the writing, and putting that discovery into the text." Perhaps this technique pertains more to how to present an argument than to how to develop one, but they often go hand in hand.

Terry Karl actually has what she calls "The NOT *Murder, She Wrote*" rule. She believes that social science writing should *not* be a mystery. "The people who are reading what you're saying are not supposed to wait until the end to get the surprise ending. In fact, you're supposed to be telling them what you're going to tell them and then giving them all kinds of sign-posts along the way to say, 'Please come with me. I want to take you with me on this journey'—which happens to be whatever it is I'm writing." This is not easy to do. For Professor Karl, writing a fairly finished introduction is crucial "because that is, to me, the road map of what's coming." So she struggles for her argument first, then analyzes and outlines how it will all piece together. "And once I understand the road map, it's easier for me to take pieces of the road." She recognizes that this is not perfect, saying she could "figure out the road map as I'm halfway down the road." But that would mean she'd have to "go back and change the map a little bit."

At some point, linguist Penny Eckert has to draw—not exactly road maps, but doodles—to see her ideas as visual patterns. She "goes for the jugular" with some bold idea to start, and she then tries to work it out. "I think I write from the inside out," she says, explaining how she writes one piece of her argument, then moves on to another part, and then another, and "eventually I'll have a bunch of pieces." She's then liable to get stuck: "I can't decide how to order the argument. And one thing I've learned is there are any number of ways you can order a piece of writing, and you're better off if you just pick one and forget it—go with it." Professor Eckert does plow ahead with that one way, and proceeds to unfold her thoughts in some kind of order:

> But then I may come to a point where I have to draw. So I take out a piece of paper—if possible a piece of newsprint, and if possible with colors—just because it keeps me interested. And I'll write one argument or one piece and draw a big circle around it—just stuff to make it out there and kind of visual—and then that helps me order my argument. Then I'll go back to writing, usually copy[ing] big chunks from here and mov[ing] them there and back and forth, and then I have the problem of making it cohere.

Of course, this is a very personal method, and it doesn't always bear fruit, at least not the first time. "Sometimes I have to do it again," she acknowledges, and she will have to draw out her ideas on newsprint one more time.

Professor Eckert is by no means the only writer to employ visual props: Rebecca Slayton has done scientific research on lasers and writes articles on the history of science and science policy, and she also feels that sooner or later it's time to pull out a piece of paper and doodle, write key words, draw arrows, sketch, and fiddle around, until the argument takes shape. I also often draw what I hope to write, and when I get to the end of a section, I'll map it out some more, extending my argument one doodle at a time.

Tom Hare writes about classical Japanese Noh drama and ancient Egyptian hieroglyphics—it may seem an unlikely combination, although it makes sense for someone who studies comparative literature and cultures. While writing his book about hieroglyphics, he sketched out elaborate drawings of his ideas—perhaps the notion of writing about a symbolic system based on pictures inspired him, but he said he has done the same thing for his other work as well. In his case, the pictures of his ideas become very elaborate, and from that elaborate graphic exercise his argument emerges.

English professor Andrea Lunsford explains that she must get the sense of the "arc" of her argument before she can write. She describes her work routine as "very sedentary; I don't get up and walk around. I do a lot of what I think looks like sitting and staring at the wall." That may seem unproductive, and she explains that it can be—but it can also be an idea incubator: "Eventually I'll make some notes." And then Professor Lunsford also moves to the visual: "It's like putting those dots—you know those things you get in cereal boxes and connect the dots and see what the picture is—and I'll start making the dots that will make the arc." Connecting all those dots makes for a cogent argument, an order or sequence, which unfolds like a storyboard for a film. "Essentially, I think of everything I'm writing as a kind of story I want to tell or argument I want to make, and so it has to have a beginning and it has to go somewhere." Once she feels she has that story, she can feel good about her arc and truly launch into her prose. Until then, she feels very uneasy.

Andrea Lunsford's attachment to the narrative character of an argument makes me understand even more deeply the way expository prose connects with fiction. A short story may not have an argument per se, but it does compel a belief of one sort or other; a poem drives at something, seeks to achieve an argument or counterpoint or language effect of sorts—even if that "argument" is very different in nature from one in an essay on social policy. Eavan Boland revealed that she does not write poems that are spontaneous bursts of inspiration: "I would certainly begin with some notes and sometimes things that are there which I would like to work with." She explained one poem she wrote when her daughter was a teenager: "Every time I saw her through a peek in the door, she had a Coke can beside her. I used to think, 'How would I ever get that into the poem? How would I ever depict a Coke can?'" Professor Boland explained that her process of composing a poem "wouldn't begin exactly with writing the poem; it would begin with the problem." And in this case, the problem was a can: "I didn't want to write the poem and leave out the Coke can."

Consciously including a Coke can is one challenge. For a lot of artists, discovering the content or theme or obsession for a piece or even for a body of work requires accessing the unconscious, using techniques similar to that of a forced five-minute deadline to articulate whatever might be hidden beneath the surface. Playwright David Henry Hwang spoke about exercises that he now teaches that help writers recognize the important messages in their work. In one, he has his students write a two-person scene, then he tells them to stop: "Draw a line across the page. And now we're going to continue writing that scene, but at intervals of between a minute and a minute and a half, I'm going to call out some random phrase—'lighting instrument' or 'water bottle'—and it's your job to incorporate that into the text." Hwang does that for some time; then he stops and has people read their work and compare the first half to the second half. While he emphasizes how individual the writing process is and hesitates to make generalizations, he is astonished at how this exercise still produces results:

> I would say nine times out of ten in this particular exercise, you find that the second half of the exercise is more interesting than the first. That is, when the writer was operating purely on his or her own kind of intellectual or cerebral steam in the first half, the work tends to be more predictable, less alive than in the second half, when the writer is really dealing with the total randomness of these phrases or words that are just kind of tossed out by the instructor.

Early in his career, Hwang started doing such exercises "to access my subconscious more." As a result, he would frequently surprise himself. "All these things started appearing on the page, you know—all these issues, whether it's cross-cultural or assimilation or East/West tension. And I began to realize that some part of me was, indeed, incredibly interested in these issues, but my conscious mind just hadn't caught up with that information yet." These exercises allowed him to experience those impulses that enable a writer to take a creative idea to another level:

> You're writing along and something comes into your head and you don't understand where it comes from, but you feel it strongly, you feel a strong compulsion to follow that, and it becomes a way to go. And sometimes you follow these seemingly irrational impulses and they lead you noplace, and then you go back to where you had the impulse and you start rewriting from there again. But oftentimes it's that impulse that really helps the work come to life.

Hwang gave the example of one of his early plays, called *The Dance and the Railroad*. Two Chinese railroad workers building the Central Pacific transcontinental railroad in 1867, one of them a master of Chinese dance, encounter each other during a strike in the Sierras: "I was writing along and writing along, and at some point I had the impulse that one of the characters should turn into a duck. And, you know, there was no actually rational justification for this. They weren't even near a pond or anything," he laughed. But because he felt that crazy impulse strongly, he went with it:

> And after a certain point, I began to realize that, oh, they're doing a sort of—you know, one is a Peking Opera actor who's been sold over here to do this work. They're off having a strike, and the other one wants to learn from him, and so they're doing acting exercises. And then the duck became a metaphor …

That metaphor was the argument or driving idea at the heart of his play, discovered by means of experimenting with an impulse.

Becoming a duck is not the same as wrestling with ethical issues pertaining to homeschooling or dissecting the social dynamic of the civil war in El Salvador. But—whether you're writing a first-hand account for an ethnographic study, or a review of the literature for a biology experiment, or a script for the theater, or a story—asserting that driving idea or theme propels an entire piece. Admittedly, it's not easy to develop an idea or a stance or an argument. Especially when life throws in a duck.

Gwyneth Lewis

CHAPTER SEVEN

∎ ∎ ∎

Thinking Modes, Writing Ways

IN THE LATE 1980s, Rebecca Solnit began to write differently after she began going to protests at the Nevada Test Site, the place where the U.S. had exploded more than a thousand nuclear bombs. "It's an incredibly rich, weird place," she explained. "It's a place where the histories of nuclear physics, of the making of the atom bomb, of civil disobedience and popular protest and direct action in American history converge with this history of physics, with the history of the Native Americans of the region, of attitudes towards the desert, of war and peace—of all these other things." How could she ever write about a place that was "so fascinating and rich"?

In academic circles, there are often distinct boundaries between different fields or disciplines, and there are good reasons these lines are drawn—as well as not-so-good petty jealousies and other trivial reasons. Knowing the distinct forms or modes appropriate for your field is crucial: a paper on nuclear physics written in the form of a poem won't get very far (although Lucretius could pull it off a couple of millennia ago). But there are constant challenges to these disciplinary borders, particularly for certain areas of the humanities and social sciences, not to mention for imaginative or "creative" writing.

But Solnit, an intellectual outside the academy, had an epiphany of sorts in the desert. She had been previously writing in three separate modes: she wrote criticism, "in this objective, godlike voice where supposedly the first person is removed to the objective," which becomes "authoritarian"; at the same time, she wrote "very subjective, lyrical essays"; and finally she was also doing environmental journalism. She found that, in order to write about the Nevada Test Site, she had to write in all three modes—in the journalistic, but also in the critical and lyrical modes.

Thinking Modes, Writing Ways 155

While in Nevada, she had very political experiences—getting hand-cuffed for committing civil disobedience to oppose nuclear weapons, for example. But as she waited to be carted away, she watched "an incredibly beautiful sunset, and smelled the creosote bush," and that pushed her to bring all three styles together and use them all at once. At that point she realized that "there's no reason why they ever were separated, and they never needed to be again." For her, a writer can't cut things off, can't compartmentalize information or segregate ways of thinking or modes of writing:

> One of the most important things for me has been preserving the range from investigative journalism to more lyrical and subjective prose, kinds of writing that correspond to varieties of awareness for me as well as to literary possibilities; or perhaps it makes more sense to say that I keep many styles or voices on hand for the subjects that arise. For me, this is about being a whole person, one who has epiphanies and engagements both—an invitation to readers to be both, to be their full selves, as well.

It would be unnatural, even violent, to cut off the different forms of awareness, "to not let them flow through these channels."

Such flow that Solnit describes disregards the fences or boundaries of these different forms of awareness, and she used her book on walking as an example: "If fields of expertise can be imagined as *real* fields, carefully tilled rectangles fenced off, then *[Wanderlust: A History of Walking]* trespasses through many of them," she said, describing one of her books. "So you think of these settled people, who have bodies of knowledge or *fields* of knowledge, which is a term we use all the time—I picture these *real* fields: these English agrarian plots with hedges around them." And with those hedges comes "a certain amount of territoriality." But her topics—and the way she thinks—cut through all these hedges, across any field that she seeks to trespass. "If walking is a subject," she explained, referring to her *History of Walking*, "it's a subject that's about human anatomy, about urbanism, about the rise of the environmental movement, about subjective and embodied consciousness, about gender politics and freedom of movement and dozens of other things. And so you have to write about all of them."

How then can the writer be identified, be situated? In writing about walking, to what field is she attached? "You're not an urbanist, you're not an anatomist, you're not an environmentalist—you're *all* of those things":

Everything that's interesting to me sprawls like that or travels like that. I use a lot of academic work, and it's incredibly valuable to me; but I feel like the academy has tended to privilege the knowledge that comes through the microscope. I'm interested in this panning, telescopic vision—that you see certain patterns when you look at something this big or far smaller. There are certain patterns that are huge, and to understand the world you also have to be free to look on that scale. That scale doesn't fit into fields. But it also comes very naturally to me. I'm interested in those associative patterns, those relationships between things.

The big picture is valuable and often hard to get. Biologist Terry Root, due to her dyslexia, could envision the ecology of continents, even though she had a harder time with smaller dimensions (such as a square acre), as many scientists do. Rebecca Solnit develops the grand vision as a habit of thought, untrammeled by borders.

Indeed, crossing boundaries comes naturally to Rebecca Solnit. That sort of trespass by an independent intellectual reminds me of one of the "forbidden" verses of Woody Guthrie's "This Land Is Your Land":

> As I went walking I saw a sign there
> And on the sign it said "No Trespassing."
> But on the other side it didn't say nothing,
> That side was made for you and me.

Most academics obey all of the signs; they rarely check out what's on the other side—and even if they wanted to, it's often very difficult to ramble across those hedges.

Rebecca Solnit writes outside of any institutional or academic boundaries, and she's well aware that her outsider status flows from what she's investigated in her work:

> In a sense, my subject has always been outside—from the outside that is the landscape and the environment to the public space of cities in which popular politics unfold as marches, demonstrations, and revolutions—but also the outside of outsiders: from the Beat artists of the West Coast, who are the subject of my first book twenty years ago, who taught me much about outside, to the ways that change and innovation often come from the shadows and the

margins—from radicals, indigenous movements, dreamers, and unreasonable people.

These are people on the margins; but for Solnit, these are "the margins of hope."

Susan Krieger is a sociologist, an innovator of feminist methodology in the social sciences who also rambles through the hedges; she also writes about people on the margins, except she's doing so within the boundaries of academia. She simply and boldly changed the nature of those boundaries. Methodology in any field often has a big "No Trespassing" sign on it, keeping strangers out; but today it's not uncommon in anthropology, sociology, or other fields to be self-reflective, to include the first-person viewpoint, to delve into the personal in order to understand the world— which are some of the features of the feminist approach to scholarly work. Yet it hasn't been easy gaining acceptance for this approach. Krieger has written widely on different subjects—her first sociological study was *Hip Capitalism*, for example—but her books are mostly about women's communities and women's consciousness. Recently she found herself losing her sight—a harrowing experience, of course—but she ended up expanding her "vision" as she was losing her sight, and wrote about that transformation in *Traveling Blind: Adventures in Vision with a Guide Dog by My Side* and *Things No Longer There*. Her approach was to explore her personal perspective as her experience intersected broader social concerns.

It can be a struggle being an innovator in the academic environment. Krieger wrote her dissertation in a novelistic style, for example, and as a result, "I had to do extra requirements to prove I was conventional enough. And they warned me, 'You'll never get a job.' But I kept going." When she wrote *Hip Capitalism*, at least one editorial reviewer suggested that she find a better topic. When she submitted *The Mirror Dance*, a study of a lesbian intentional community, publishers threw it back at her because she employed the voices of her subjects, having them speak for themselves— sort of like a documentary without a narrator—and the editors "wanted an authorial narrative." She wanted a chorus; they wanted a solo performance—and her unconventional style did not appeal to them.

She finally found an editor at a university press who was a playwright. "I like the multiple voices," he confessed. "That's what a playwright does." So it was published. *The Mirror Dance* turned out to be very popular among people "who like somewhat unconventional things." Her next book was more conventional, "a little more straight social science, because I was making an argument; I wasn't just playing with all the voices." But then some of the people who had liked her previous book said they were "disappointed it was linear." She relies on the feedback of her readers, but it was clear that she would constantly perplex or disappoint at least a certain number of people.

Then she began writing about memory and insight, about inner vision—and coincidentally, at roughly the same time, she began to lose her eyesight. She found it fortuitous that she discovered insight just as her ability to see outward was becoming impaired. That made her realize that what was unconventional about her work was not any of the topics, but her method. "To me, method, how the thing is done—the 'how'—is most important," she said. "How I structure a study, how I structure a book-length piece, how the details are organized, how the voice goes along with what it says, what it does, how the pieces are put together—this is the crucial thing." She was always interested in method, and her realizations about vision seemed a continuation of that interest: *How* does one see?

What makes her writing new, as she goes on with her research studies, is that "my degree of intimacy increases, I think, and it broadens in some respects; I take on new subjects." Her more recent work, she believes, "has a much greater sense of intimacy, honesty, presence":

> I'm always trying to draw great honesty from within myself and describe many details, let's say, that in my mind are throwing light on the experience of blindness, or what vision is about, or trying to convey in that book through my writing what happens with blindness. I'm using the writing to do that without even saying that the writing is doing that.

She noted that someone who's outside of academia can read *Traveling Blind* and say, "Oh, but it's so detailed. The pace is so slow. You're telling us about every this and that." She pays a lot of attention to those details because she tells the reader about the world as perceived by a blind person traveling with a guide dog. "You *have* to notice every this and that, or you're going to trip over and fall. And I'm trying to figure things out anew and figure out how to be safe when traveling blind. And you do this detailed little work. I'm not telling you the story in order to entertain you and give you the conventional smooth read." As a consequence, *Traveling*

Blind is not mass-market literature: "It's really a very studied, very disciplined presentation of an experience, and I know that. So in a way, people in different places will like and appreciate it very much, but I won't appeal to the popular audience as much as they might have first hoped because it is unconventional. It is a unique creation."

Other writers, such as Fred Turner, have also crisscrossed the boundaries of genres and methods. Fred Turner began as a poet in college, then went to graduate school to become a literary scholar, left school and began writing theater reviews in Berlin, and then wrote reviews back in the U.S., where he got experience in more types of journalism, including investigative reporting, before eventually joining Stanford's Department of Communication. When he started to write for newspapers, he learned to cough up very brief, 600-word articles; and he found that his previous experience writing poems was actually a valuable skill, since poetry demands that the writer be very concise in order to create tight images or other literary effects—and he brought his journalistic experience of writing in this very economical manner to his academic work.

Today Professor Turner writes cultural history—such as *From Counterculture to Cyberculture,* a study of the relationship between 1960s social experimentation and the rise of computers—and he finds himself tramping across the multiple fields Rebecca Solnit describes. This multidisciplinary approach draws from his previous career as a journalist: "I still operate full on in the faith that the best thing you can do around a problem that you're interested in is to attack it from every direction, use every available tool, and trust your own instincts." For Turner, a professor of communication, that is not an impediment; given his experience, "academic work is journalism on steroids—what journalism is supposed to be. It's sort of journalism done with enough time to really do the research, enough analytical training and enough analytical tools to do really rich analytical thinking. So I still think I'm a journalist."

As a journalist-academic, Turner draws upon diverse intellectual sources beyond the strict boundaries of his department: "My intellectual home is on my bookshelves, in some of the books that are there. It's in the social and professional networks that I travel in." He considers himself part of a scene, and not an individual genius. He employs a phrase coined by Brian Eno, describing himself as a "scenius": "*Genius* is this thing that we imagine bubbles up out of us individually," he explained. *Scenius* is the kind of smarts that you get being a part of a really good *scene.*" In his book on the development of cyberculture, he draws upon the work of that broader scene: "I'm using a lot of good science technology studies and some good sociology and some good history. One of the challenges for someone starting a new book, as I am now, is: what scene can you place yourself in that will feed you richly? And that's a challenge wherever you are."

Even though Professor Turner feels that his academic books are a lot like investigative reporting, it's still a strain to write for the academy, even if the number of readers is limited. It can be a small world, with sometimes twenty or forty people at the core of any particular field: "In the academic setting, I feel like I'm often writing at a cocktail party." It's as if those few people are all at the same party together, each one listening to you, and each one eager to see if you mention their name in your conversation so they can feel good about themselves. That can be tough, and even a possible source of writer's block:

> It can be quite crippling—if you hear them all waiting for you. And so part of the challenge I've found in an academic setting is learning how to speak from within a discipline, and speak to that discipline, without being crippled by the sense that everybody out there on whom my dissertation, Ph.D., then job, and now tenure, depend, is listening. And that's quite hard to do.

There's a lot at stake in this "cocktail party," since in academic writing any field's lingo or jargon "is about asserting membership in groups so as to claim power and go forward institutionally. When you speak in a plain speech style you forfeit some of that power." Susan Krieger, for example, seemed to violate or push beyond her field's accustomed boundaries, as previously determined by sociologists, and did write in accessible prose.

These divisions are made even more troubling for any interdisciplinary approach because there are also great divisions between types of writing, such as between "creative writing" and "creative nonfiction." For critic of American poetry Albert Gelpi, all good writing is "creative writing, not just poems and stories and plays." The writer finds something that "calls out to you, that calls you out; it's the calling or vocation of writing. In my case, it was writing about poetry, especially about American poetry." Even in an assigned writing job, you can find:

> … something that grabs you, sparks you, draws you out. The engagement between writer and subject matter works both ways:

as you explore and clarify and give definition to the topic in the combining and shaping of words, you are in that process exploring and clarifying and giving definition to something in yourself, something of yourself.

In this creative calling out and pulling in, content—"the synthesis of craft and subject matter"—plays a critical role. Professor Gelpi quotes poet Robert Creeley: "Form is never more than an extension of content." And, as Gelpi points out, "Content is never more than an expression of form." Another poet, Denise Levertov, revised Creeley's dictum, "to give it another inflection: 'Form is never more than the *revelation* of content.' Form, in other words, both explores and contains content; craft both defines and discloses, and sometimes even discovers, meaning. It opens to close; it closes to open."

All of this flow of craft and subject matter, form and content, closing and opening, sounds right; but it can be difficult when you cross those accustomed boundaries, particularly when there are those people impatiently waiting at that cocktail party who are not as broad-minded as Albert Gelpi when it comes to understanding the nature of creativity and writing. Susan Krieger, writing as a sociologist, produces unconventional work that in many respects approaches the personal essay; Rebecca Solnit crisscrosses journalism, history, personal reflection, philosophy, science, sociology, and ethnography as she wanders through all the hedges and stone fences from one field to another without the constraints of academic enforcers. For lack of a better word (or of imagination), Solnit's work often gets labeled as "creative nonfiction."

"Creative nonfiction is a terrible word," Solnit observed; it's a kind of closet in which to shove certain types of writing, particularly a lot of her own work. "Creative nonfiction" is a descriptive term defined by its negative being, since *fiction* is so privileged in the eyes of so many in the literary world that it has become "the measure of all things." For her, creative *non*fiction "is the literature that is *not*." Because creative nonfiction is something other than "fiction"—and fiction is valued as the height of literature—it's been given "the embarrassing epithet 'creative.' Creative nonfiction is an amorphous term for amorphous literature, from experimental prose to journalistic reports. And perhaps that's good. Perhaps it's better to be free-roaming on the open prairie than held captive in the castle."

Literature as a castle with many rooms is yet another figure Solnit employs to describe the tyranny of categorization: "Picture literature as a castle with a moat, with its ivory towers, dungeons, bedrooms, and thrones," and the castle with many rooms describes the ways different types of writing are regarded:

> Most of my life, the castle was meant to be for poetry and fiction, and something about the way the two were constantly grouped together suggested that they were akin: the Duchess and Earl of Literature, perhaps, or King and Queen, though it's terrible to think of them as married. Surely, poetry would be a slender, quiet person overwhelmed by the noisy novel. Let's give them separate quarters.

Being inside the castle is "an equivocal fate," since one is confined "and a lot defined and studied and dissertated upon." However, that castle, like a fortress, is a gated community, defined "as much about who is outside" as on what's locked inside. It's true that her own "nomad literature" can be seen "as a camp outside the gates of the castle," and as a result "have fewer official rewards and less prestige."

With attention in literary circles more focused on fiction and poetry, what could be said about the lowly essay? "Who ever wanted to grow up to be the great American essayist, after all?" But, as Solnit points out, "Montaigne wrote his essays a century or more before the novel was born, though the romance had flourished earlier." And much early poetry was essayistic: "You can consider poems like Lucretius's *On the Nature of the Universe* or Virgil's *Georgics* as earlier ancestors, and as reminders that even instruction manuals used to be written in verse. Once upon a time, everything was poetry," and today, "a lot of the contemporary poetry I like best is essayistic, often autobiographical—a crossroads of emotions, ideas, experiences, reflections, and descriptions." And much poetry is "non-fiction" —but, again, by using that term, "fiction" becomes the defining genre; a piece of writing is categorized as something that it is *not*.

But Rebecca Solnit weighed alternate ways of regarding the whole process. Imagine that perhaps "there is no castle, and that we're free to map literature and writing in myriad other ways. If literature were a castle or a palace," she mused, "I snuck in its back entrance as an editor, a critic, and a journalist, being cautious about which doors I knocked on and what claims I made." No matter how she got into the castle, she's there—and her claims are increasingly accepted.

■ ■ ■

Susan Krieger's observation about "plain speech" and academic power has a lot of implications that political science professor Terry Karl has considered in depth. Karl writes in a wide range of styles as an academic (lately writing about the problems of the "oil curse" affecting developing nations), but also as a consultant for nongovernmental organizations dealing with human rights, and as an expert witness in trials bringing to justice people accused of death squad murders in El Salvador, testifying before congressional hearings. Because of her experience writing in all of these arenas, she developed a rule. She already had her "Not *Murder, She Wrote* Rule," which is: Always state right up front who actually did commit "the murder"; there's no mystery about it. That is, always put your argument or conclusion at the top; there's no need to build to a climax for a basic political science essay: tell them what you know, explain how you know it, then tell it to the readers again.

Her second rule is a bit different. She calls it "The Fidel Castro Rule," choosing that moniker after an epiphany she had while doing research in Cuba. She described watching the revolutionary leader give one of his famously long orations on a very complicated political issue:

> There were thousands of people listening to him, and I realized that they were all kinds of people—people from the University of Havana, whom I happened to be with, and a peasant who looked like he had come from a rural area outside Havana, who told me that he was very proud because he had just reached the sixth-grade level. He was an elderly man and had not been educated prior to the Cuban Revolution. So I was looking at this range of people, and I was realizing that Fidel Castro was able somehow to explain an extremely complicated political phenomenon that we teach courses on at Stanford in a way that everybody in that particular space understood, in this range of people. I never forgot that, and to myself I say it's the "Fidel Castro Rule"—and that means that we ought to be able to take, in our writing and in our talking, the most complicated things and make them understandable to all kinds of people.

The academy, Professor Karl noted, is often where "we're rewarded for being as obscure as possible," but the "Fidel Castro Rule" is different: "If my writing is too complicated or if I am not expressing myself as clearly as possible, I actually think that's *my* problem and not my reader's problem."

The "Fidel Castro Rule" means aspiring to write in such a way that your work can be available to a broader public (such a goal is not about politics, despite invoking the Cuban revolutionary's name—unless accessibility is political). Sometimes academics do pump up the arcane language to give themselves a type of magic power; but in a lot of fields, especially the social and natural sciences, there are often simply too many technical terms that are needed for an essay to be made easily available to the uninitiated public. Psychologist Claude Steele explained that he would write an article for professional journals after he completed an experiment, and he would produce, quite simply, a report. "Most of the time that's what you're doing," he explained. "You've done this piece of research. You've talked about it with your collaborators. They're sick of you. You've analyzed the data, you've gone back and forth, and now you know what you've found, and you're reporting that." Hazel Markus, also a psychologist, concurred, explaining that writing is often secondary:

> The main process is doing the research. It's doing the science. So all of your effort is focused on designing the most elegant experiment that you possibly can and then executing that experiment. And then hopefully your results have something to do with what you predicted, what you hypothesized. And then there's this final stage of writing it up. And we tend to think in the social sciences of—well, that's just the last step, the way to convey the results of your science, get it out there into the world.

Poor writing, lack of clarity—all of those things will interfere with such a report, but what's central is the scientific results of the research you're reporting on. "It's easy to be a scientist and not worry very much about writing—to worry a lot more about the nature of the research and the design and the statistics and those kinds of things," according to Professor Steele. Still, while the experiment's design and results are crucial, "getting it out there" is also basic. As chemist Richard Zare points out, if you don't communicate your findings well enough, if people can't understand what your discoveries may be, your work might as well not exist.

But then there's the scientific or academic mode—prose filled with technical terms and concepts that have all the appearance of true science but can sometimes be exceedingly difficult for the uninitiated. And that doesn't count prose that's been purposely made murky in order to show off some kind of superiority. Claude Steele only half-jokingly said that sometimes the notes that students leave on his office door are better written than the papers they end up handing in to him in class. "They just write the note—just write it, you know. And it's clear and good and it says just what they wanted to say and it's cool. But the paper they write—they want to get in that scientific persona and *sound* like a scientist to be credible." For good science writers it's a phase to pass through, to *sound* like a scientist. But there is a payoff for clarity: As Hazel Markus noted, for scientists who can write well, "their work has a lot more impact, because if it's written well, the article will have legs. People will give it to somebody else to read, and they'll start reading it; and being able to follow it and finding it interesting, they'll continue to read it, and that work will just get much more broadly disseminated"—and with much wider impact than something poorly written or unnecessarily difficult. Richard Zare, for example, writing about lasers, employs vivid metaphors, not distracting but lively, when talking about concepts. And even someone outside of the field, like me, can at least engage in what his report may convey, if not understand it completely.

The writing, however, needs to stay within accepted bounds in terms of metaphors and other conventions. Don Barr, a physician who is also a sociologist, pointed out that a journal article makes only one or two major points based on the research, that it's basically restrained—or constrained—by the limits of the data. Typically in natural or social sciences, the conclusions stay close to the vest. He related that several editors chastised him for going "a little too far" when he went from presenting his findings without much discussion or interpretation to extrapolating from them "what I think the implications of this knowledge are." The article is evaluated on the presentation of that new knowledge—the results of an experiment or analysis. "Don't tell us what you *think* about the world," the editor would discipline him. While you can describe what you think the importance of the knowledge may be, "if you start taking yourself a little bit too seriously," you will get a rap across your knuckles. "In one paper I pointed out that if you apply sociological theory to the issue of managed healthcare, you conclude that HMOs are never going to solve the problem of American healthcare. What you really then need is the government to step in and solve the problems." If he had only said that HMOs will never work, he might have gotten the article published. But he kept on going, saying, "Now that I've shown you that, let me tell you what I think about it," and what to do about that fact. It's at that point that he crossed over the line; he transgressed, and the field took out its whip to enforce some discipline. There are proper places for opinion pieces—biologist Donald Kennedy was editor of *Science* and managed to regularly put out policy opinions in tight 800-word editorials—but most research-based articles keep their conclusions very modest.

Empirical researchers do write broader articles, drawing from previous work. After reporting on a series of experiments, a scientist can, according to Claude Steele, try "to integrate this into a theory—a large theory that's got a couple of simple ideas, that's going to explain a lot of things." The theoretical paper involves a very different kind of writing than the report on research, "and there, I think, your writing is a lot more important" than in the report on empirical findings from one place. Professor Steele had done many experiments on how socially constructed images affect performance, and he gave it a name: "stereotype threat." "It's interesting, but the name for that phenomenon didn't come until the article was all written and accepted and it was in galleys," he explained. "I can remember calling the journal and saying, 'Is it too late to change the name?' So the name for it came after that kind of long, delayed process." In such a way, the search for one theoretical concept—and the apt name to describe it—resulted from the range of multiple empirical studies.

Interestingly, writing isn't even the main vehicle for a lot of scientific reporting; charts, numbers, diagrams, graphs are far more important. Scientists and engineers are very data driven, according to materials scientist John Bravman. "We're writing about data, we're writing about how we obtain the data, what the data is, and what we think it means. And then sometimes we make models of the data, too," he explained. In a nutshell, that describes a lot of scientists—crunching numbers and measurements. Many, like Bravman, are visually oriented as a consequence:

> When you write your paper, the first thing you have to do is to assemble the sets of data, be it numerical, be it pictorial, micrographic, what have you—assemble the data that's going to carry the story forward. Make sure you have that, not necessarily in

final form—but assemble your story in pictures, because so often one graph, one micrograph, will replace hundreds or even thousands of words. So, get the illustrations lined up and ready to go, and then write the story around that.

For John Bravman, it's a story—with beginning, middle, and end—that gets first established with the illustrations. He and other scientists and engineers confessed that they don't read a journal article in a linear fashion; they skim the abstract and the conclusions, and then skip to the charts and diagrams before reading from the beginning.

Of course, this data story has to hold together. Philosopher Debra Satz observed that it seems as if the norm in social science papers, such as in economics, is "to have almost as little prose as possible, and as many formulas. Sometimes you're trying to figure out what work is the formula really doing in this paper." And the formula may only be a type of orientation. "It's not clear that the formula is doing very much work. You could actually say in words what the formula is doing, but the field values technical writing." In a lot of disciplines, numbers trump words in terms of style as well as content.

But let's get back to the "Fidel Castro Rule." A lot of academics want to write for popular audiences, despite all the slanders that academics love to be obscurantist snobs. When you have an insight or idea and "you want to take that idea and tell your family about it or the lawyer on the train about it, that's a different kind of impulse" than one for writing a psychology journal article, Claude Steele said. "For me, it's a very different type of space to be in," and he actually moves to a different room to write this type of essay. "You're much more worried about making sure the sentences are being clear and being understandable to a broad audience in that kind of work than, again, the scientific stuff. You want that to be really clear and good, solid and coherent." As Hazel Markus explained, "I've come to realize that the writing component is not just a way to communicate what you've found. It's really a way in which you can light up aspects of reality that weren't available to you before, that you couldn't see."

Writing to reach a mass audience doesn't come without effort to many scientists, and sometimes it results in unintended consequences. Biologist Robert Sapolsky has been able to write for the broader readerships of *The New Yorker* and other magazines because, as he says with some irony, he wasn't "terribly well trained as a scientist." He described himself as "the social science type" who never took any chemistry or physics in college. "I don't have a very good fundamental grounding, so I am easily panicked and can easily imagine how somebody else can be too." Obviously, he did catch up on his science education, but he also did his graduate work at a school that didn't have any teaching assistant positions, as they do in a lot of universities. "So I figured out how to moonlight," he said, which meant that he taught at The New School for Social Research in New York. Right at that time, a fashion school in New York had just lost its academic accreditation, "so they shut out all their tenured non-design faculty and forced their students to go to The New School to take their non-design courses." The fashion school had a science requirement, and Sapolsky ended up teaching one of the required science courses: "So I would get these classes full of these unbelievably hostile, phobic, teeny-bopper textile designers, and this forced an enormous pressure to be clear, to learn when to stop and use an anecdote or a metaphor or something. I think that in retrospect it was very good training."

Eric Roberts teaches computer science, and he learned the equivalent of his own "Fidel Castro Rule" when he taught for the first time after getting his Ph.D. He taught at a women's college outside of Boston for five years where he learned "to inverse the gender stereotypes. All my best students were women—ALL my students were women—and you can't use male-oriented examples; it doesn't work," he explained. When he came to co-ed Stanford, he still ditched all male-oriented examples in his lectures: the football metaphors were gone, along with "any third-person pronouns whose gender can be identified." He developed all sorts of strategies in his teaching that he then applied to writing textbooks, "to adjust the writing to make sure that you avoid putting anyone off, and those are things you acquire with practice, certainly the non-gendered language. The lack of examples that would be likely to alienate any particular audience is something I've worked very hard to achieve," he said, and he employs all of these practices in his textbooks to make complicated ideas about computers and programming accessible to everyone.

John Hennessy, computer scientist as well as president of Stanford, coauthored a major textbook; and he, too, found ways to reach the uninitiated. Like Roberts, he and his coauthor used a wide range of cultural references. Each chapter typically begins with a quote to illuminate a major concept. He gave an example of the epigraph for "a chapter that talks about computer languages and how they're translated into machine languages." Hennessy recalled the quote, attributed to King Charles V, which goes something like: "I speak Spanish to God, Italian to women, French to men, and German to my horse." That analogy seemed to capture the relationships between computer and machine languages. For Hennessy, employing examples or analogies is key to explaining the science, and he noted how he uses "either very concrete examples that use particular situations, or they're analogy examples where we're trying to give the reader for a very complex topic a simple way to understand it." He emphasized how critical these types of analogies are in helping students to master the conceptual frameworks. With this groundwork, they can then go on to more advanced work.

When physicist Leonard Susskind writes for readers who are not scientists, he produces a first draft in what he calls "journalese"—the esoteric scientific language of a science journal. He read out loud the first draft of a paragraph on entropy from a book he was writing at that time, which revolved around the scientific exchanges he's had with Stephen Hawking and other physicists. His first shot at "entropy" was, "Entropy is the logarithm of the number of configurations of a system subject to a set of constraints.... For a classical system, it is related to a volume ... while for a quantum system ... the number of discrete quantum states...." He went on like that for six or seven pages in the first round. "By this time I had already written enough to know that it was very boring," he explained. "But also by that time, I had confidence in my ability to do something good with it or something at least decent with it." So he estimated that he revised that description of entropy a hundred times before he finally found a way to explain the concept in a highly accessible descriptive style:

> It's a bad idea to park your BMW in a rainforest for 500 years. When you come back, you'll find a pile of rust. That's entropy increasing. Leave the rust pile for another 500 years and you can be sure that it won't turn back into a working BMW. That, in short, is the second law of thermodynamics ...

He went on in his explanation, but you get the idea.

Again, not every editor likes scientific prose to be approachable. Professor Susskind had an encounter with *Scientific American* years ago that he described as "bizarre." He considered the quality of writing in the magazine at that time to be terrible and boring overall, although the first introductory paragraphs in most articles were often very interesting. "Then they sink into this 'Scientific Americanese'—not even journalese—and they all sound the same." He asked a friend, a scientist who can write well, what had happened to his writing after one of his articles appeared in the magazine:

> Sure enough, first paragraph is great and then it sinks into the usual stuff. I asked him, "What goes on here? Why did you do this? I know you can write." He said, "No, you don't understand. The editors force you to write that way." They do not allow you to write to allow your own soul to come through, except in the first couple of paragraphs.

The time would come when Professor Susskind would have his showdown with those editors.

Scientific American invited him to write an article, which he crafted in the narrative style he prefers, beginning with "an amusing courtroom battle between two physicists, one who threw the other one's computer in a black hole and ..." But it came back from the magazine radically changed, with all of the narrative explanation taken out of it. "They already had sent me $1000, so I was caught—and I wasn't going to be caught. I sent it back and said—I wrote one sentence—and the one sentence said, '*You puncture my prose, I break-a you face.*'" A little bit of his Bronx had slipped out, and he laughed as he told the story. That wasn't the end of it; he kept wrestling with the editors, again and again, and they eventually gave up. He noted with satisfaction that the article ended up winning a major prize for scientific writing, "and now they go around boasting about it."

What sweet revenge. But perhaps because Professor Susskind is a renowned physicist, he doesn't get anxious about trying to reach the layperson in addition to fellow scientists. But others, especially in the social sciences, have to deal with doubters. As psychologist Hazel Markus put it, social scientists "have worried so much for so long about being identified as 'real scientists,'" and I actually witnessed a social scientist and a natural scientist almost come to blows on a panel because the natural scientist did not think her colleague was doing "real science." To compensate, many social scientists feel forced "to write with a jargon that will show that you're a scientist. And if you pull back and have it in everyday language, that somehow makes you *not* as scientific, *not* as smart as the others." Philosopher

Debra Satz notes, "Some of the humanities—maybe English at times—have tried to emulate that in having very technical-sounding writing that's very hard for a layperson to just pick up." Murky, obscurantist prose often grows from anxieties, not from the subject.

Many scientists don't write for lay readers at all, simply because they don't want to reach the nonspecialist—or, as Robert Sapolsky noted, they feel there's no way they could explain what they do "without becoming totally simplistic and distortive." And if they try to write to educate the masses, they're liable to be scorned in even more ways than Hazel Markus described. According to Sapolsky, "There's even a snotty term in science for what this is about":

> Carl Sagan with his billions and billions of stars—he's like the most successful science writer of his time, and, as a result of doing that, he totally destroyed his scientific career. And the snotty term that's used for it among scientists is that one gets "Saganized." There's a presumption that if you're spending so much time doing this that you can't possibly do good, serious science anymore. And it actually did quite literally damage his professional career.

I was shocked. The late Cornell astronomer and TV host of the PBS hit show *Cosmos* was beloved by millions, yet Sagan was dismissed by many of his peers. Astronomers assume that the cosmos cannot be simplified, and that by trying to write for a broader audience the work becomes distorted—and the scientist is distracted from his real research. (I suspect that Sagan may have also been belittled because he was so lionized by the public; a little jealousy may have been at play.)

As a result, while Robert Sapolsky has great fun writing for nonscientific publications, he purposely restricts that writing time to the duration of his commute by train between San Francisco and Stanford. That way he limits his *New Yorker* output so he doesn't get Saganized by producing too much for readers outside the neuroscience universe; he would not want to be known as a *mere* popularizer and not the expert on stress and stress-related disease (with lots of fieldwork with primates) that he is. Still, he can't help but enjoy himself producing essays with mass appeal: "I constantly crank out pieces that get back to the same theme: 'Genes do not determine behavior; genes do not determine anything; there's next to no genetic determinism; this is politically dangerous—blah, blah.' And these articles wind up being really preachy and irritating." But he tries to break away from the sermonizing, and one essay he thinks was very effective was a response he wrote to something he'd seen in *People* magazine.

Professor Sapolsky had become an avid reader of *People* magazine in order to tune in to the gossip that constitutes much of popular culture, and he was delighted with their annual issue listing the fifty most beautiful people in the world:

> What they do is they have sort of a theme each year. And that year their theme was "nature or nurture—what explains the secrets of the fifty most beautiful people on Earth?" And they asked each one of these people where they thought their beauty came from. This was like to die for; you could not have asked for more ludicrous, fabulous stuff. And the people had these utterly bizarre environmentalist stances. Ben Affleck said it's all due to his cosmetic dentistry. This was his explanation. And then the other extreme: Gwyneth Paltrow had her grandfather come in, and [he] says, "She was like this from birth"—which makes sense of probably why the two of them [Paltrow and Affleck] didn't stay together as a pair (and I actually know that because, if *People* magazine didn't write it, I'd have no idea who these people are). This was perfect, and I wound up writing this very sarcastic piece about the fifty most beautiful people in the world who debate the nature-nurture question.

In this debate, someone came up with what's currently accepted as the scientific position, "which is, genes affect how you interact with the environment and the environment affects how you interact with your genes." It was a pop singer's mother who encapsulated this idea: "Her mother was explaining, 'It's all due to her cosmetics skill'—and then she says, 'She was just born knowing how to put on makeup!' A gene/environment interaction exactly!" Sapolsky got excited: "This is great—Can you believe this?—I think this is fabulous. Too bad people can't think about this when they think about what genes have to do with IQ or aggression or criminality"—and something along those lines was how he concluded his essay. He hoped his article served a purpose by explaining this concept, but he realized that he had had to simplify it, and lots of scientists would get on his case for doing just that.

So, was he Saganized? Was his scientific reputation jeopardized? Most of the scientists I spoke with didn't think he would have a problem. Donald Kennedy, biologist, former Stanford president, and the editor of *Science* at that time, believed his reputation was secure. But Professor Sapolsky wasn't so sure: maybe it's "just my rationalizing every time I get a crappy grant score [the evaluation of a grant proposal]. But every now and then I do get evidence that this is the case." It makes him nervous, and he explained the example of how the articles submitted to professional journals are reviewed anonymously—the author never learns the names of reviewers, and such professional anonymity "allows people to be just total shits to each other in this business, and it's really brutal. I am guaranteed if, in some paper of mine, all I need is like one incoherent sentence in there, and there is going to be a snotty comment: 'Boy, for someone who publishes in this and that, that was sure incoherent; I have no idea what you're saying!'" He concluded that the anonymous review was "a really good realm for settling scores and undermining stuff.... It's a very childish arena of science." It sounds like the anonymity that the Internet allows for a troll, or that a windshield provides so that one irate motorist can give another driver the finger.

Hazel Markus believes it's absolutely critical for people in psychology and social sciences to reach the broader public. She noted that in the current political climate there are lots of people who talk about issues pertaining to education, the family, employment, and welfare, and these pontificators are people "who have no clue at all; who have no social science at all." As a consequence, those who do know what they're talking about need to inject their views or else the policy outcomes could be terrible. Just think of climate change or embryonic cell research or teacher evaluations:

> I think the social scientists almost have to just say, "Okay, we're going to go right into the fray and use as much everyday language as we can and try to popularize our ideas." I mean, some of your science colleagues may, you know, wonder what you're doing there. But I think we have to do it. The responsibility is on us.

She admitted that she had previously held a very different idea of what it means to be a scientist:

> As a scientist, I grew up with the idea that you do the science, put

it in the journals, and then there would be sort of a cadre of people who would come along and read the journals and then turn it into nice, interesting, everyday, very user-friendly language. Well, guess what? Those people don't exist.

Hazel Markus realized that, with the cadre of explainers not there, she has to do the explaining herself. She's no longer worried about being Saganized; she believes that "it's better to get your ideas out there" than for them to be ignored or abused.

Philosopher Debra Satz has her own "Fidel Castro Rule"—she writes for her mother:

> The good virtue of philosophy is, because of the intention of the argument, it's very clear. So clarity of expression is really valued. Philosophy has a very clean, clear way of writing. My mother could pick it up and understand it. My mother didn't go to college. And I write with her in mind, that I want her to be able to understand what I'm writing.

Because philosophy, especially analytic philosophy, emphasizes argument, plain prose is regarded as a suitable vehicle for expressing that argument, and there is less attention or value placed on style. "John Rawls, who is probably the most important philosopher of the twentieth century, is not a very eloquent writer." In fact, there is a long-standing suspicion of eloquence or rhetorical effects that goes back to Plato. Will the reader be swayed by sweet palaver or by clear reasoning? As Professor Satz emphasized, "The bottom line is, do you have good reasons for your positions?" Eloquence or literary felicities are not encouraged.

While reasoning is crucial and clarity considered basic, philosophy also values complexity. Troy Jollimore, analytic philosopher as well as poet, shared the story of a friend who had sent an essay to a journal. This philosopher's essay was rejected with a surprising comment from one of the submission reviewers: "It's too clear. This paper is too clear." Jollimore and his friend were astonished. How could something be *too* clear? This reader, however, expected that use of complex language was necessary in order to convey complex ideas—and perhaps by "too clear" he meant that the language was lucid but simplistic, and might not effectively carry the logic of the complicated argument. When I suggested that complex ideas do not need to be expressed in convoluted sentences, that these ideas can be "unpacked" and presented in a series of simpler sentences, a philosopher in our conversation's audience disagreed. She insisted that multiple clauses and subordinations and other stylistic gnarls were necessary to convey qualifications, objections, counterarguments, and other subtleties of logical thinking. "You want to make the point so specific that it's not misunderstood or taken to mean something else," according to that philosopher in the audience. "This is a characteristic of philosophy. You have to be very precise. And so sometimes precision cannot be put in a very simple way."

Preference for this knotted way of writing flows from the way some philosophers regard their field. Philosophers have a "scientific notion of progress," Jollimore explained. "We have this idea of an ultimate goal, which is a complete, thorough understanding of whatever the subject matter is, that will be comprehensive and it will take everything into account. And everything true that's ever been said about this thing has to somehow be incorporated into that and be reconciled into that." All of this creates a set of responsibilities and constraints, taking into account the tradition and possible objections, but also trying to explore ideas in new ways—by not saying something that's already been said, and at the same time not being superficial. "So that leads, sometimes, at least in my writing," one philosopher explained, "to the tendency to pack sentences with a lot of qualifications to avoid possible objections, to define the point so it's not a simple point, to take into account all those people who have come before. So as you go along writing your article or your book, more points come in—the possible qualifications—so that sentences start to grow exponentially." Consequently there's a real tension, and what passes for clarity may actually be oversimplification.

Of course, not every philosopher works in this way. Richard Rorty remembered how, in graduate school, he "had to throw in a lot of symbolic logic, and break down arguments into numbered premises. So I dutifully wrote that way—and the result was pretty awful. I remember one paper I wrote on [Ludwig] Wittgenstein that had forty-seven numbered propositions. It read like a parody of itself." Rorty eventually "boiled it down to twenty-two and published it." But he went through a period of "trying desperately to sound properly professional because philosophy was going through one of its spells of hyper-professionalization. I wasn't good at it, but I tried."

Rorty's writing style took a radically different direction after his friend from graduate school, Harold Bloom, published a groundbreaking book of literary criticism. Bloom had produced "standard-model books the first couple of times around" about Wallace Stevens and other writers, but in 1973 he published *The Anxiety of Influence: A Theory of Poetry*, a book that:

> … was like nothing he'd ever written before and like nothing anybody else had ever written, except maybe Nietzsche. I thought: Geez, if Harold can do it maybe I can do it too. So I loosened up a bit. It was the spectacle of Bloom breaking out of the English professor's mold and writing to please himself that encouraged me to write more to please myself.

Indeed, Rorty did break the philosophy mold. It was a gamble that paid off, at least in terms of readership. As he veered from the standard model in his field, his audience expanded as a result. He was able to play a role as a public intellectual, jumping into debates, influencing readers far beyond the bounds of academia.

Richard Rorty never wrote novels or poetry. But Troy Jollimore is a poet as well as a philosopher. It's typically hard to write in a completely different mode or genre from what you've been trained to inhabit, with each mode and each field demanding very unique ways of thinking and writing. But I've learned that Jollimore is not the only writer crossing into different realms: for example, Welsh poet Gwyneth Lewis recently started writing plays, and she thrilled at the idea of "using someone else's body," feeling a type of megalomania—and then of course there's anthropologist Renato Rosaldo's stroke-induced awakening to verse.

Still, poetry and analytic philosophy seem like two very radically different approaches to thinking, much less writing, despite the fact that "they are both about, in some sense, understanding and coming to understand the world better than you did before," despite the chasm between the two. "A poem can get away with a lot more than a philosophical text can," Jollimore noted:

> If you're partway through a poem and it's been a good reading experience up to this point—which is what you want a poem to be, right? That's its raison d'être. So you get to a certain point and it's good; what do you do to keep it good? You can do anything. Anything that works is fair game. So you can follow up what you have so far with an utter non sequitur, which lots of poets do

these days. Just an utter non sequitur or some sort of joke, some sort of funny observation; all sorts of different techniques are options, which wouldn't be options in a philosophy paper. You can't get to a certain point in a philosophy paper and think, "I don't know where the argument goes from here; I'm going to make a joke." You can't throw a non sequitur in; you can't throw in a good observation or start telling a story of some sort unless it serves the purpose of the argument.

Poets are quite serious about those options and all that a good poem requires, but Jollimore believes that poets are "a lot more comfortable with pluralism, in a sense, than philosophers are." Philosophers want to reconcile ideas, pull them together, make things logically consistent, and come up with one sustained story—not multiple options. Poets, on the other hand, "are happy to keep tossing out different metaphors and looking at things in different ways. And the more we get of that, the better. It's an accumulation. And if it's diverse and it doesn't really all go together, that's great; the poet is happy. The philosopher is miserable, but the poet is happy."

You might consider the miserable philosopher and the happy poet as coming from two completely different writing cultures. But when writers are shaped by broader cultural assumptions in radically different ways, the whole notion of different styles or modes moves far beyond genres and fields. We're not even aware of the way we are all products of our cultural practices. These practices "are like water to the fish, the air that we breathe," according to Hazel Markus. "You don't see them. We use them, but somebody else has to point them out to you."

Professor Markus gave the example of the ways American Indian students write and speak, especially if they've come from a reservation setting and the university is their first time away from it. She's observed "a very circular way of writing. You don't get to the point. You start way back from the point, and it sounds like a joke, but it's actually true.... You tell the context. You tell the story of how you got to where you are." With such apparent meandering, the teacher may get impatient, exclaiming, "Get to the point!" It appears to the teacher as if the student wants to avoid getting to the heart of the matter. Put your cards on the table, get right to the point, is the common approach of a lot of American and European writing. She observed a similar dynamic when collaborating with Japanese scholars.

The writing would seem "very circular":

> This would appear, from [the usual] American perspective, as beating around the bush. You don't get to the point. If something's important, you don't say it. You're indirect. The important things are implied. They are inferred. It's really important that you don't say it. You're very careful with the words you choose. You set the context. So it's just such a different task than the very analytic style that I have more or less been taught to write in, where you figure out what it is you want to say, and you get to it right away—especially in scientific writing.

A university needs to be aware of these very different writing styles that "students bring with them—the various contexts they've come from before coming to Stanford." Students arrive with different ideas about why and how they're writing—and difference is not an error.

Meandering or getting straight to the point, happy or miserable, zany or serious, writers cultivate their own truth. No matter the methodology, no matter all the non sequiturs of poets and the rigid empirical methodologies of research scientists, writers try to communicate what they know and feel with urgency. Literary scholar Shelley Fisher Fishkin admired Hemingway's dictum that a writer needed a "built-in, shockproof bullshit detector." She took to heart Hemingway's "impatience with superficiality," and as a result she has "very little patience for jargon or ostentation." Although she didn't exactly have a "Fidel Castro Rule," her experience as a journalist was helpful to her, as it was for Fred Turner and many others: "No matter how complex the idea is," she insisted, "there's no excuse for obfuscating it in order to prove how smart you are or how specialized your knowledge is":

> There are many, many levels at which you could talk about something. You should always be able to talk about it in a way that anyone who is not a specialist could also understand it. When I became a scholar, I didn't change my demands: lucidity and clarity.

And then she chuckled at "lucidity and clarity." She realized that she had just violated another old rule of journalism: "Two words aren't necessary if one does the trick."

Rob Reich

CHAPTER EIGHT

■ ■ ■

Styles of Writing, Methods of Knowing

"Eschew surplusage," Mark Twain advised, violating his own advice to illustrate the point. Twain objects to "surplusage"—the use of overblown words that create a pompous style—although that little sentence does not contain a grammatical or mechanical error. Using a phrase, selecting a word, determining the shape of a sentence, chasing down the right verb— all these are choices and not errors. Twain offered yet another maxim of what's at stake: "The difference between the right word and the almost right word is the difference between lightning and the lightning bug." A writer makes stylistic choices, and even if a choice is a lightning bug that's not up to the task of shooting huge bolts from the sky—even if that choice is weak, ineffective, or wildly inappropriate—it's not necessarily incorrect.

This is important, since some teachers, for example, hector their students that passive sentences are "wrong," and that they should never use them—even though a passive sentence is not at all grammatically incorrect. Overuse of the passive form may make for weak passages with dull prose in which it's unclear who's doing the action, but … Passive sentences *must* be used; and when they're used judiciously and appropriately, those grammar cops who issue tickets don't even notice. Besides, the God of Language would not have invented passive structures (or overwrought vocabulary like "surplusage") if they were always forbidden; and in some modes of writing, such as lab reports, passive is always expected: the genes were spliced, and we don't care who did it. The upshot is that making choices is the realm of style: such things as diction and word choice, the shape of sentences and paragraphs, the way voices and material are incorporated, and more. Sometimes there's resistance to the whole notion of style, but readers do respond to vivid writing, especially if they don't even seem to notice that the prose is effective or streamlined or even beautiful but simply carries them along.

"Writing is a language act," explains literary critic Albert Gelpi. "So is speaking, of course; but writing is a much more conscious, self-conscious, much more reflexive, self-reflexive language act." For Gelpi, good writing is a craft, and the writer respects words—loves them, knows them, relishes how they work individually and in concert, practices how they can be arranged into "larger and more complex forms." Writing is not something that can happen thoughtlessly or casually. "It demands concentration, discipline, practice, persistence, revision. It combines spontaneity and control, intuition and analysis." And, with all of that, writing can also be pleasurable, no matter what the field.

"A lot of *engaged* writers seem to believe beauty, the pleasures of prose style, amusement, and epiphany are what you check at the door when you go to the committee meeting," Rebecca Solnit observed of some responses to the idea of style by writers engaged in social justice struggles. Her own writing certainly engages in the fate of people and the survival of the planet with great passion; and her prose is well crafted, her language exciting yet controlled. Wooden writing is not a requirement for social action—and encountering epiphanies is at the root of Solnit's intellectual project. Few of the writers I've spoken with believe they are disconnected or aloof, although they may regard how they engage with the world very differently. Even the more esoteric or specialized scientists are likely to feel they are part of a larger purpose, although their work may not seem so pointedly political. For example, biologist Terry Root's interest in birds connects with her concern with global warming. Few writers want to crank out dull prose, empty rhetoric, or mere fluff. Style does count.

Style is learned—even the style George Fredrickson mentioned earlier: that is, writing with such clarity and lack of affectation that the reader pays no attention to any literary qualities but only to the historian's meaning. Style is often learned by imitation and by the timely intervention of a teacher or editor. But style may also develop out of a clash of cultural expectations. Biographer Arnold Rampersad explained how he attended "a kind of neo-Victorian high school" in Trinidad, where he developed a "Ciceronian, Latinate style, pompous to some extent." This was the hothouse that was British education. Then a kind woman in the neighborhood handed him *The Great Gatsby,* and he was astonished. Next came *Look Homeward, Angel,* and he was so affected by that novel he could not read the book again for fifteen or twenty years "because it so ravaged me." But American plainspoken prose immediately made a big dent in his Latinate armor. All his discoveries in literature came just before Trinidad attained independence from Britain, when the West Indies was developing "a very cosmopolitan approach to culture." That encounter between British "superiority" and the Caribbean embrace of the world created a special excitement: "It wasn't really colonialist so much as it was colonialist with *independence in sight.*"

"We thought 'American culture' was an oxymoron," Arnold Rampersad explained. He was "so obsessed by the superiority of British standards" that it took him some time after moving to the U.S. to fully "recognize the gloriousness of American writing." He began to admire a completely different style than the Ciceronian; he appreciated "clear, unaffected prose," particularly the work of "one of the greatest American prose stylists, Langston Hughes, who's often thought of as writing all the time for children; but the absolute lucid clarity, the simplicity of his sentences—it's just miraculous." He knows, too, that under pressure, he could easily regress. He could find himself resorting to that somewhat ornate neo-Victorian mode: "Ornate is not a good word to attach to almost anything. It suggests excess." His tactic was to find a balance between "the great clarity that marks the prose of Whitman or other American writers and the complication that you almost always have to bring to a significant subject." Striking such a balance is not easy, but Professor Rampersad has been producing particularly lucid prose about complex characters over the course of many books.

Abraham Verghese, physician and writer, also found models; he discovered his inspiration in French literature. He became a big fan of Émile Zola, especially his books about Paris. "They are incredible, because you start reading the series, and you can smell and breathe Paris on every page," he reminisced. "It's quite remarkable how that happens, and that was my ambition." As a doctor, he wanted to emulate Zola's vivid descriptions of urban scenes; he wanted to do for medicine "what Zola had done for Paris." In his novel *Cutting for Stone,* he worked to have every page "imbued with that sense of a medical environment, and Dettol and Lysol and pus and blood and urine, just to have all those miasmas in the air on every page." But he also wanted "to capture the very things that I love about medicine. I think I always felt that the study of medicine, as a medical student, and even now as a physician, was incredibly exciting. It was really a romantic sort of pursuit, and I very much wanted to fill the book with that."

Dr. Verghese heard an aphorism in medical school that he heard again in the University of Iowa Writer's Workshop, and it sounded the same note that inspired his fascination with Zola. "I was struck how two different kinds of teachers were saying the same thing: 'God is in the details.' And I say that in medicine a lot, but I think it's true in writing—that I think detail allows the story, or allows us, to be as realistic as [we] can be." Again, an author's work inspired him: C.S. Forester's "Hornblower" series of sailing novels:

> When I was in my teens or even earlier, I discovered Hornblower one rainy holiday. And this was taking place in the Napoleonic era on a sailing ship, full of nautical terms, none of which I understood; but I had the great sense that even though I didn't understand them, this was authentic detail, and it was so vivid. And very recently, I reread the whole series again and found that it remained utterly captivating. I still was clueless about port versus starboard versus aft deck versus poop deck and so on, but it didn't really matter. One sensed that the detail was authentic.

Dr. Verghese sought to recreate that sense of authenticity via detail in terms of medicine. He was conscious that the ordinary reader would not know all the terms, but that "they would be able to guess, or at least it would not interrupt their flow."

Along with detail comes precision. Reverend Scotty McLennan writes about spirituality, religion, and ethics. As I've described earlier, he posts above his desk little signs with words of wisdom—a list of mottos to encourage him to stay on track. One of them is, "Write poetry: make every word count." Like Arnold Rampersad, he too admires F. Scott Fitzgerald's *The Great Gatsby* "as a beautifully constructed piece of work." Consequently, he put up another slogan: "Think Fitzgerald." Copying the style of other writers is one way to learn—trying to imitate Fitzgerald can help, if you can do it; or Mark Twain or Susan Sontag. In all of that effort to internalize the style of the master, you pick up some skills and your own "voice" emerges. At times I've asked students to write parodies of writers they like—that's one way to dig into a writer's style. Eventually, I ask them to write parodies of their own writing—and that's another revelation, often a performance of their own excesses.

Short-story writer Nancy Packer learned to write literally at the feet of her master of fiction, Wallace Stegner. He profoundly affected her style of fashioning stories when she attended his workshop at Stanford:

> On page three of one story, he wrote, "This baby is a long time learning to walk." You know, that was a wonderful thing to say. I understood the short story in a way I had not understood it before. And my stories now start in the first paragraph. Something is moving in the first paragraph—none of this New Yorker stuff where they've got two or three pages of background and then something really important happens. But my stories start. Why? Because Wally said that.

Stegner never scribbled many responses on her manuscripts, just a few choice phrases at strategic moments: "His little comments were so particular and so right-on, they were just absolutely bull's-eye."

Through a serendipitous twist she was hired as a lecturer at Stanford. "Philip Roth was supposed to teach, had accepted a position at Stanford as a lecturer, but something better came along, and he didn't make it," she explained. "They were desperate, so they asked me." Her husband was an administrator and they lived by the campus, so she was definitely available. But there was a scarcity of office space. "Wally had a great big office, so he said, 'Okay, I'll move a desk in. You can share my office.' So, I shared his office." As a consequence, she was in a position to overhear a lot of his conversations with students, which allowed her to learn from him by means of eavesdropping—which gave her little workspace big impact. She also learned that Stegner was "a marvelous man, a truly great human being"—not often the case with office mates or, for that matter, literary mentors.

Nancy Packer is stylistically very precise and very sharp. I noticed in her classic composition textbook *Writing Worth Reading* that she's very conscious of what she's doing; she has a lot of the control that Albert Gelpi emphasized. For example, there's a great passage on the sentence: "Short sentences are fine. They say what they come to say. Then they leave. They are clear. They are direct. They are efficient. They can be punchy. But they can become exhausting. Too many in a row will not do." That paragraph goes on for a while, and then she speaks about overlong sentences, writing a comparable string of elaborate elongated ones. She displays in that passage a consciousness of what she can control stylistically—the fact that style is beyond grammar or correctness but is a matter of choice, and that overuse of anything can be deadly. Short sentences? Or elaborate Ciceronian avalanches rumbling down the page in subordinate clauses and appositional phrases and absolutes? Or both?

I asked Nancy Packer what influenced her style besides Wallace Stegner's short-story wisdom. "I was weaned on the works of Ernest Hemingway," she replied, and many writers who came of age during Hemingway's ascendancy mention the same thing. "You weren't allowed any adjectives or adverbs. You just had to get it down in nouns and verbs, all said in nouns and verbs." It took her a long time to move away from that influence: "I threw off the incubus and started trying to have an occasional adjective or an occasional adverb, but I still am pretty particular about the language. I don't know that I'm a great stylist; I'm not, but I am as particular as I can be about the language."

Andrea Lunsford struggles with style as well. "I'm not satisfied with myself as a prose stylist," she confessed. "I'm good at certain kinds of style and then I'm not very good at others." Professor Lunsford has studied writing and rhetoric for decades, and like Nancy Packer has written composition textbooks used in thousands of classrooms, so consideration of style is clearly in her portfolio, and she's always very attentive to it: "I learned really early that I loved these big left-branching sentences that just start out and go off here forever and might be sixty or eighty words long and still haven't gotten to the main clause—well, that's no good. You can't do that very much, so you can learn to pick out stylistic tics that you have and identify them, and then learn to try to work around them."

Andrea Lunsford tries to get a grasp of style by taking a few pages and closely analyzing them, whether her own prose or someone else's writing. As she describes it, she makes herself sit down "and count numbers of words in sentences—something as silly as that." Or she examines how sentences open, what kinds of clauses and phrases she could use. "Do I have any metaphors, what sorts of figures of speech, am I quoting other people, what kind of people are they, why am I quoting them?" Professor Lunsford poses these types of questions, zeroing in on her own work: "I just really take that nitty-gritty look."

Other people often ask these questions, but the trick is trying to read your own words as if they were utterances by someone else. Stylistic tics often reveal themselves when you write a parody of your own work—that's a distancing strategy. Or someone else does you the favor of pointing out those habits. One student leaned so heavily on "clearly" in her sentences that the word was showing up three or four times in each paragraph: "Clearly, the business climate in Costa Rica was conducive to ..." If it's so clear, why do you need to say it? We went through her thesis paragraph by paragraph deciding how many times "clearly" could go. "Clearly" is good for emphasis, to underscore something, so we kept a few; but to have used it so many times was maddening. She, of course, didn't even notice it. Keep in mind that it was good for her to use "clearly" copiously in her early drafts, since it acted as a "trigger word" that gave her permission to say something—but then she needed to chuck most of its appearances in her revisions. There are other quirks, such as "I think that ..."; or sentences strung together by semicolons because the writer feels they are naked on their own; or "In this chapter I will explain ..."—and other often unnecessary meta-rhetorical markers. Indeed, with a good "clearly" or "I think that," a writer can get her engine up and running and then comb most of those words and phrases out during revision. Indeed, my own tic is the overuse of "indeed"—and I often have to cull them from drafts.

Literary scholar Ramón Saldivar makes a point of reading his work out loud, as do many others. Thomas Hare has written on classical Japanese Noh drama and ancient Egyptian hieroglyphics. These topics seem as distant in time, place, and culture as anything you can imagine, but Japanese Noh (and language) and Egyptian hieroglyphics are both complex symbolic systems, and that interests him. He wrote a book that also drew upon the theories of Jacques Derrida and other difficult thinkers, so he made a point of taking long walks reciting his drafts out loud, even memorizing sentences. Generally, what I've found is that if you read out loud and you find yourself having a hard time catching your breath or the rhythm seems off, you may want to check the length of your sentences or the punctuation. The reader always needs to breathe, even if silently. Also, when reading out loud, you can often hear whether or not something actually makes sense.

Voice, the reverberation of actual speech, is important in most writing; but it's always essential, actually palpable, in writing plays and film scripts. "The big difference between playwriting and everything else is—to state the obvious—when you're writing plays, you're writing human utterance only," explained playwright Amy Freed. "You're writing only language that is based on need or want. So a character speaks because they want something from another character. You don't get to use any description, normally speaking. You don't get to use a whole lot of reflective or passive speaking, so that's a huge style imperative." What's said between human characters is mostly what the playwright works with, even if the play is filled with talking vegetables and singing household appliances; but even then the language is captured, heard on the streets or on the media, and brought to the page and then the stage.

"There are some things that are different about playwriting from other forms of writing," David Henry Hwang explained:

> I often think that there's sort of a continuum. And if on the one end of the continuum you think of novel writing, playwriting is somewhat like novel writing in that it involves structure, it involves words. But at the other end of the continuum, there is music writing. And playwriting is also somewhat like music writing.

For Hwang, "the words on the page are only as important as the notes on the staff of a musical piece." Music is not really written in scores to be read but to be performed; likewise, a playwright does not write a script to be read:

> We read plays because we can't go see everything. But essentially, the play is a score. And what that means is that there are specific requirements that playwriting demands that are different from novel writing, because you're dealing in an art that takes place over a specific period of time. And individuals do not experience it alone; individuals experience it in a collective.

This collective experience changes naturally over time in speech, as all language does; and it's not necessarily always interesting. "We're in a modern era for talking," Amy Freed observed. "If you listen to … how language has changed since the advent of television and electronic media, there's a flattening of the human voice that's happened all over the world. For example, dialects are disappearing. There's a universality of expression because we're repeating catch phrases [and] slogans and adapting characters from media, so in a funny way, our lives and our personalities are imitating art." She recalled a friend who teaches dialects in the theater, and her friend would go to Covent Garden to collect the kind of Cockney that would get performed in *My Fair Lady*. But, "It's very hard to get good

Cockney anymore on the street because TV has gone everywhere, and Hollywood is shaping the access to the English-speaking world." Every writer in the theater now has to confront "this flattening of language," and it is a critical style choice. Does the playwright work in the vernacular of people who learned to talk from watching television, or are we "writing from a slightly earlier, more literate, less visual era?" As a result, Amy Freed feels that writers for the theater are forced to make a choice between the voices of the present flat moment and the more richly accented voices of earlier time periods.

Style involves other facets as well, such as how one explains a reality or tells a story. "Some people might accuse me of being old-fashioned for this reason," observed historian David Kennedy, "but this is a very settled conviction of mine: that history is best done in the narrative form." The earliest historians, such as Herodotus, were rooted in the narrative form. Professor Kennedy recalled the insights of a psychologist who discovered:

> … there's something genetically hardwired, innate, in our recep-
> tivity to the narrative form; from such an early age, [that] we are
> acclimated and accustomed to storytelling, story hearing—that it
> is a way we make sense of the world. It's just the way we organize
> our experience: the way we render the world intelligible to us is
> to tell ourselves stories about it.

There's been a lot of controversy among historians about other vehicles for relating history, but Kennedy believes "it's very difficult to do without narrative in historical exposition."

Historians always have the forward motion of events through time as a skeletal system. Middle East historian Joel Beinin pointed out that, with any large project, the first thing he does is to make a chronology: "It's really mundane, nitpicky, empirical stuff to get the dates and the actors and the very traditional, political-history narrative line down." But that isn't the end of it; no event travels through time without significance: "The dates, the names, the events—they could mean many different things, or they could be totally random and mean nothing. It's the historian's job to figure out what they mean." Consequently, it takes a long time "before I'm happy with a working hypothesis." Narrative sets the basis for analysis, and analysis leads the writer to highlight one event over another.

David Kennedy may be a little old-fashioned in other ways, such as employing the development of characters, which is also controversial in the field. In *Freedom from Fear*, his sweeping Pulitzer Prize-winning history of the FDR administration, he very self-consciously "used the good old novelist device of characterization at many points in order to attach an analytical point or a line of argument or some important consideration to a biographical figure." In that way, he explained, "the reader would have a vivid sense of a human embodiment or incarnation or representation of this otherwise abstract phenomenon." Kennedy gives the example of General Curtis LeMay; he pays attention to LeMay as a character "because he embodies the most excessive logic of the doctrine of strategic bombing. He's the guy that oversees the fire bombing in Japan, for example."

Kennedy's mentor, so to speak, is Charles Dickens. He reads Dickens periodically to refresh his sense of how the novelist creates characters, and how well characterization can work. But he cautioned that characterization could be dangerous for a historian "because it's easy to slide off into stereotyping, or to slide off into creating the impression in the reader's mind that these people made history. Most working historians are very skeptical of the power of human agency in history." Contemporary historians don't focus so much on "the heroic, titanic individual," as was the approach in the past. Instead, they consider "the circumstance and the situation, vast impersonal forces that are driving the action." Consequently, characterization "is a tool that has to be handled in historical writing very, very carefully."

When an author mixes modes or intellectual approaches, he can produce unusual effects. Joel Beinin wrote *The Dispersion of Egyptian Jewry* in ways that were different from his other, more conventional histories: "A small part of it is literary criticism, and part of it is anthropology, and part of it is social and cultural history. And those things, those parts, were conceived of separately." He wrote the book intentionally "in different modes that didn't appear to connect with each other, because I had a certain argument about how they really did connect to each other." Paradoxical, perhaps; but to tell the story and paint the portrait of the sensibilities of Egyptian Jews required a wider set of tools, so Professor Beinin's approach was different from the typical historical account.

Arnold Rampersad described the attraction of biography much as Kennedy and Beinin did. With biography, he saw an opportunity "to use fictional techniques while at the same time adhering to what I sincerely believe are strict standards of evidence. I don't cut corners in that way."

But he does feel "an absolute obligation to hold the reader" by telling the story." The challenge, he explained, is to tell the story in a compelling way, including using fictional techniques "while absolutely believing in fact and the sanctity of fact."

▪ ▪ ▪

Research is crucial; accuracy is essential. But sometimes you can only go so far—and even go *too* far—with facts in the writing process, despite their sanctity. "You can do more research than you have to do," historian George Fredrickson observed. His own dissertation advisor told him that "at a certain point you could go out and do more research, but if you've got enough to make your case, then go ahead and make it. And that's what I try to tell students as well—that if they've got enough to make a strong argument, they don't really necessarily have to cover everything there is on that topic." He found, in his own work, that there are "diminishing returns" with unrelenting digging through archives.

I've written historical fiction (or, as I call it, fictional history), and I know that if I know *too* much about something, I won't be able to imagine what took place no matter how vivid my vision. I call it being "creatively naïve": when I know just enough to be foolish, I can take a stab at an attitude or a character, I can go out on a limb without getting paralyzed—and then I can catch myself later, deepen my knowledge, do further research, discover that I've created something true through intuition, or decide that I'm just cranking out baloney. Just as in fashioning an argument, you don't want to stifle a direction, a thought—and you can always check it out later. You have to be able to feel unencumbered enough to create something; you need to take the risk to imagine a world, what it was like.

In order to write his novel *A Working Theory of Love*, which involves artificial intelligence creating a personality from the journals of a dead father, Scott Hutchins had to do research. He even served as a judge for a Turing test—a contest in which computer enthusiasts make talking computers sound as close to human as possible. "It's fascinating to see these programs that try to pretend to be human," he said. But he didn't need to become a software engineer himself in order to learn how to create his computer character.

There is knowing too much, deciding that you know enough, and resigning yourself to the fact that you'll really never know. Diane Middlebrook recounted a dinner conversation she had with Arnold Rampersad just as he was about to undertake his biography of African-American novelist Ralph Ellison. She was "dumbfounded that the theme of this dinner party was his dread of this book, the fear of writing." But she understood his feelings, "because it is horrible to be at the beginning of the biography project. You know that you are ignorant *and will remain ignorant*—you will find a lot of things to say, but there is always the fact that people are really unknowable." She acknowledged that only the experienced biographer "would have the kind of dread that Arnold had," because the novice biographer would be deluded into believing she could really plumb the depths of someone's life.

Diane Middlebrook understood very well what it is like to wend through thickets of the unknowable as well as through brambles of forbidden knowledge. She had written a biography of poet Anne Sexton, and was caught in a furious scandal because she had been given access to hundreds of hours of audiotapes of Sexton's sessions with her psychiatrist that provided her with unique knowledge of the poet's emotional life. Sexton's children had allowed her to use the tapes, and had thought that the confessional poet would have approved, as had the psychiatrist; but many in the medical profession and beyond were horrified, believing that guarding a patient's confidentiality continues even after their death—and there was a huge uproar. But the biographer had a precious resource: unprecedented access to the poet's sense of self. In this instance, with such unique material, she was keenly aware that "the biographer is in the privileged position of knowing more about the life than the subject does."

In fact, Anne Sexton's daughter called Middlebrook up once, asking for information about her father: "Diane, we were having a debate the other day: when did my father change jobs?" One of Middlebrook's multiple notebooks holds day-to-day information on her subject; it's a particularly raw version of what would become the book—the logbook of evidence. It's "one of the great satisfactions of biography. It is like a photograph that begins to develop; you are so surprised to find juxtapositions: this day, *this* happened; this day, *that* happened." She would go to the notebook that held that sort of information to find out when Sexton's husband changed jobs. This is the notebook in which she logged the facts of each day of her subject's life in order "to remind myself of all the things I have left out" when she "formulated this particular era" of Sexton's life. "Was there something that I overlooked when I was selecting, and do I want to put it back in?" she would consider as she reviewed her notes.

Still, her manuscripts often overran the page limits, and she would also look through this and other notebooks for "things that can be left out, or crucial inflections that can be given to what is already there"—echoing George Fredrickson's caution that it's possible to research too much or to throw in every detail without differentiation. During our conversation, she pulled out several notebooks, each with special binders and in different colors, and each for different purposes—a complex system of research materials. A brief perusal of her logbook notebook, and she was able to tell Anne Sexton's daughter what she wanted to know.

Nonetheless, there are limits: "With a biography, there is no straight line; all is muddled," according to Professor Middlebrook. "You don't know what you know, you don't know what you don't know; if you find anything, you make a note about it, because someday it may find its partner. You have to have very good ways of keeping track of what you have found and where you have put it," she said, explaining the rationale behind her elaborate system of using different notebooks for different material. With biography, "your readers expect a story," but they also expect "a story that answers the question: 'So what? Why do we care about what this person has done?'" As with history, you need to present the significance of the story; you have to be willing to offer your judgment about things while trying to be right. "Not to have an axe you are grinding, but to be that poised intelligence in the present looking at the past. You are the transmitter, in a way, to the future."

Making these judgments about a subject is not easy. Richard Roberts, who studies African history, was writing about an African leader, Faama Mademba Sy, who'd had complex relationships with his people and with the French occupiers. The French had anointed him king in an area that had never had kings, but then accused him of abuse and malfeasance in 1899. Not only did Roberts have to extrapolate or create narratives through inferences because of limited textual evidence besides legal records; but he also had to deal with the starkly different ways this figure had been regarded, negatively and positively, by the colonizers and the colonized—all the while trying to avoid grinding his own (or anyone else's) axe. This is tough: Remember Carol Shloss writing about Ezra Pound's daughter, respecting her subject's understanding of her father's innocence while contemplating the meanings of treason for her own project? Pound's daughter is very much alive, which hands to Shloss an even heavier responsibility to present her subject's voice accurately and honestly (and for her to sort out her own understandings of the issues). It's for this reason that Diane Middlebrook liked to write about dead people: "They can't read your book." She was writing about long-dead Roman poet Ovid at the time of her own death—but she knew she still needed to be accountable to her subject's actual worldview.

"You always have to be on guard against the treachery that is subjectivity," Arnold Rampersad advised, "and just try to be honest at all points." He pointed out that, according to Freud, "Biographical truth is not to be had. Anyone starting a biography is just simply handing himself or herself over to the telling of lies." Of course, Freud wrote biographies himself; "so perhaps he knew whereof he spoke." After all, what did Freud really know about the life of Moses in *Moses and Monotheism*? Rampersad regards Freud's assertion as a cautionary statement, since the writer is always bringing "your own judgment, your own prejudices, your sensibility—which you can barely control and understand, yourself—into this business of creating a life, creating a story" that readers will take to be the truth. "One has to be very, very careful. ... Truth is absolutely impossible to gain, to settle," Arnold Rampersad explained. "You're dealing with *approximations* of truth."

Adam Johnson, writing *The Orphan Master's Son*, set in North Korea (one of the least-known places to an American writer), had to fashion a believable North Korea and North Korean characters while attempting to achieve some kind of approximation of truth with extremely limited resources. And he found himself in a quandary about representation similar to that faced by biographers and historians. "Who am I to write about the lives of people on the other side of the world, let alone to profit from it?" Johnson asked. But he determined that "If there's a place where fiction can tell a story," North Korea is that place. "I won't say that journalism has failed us or that nonfiction has failed us, because they have to confirm everything; everything must be verified." But, "Very little can be written about that country—a country that doesn't have a census, even. It won't state the population of the capital; it won't release birth or death records—very basic things." He believed fiction could allow him to understand that world in ways that nonfiction could not: "I think this is a case in which the extending arm of imagination can provide something that the historical record can't." But he also knows that "Trespass is inherent when you write outside your own experience. Who am I to write across my race, my culture?" He's sure he must have gotten some things wrong in the novel, "but there are no other portraits; there are no other voices. I won't know if I've got it right until North Koreans are allowed to tell their own stories. And I think even after freedom comes it will take them a while to come to grips with their story and to be empowered to tell it."

In order to check his accuracy, Johnson showed his manuscript to Korean-American friends, but they demurred: "They were, like, 'Bro, I'm from California.'" He showed it to a friend from Seoul, who said she didn't know anything about the North: "I don't know who those people are." And when he showed a part of the manuscript to someone who had fled North Korea, "the American aesthetic of it was very strange to him. The engaging of the artifice was not something he was used to." In fact, Johnson discovered, no one is really a writer in North Korea (the way Soviet dissidents would have been); people don't read books widely; there's only one narrative, and it is the story of the leader's glory.

Johnson drew upon the few books he could find about North Korea, accounts by defectors, and even online English versions of the official newspaper—and he did get a chance to travel there, albeit on a carefully monitored tour. He found "books about the nuclear dimension, economics, military, and geopolitics in that region, but there were no stories of just people." He studied the agriculture, the mountains, the mines, the military, the elites, "and their crimes were fascinating—the assassination teams, the tunnel teams, the counterfeiting teams." But he still had a hard time finding out about the lives of ordinary individuals and how they thought and felt. Even defectors have problems telling their stories, needing the help of journalists "because their whole life experience goes against that kind of revelation and communication." All of North Korean life was fascinating, and he felt "a Dickensian urge to pass my gaze" over all the strange aspects of the place. For example, there are kidnappings in his novel, and each one is based on an actual kidnapping; there are tunnels under the DMZ; and because of embargoes, they use their fishing boats for secret activities like moving weapons and missile parts, counterfeiting money, and dealing crystal meth, morphine, and heroin. Everything is done by means of the simple fishing boats. "The fiction of my book is that one character would do all of those things, which would be impossible," Johnson explained. "Those would be very sequestered lives in North Korea. But I decided artistically the larger portrait merited breaking the verisimilitude of someone's existence there."

Adam Johnson did initially try to leave out the grand scriptwriter himself, Kim Jong-il (still alive at that time); but he realized he had to include him in the narrative. "I had to betray my initial urge to keep him out; and instead, then, I had to humanize a dictator, find his strengths and weaknesses, his humor. [Former Secretary of State] Madeleine Albright was my great source on all of that," since Albright wrote about her encounters with the leader. Johnson would write until he didn't know if he believed that what he was writing was truly North Korean, and he would go and do more research. "It just was a conversation that way, extending my imagination as far as I trusted it and then going back to sources and researching a great deal," until he felt he could imagine the mentality of North Koreans and the reality of their lives.

■ ■ ■

Scott Saul drew upon a whole treasure trove of sources for writing *Becoming Richard Pryor,* a biographical study of how a black boy growing up in his grandmother's bordello in the rough, segregated red-light district of Peoria, Illinois, became the radical comic who drew upon the dark sides of life and the ugliness of American racial attitudes. No one had yet written a researched, analytical biography of how Pryor grew to become such an original success, and Saul delved into court transcripts, journals, screenplay drafts, videos and audios of performances, and interviews with family and friends to reveal that mystery.

Interviews are a bit different from the participatory observations that anthropologists make; and many historians don't trust oral history at all, since memory is so elusive and people do love to bullshit. But if he were alive today, Richard Pryor would only be in his seventies, which means that it would still be possible to talk with people who knew him throughout his childhood and beyond. In the course of his work, Scott Saul "interviewed people who were at least sixty to people who were over ninety. And I got a glimpse of these people before they vanish from the face of the earth." Such research becomes a type of detective work.

This detective work is very exciting when it comes to Pryor's sojourn in Berkeley. He had been an Ed Sullivan-type of comedian, imitating Bill Cosby's anodyne non-confrontational style; but he had a breakdown onstage in Las Vegas in the late sixties, feeling that he was not performing as his true self—and he walked off the stage. Sometime in the early seventies, a little-known period in his life, he escaped to Berkeley, where he hung out with black writers like Ishmael Reed and Cecil Brown and with Black

Power radicals like Huey Newton. During this Berkeley "moratorium" he totally transformed his comedy. Saul had known from Richard Pryor lore that the comic had done a radio show for KPFA, which was the flagship Pacifica Foundation community station in Berkeley, and he wanted to find out about this show. If Saul could find out when this show had been broadcast, he'd find out when Pryor had been in Berkeley. Saul went through the radio station's archives, going through all of their monthly newsletters, looking for every mention of Pryor. He discovered that, starting in 1971, one person had a column monitoring the media for KPFA—Alan Farley. "And he wrote of Richard Pryor, really loved his work, and he would write in the newsletter, 'Richard Pryor's in town; go check him out.' Then he would say things like 'Richard Pryor's appearing on my show,' and then 'Richard Pryor's got his own show.'"

"I've got to track down this guy; who is this?" Scott Saul decided. It turned out that Farley was still involved in public radio, producing shows. Saul had not realized just how valuable a source he was until he met him and learned that he had not only known the comic, but he had also been the one who had actually "driven Richard Pryor up from LA to Berkeley. Richard Pryor [had] slept in Farley's car on the way up; they had lived together; Farley had cooked meals for him; and they were roommates." And because he also loved recording things, he recorded everything that Richard Pryor did—performances, appearances on KPFA, even Pryor's brief show on the station: "Farley had ten hours of audiotapes that no other biographer has really thought to poke into, and they were really remarkable. That's kind of how things work. You sort of pull that thing and push this thing and keep on pressing, and you meet the right people eventually."

Scott Saul interviewed Alan Farley as well as many others who had known Pryor at various stages of his life. Even though valuable, interviews are tricky. "Good research is key," he explained. "Before I go into the interview, I want to know as much as is humanly possible about this person in ways that will affect the interview, because they don't know what they know. If the interviewer has mementos from that time, he can ask very specific questions, and new memories will be jarred loose." But memories must also be checked against the historical record. "People tell a lot of stories, and I want my biography to be grounded in historical fact as much as possible."

Arnold Rampersad relies on letters as "the most reliable single instrument in trying to understand a life." This resource works well when researching Langston Hughes or Ralph Ellison; but it may be problematic with those alive today, since so many no longer write letters and not many of us keep our emails. Nevertheless, for his subjects, Rampersad works through their letters first, trying to get them "under my belt, so to speak; to have some core of fact, even though every letter we write is strategic in intent: we write it for a purpose, we change guises, we change personas in writing letters." It's the job of the researcher/detective to understand why a letter is written in a particular way. "What is desired in the letter? So at every level, you're examining and examining again, searching for the 'truth' behind the particular document in front of you." Once Rampersad has that body of knowledge, he can go and interview people, although over the years he too has discovered how unreliable interviews are. Sometimes people don't want to help and they keep information back, or they really want to help and invent information without, perhaps, knowing that they're inventing it. "The good thing about starting out with the letters," he explained, "is that you can tell almost immediately whether the person who's speaking to you is reliable or not, and the degree of reliability."

Scott Saul agreed, commenting that an interview is "always a delicate dance, because sometimes people are attached to stories that seem utterly, historically impossible." There are dramatic variants: it's possible that the historical record is flawed and that the apparently impossible is true. Consider the many years that academic historians derided the African-American oral tradition for its claim that Thomas Jefferson had had children with his slave mistress, Sally Hemings. It was only much later, with the application of DNA evidence, that what had seemed "historically impossible" had become possible—even probable. In addition to the possible waywardness of accepted history, there may also be some "emotional truth in the story, so you have to let them go with what they think, and challenge them when you have other points of view. But," as Saul observed, "it's that kind of clash of points of view that makes for a great story as well."

"Thucydides ran into this problem 2,500 years ago in writing the *History of the Peloponnesian Wars*," explained David Dunaway, a radio documentary producer and oral historian who literally wrote the first textbook on doing oral history. According to Dunaway, Thucydides complained that he "would go out and do interviews, and everyone tells me a different story, and I suspect none of them are completely true." But the Classical Greek historian figured out how to address this. If you do a lot of interviews on a topic, "you can use a kind of triangulation, which is very similar to the way the old sailors used to make their way through the night without all our fancy GPS." One interview tacks one way, another tacks in a different direction, and "the sum of these interviews [is] a straight line. But it's not a straight journey to get there": even when three or four people are all in the same room on the same day, or even in the back of the same car, they will very likely tell very different accounts.

Dunaway gave the example of a moment in his biography of folksinger Pete Seeger, when Seeger and Woody Guthrie were traveling with the rest of their band in a car. Pete Seeger got angry with Guthrie and "blew up and put his foot through Woody Guthrie's mandolin. Pete has a temper—it takes a lot to get his temper going, but once it goes, it *goes*. I never heard of Pete getting mad like that." Dunaway asked other people who'd been in the car about this scene, and each one told a different tale. Then he asked Pete Seeger, who told him his own version. None of the versions were exactly the same, but they were close enough that Dunaway could understand the situation, "and there isn't any doubt in my mind that this happened."

As I noted earlier, many academics are not at all comfortable with oral sources, except in fields like ethnomusicology, folklore, descriptive linguistics, and anthropology. "The oral text is a complex text," Dunaway said. "Because it's spoken, it depends on who's in the room; ultimately it's a performance—the audience comes into it, the performance comes into it, the mood of the individual—it's not a fixed text. There are multiple viewpoints." This means venturing into a world of ambiguity and conflict. "Oral history implicates historians because it forces them to become field workers, to leave their offices and their stacks and interact with the raw material of history—and that is scary for some people."

Scott Saul gave an example of the thrill of going out in the field and interacting with that raw material. He met Richard Pryor's first manager in New York, Manny Roth, who had become the manager of the Greenwich Village club "Cafe Wha?" before Bob Dylan and others performed there. "This guy was incredible," Saul said. "He's ninety years old, and he asked me to meet him at ten o'clock at night on a Saturday night, and he drove himself." He wanted to meet at Starbucks but the coffee place was closed, and they ended up sitting in a car talking from 10 p.m. to 1:30 in the morning:

Roth grew up in a very poor family, a dirt-poor family, in southern Indiana, not far from Ku Klux Klan territory. Which is one of the reasons why he, as a Jewish person, bonded with Richard Pryor, given his struggles; and we talked about everything from family life to why he got interested in theater, why he founded the Cafe Wha?, what Greenwich Village was like—and then we talked about the time he had with Richard, serving almost as a surrogate father figure.

This was a powerful experience for Saul. He felt fortunate to find all those connected to Pryor, to have "the license to track down these people—they're not always easy to find—and get thirty minutes, two hours, sometimes as much as ten hours or even more of people's time to parse their lives in great detail." It is, as David Dunaway observed, a complex performance that reverberates in multiple directions. Scott Saul learned that, "In a weird way, you find yourself dissecting their life with greater scrutiny and attention than maybe anyone had ever asked them to do, unless they'd done psychoanalysis."

As with many biographies, histories, social criticisms, fictions, and other genres, a life (or a business, social movement, war) is not necessarily pretty or easy to write about. Abbas Milani, a scholar of Iranian history, culture, and political policies, recently published a biography of the Shah of Iran. He had spent some time in one of the Shah's prisons before the 1979 revolution, yet he had to write objectively about the monarch's life. He had to be dispassionate even when the Shah was being thoroughly decadent, ordering planeloads of European women to fly in to service his needs; or when His Highness was being completely cold-blooded, engineering the torture of his opponents. Remember Adam Johnson's task: he had to make the North Korean dictator into a human and not a cartoon character.

Scott Saul didn't have to deal with a monstrous monarch or autocrat, but he did have to come to terms with Richard Pryor. The comic did "a lot of horrific things in his life … certain things that are inexcusable by pretty much any moral standard. The domestic violence is pretty difficult to take." But Pryor would bring these moral failures and abuses to the stage and into his act. "He had the courage to talk about it, and to present himself as a deeply flawed or deeply human person, on the stage." His confessional approach "gave me license, in a way, to ask pretty much any question of anybody I talked to, because he was so ruthlessly candid onstage. I can ask somebody, 'When he beat you, how did that change the relationship?'" You would normally have to have an intimate relationship with the person to ask such a question, but Pryor had already presented this onstage as an example of how one should "talk about one's flaws and one's most unlovable parts."

The more that Saul worked on the material, "the more in awe I am that Pryor was able to come onstage, act as he did, do the films he did, given how difficult his childhood was." He was impressed by how Pryor was able to overcome the tough things in his life—growing up around a brothel that his grandmother ran, his father a pimp, and his mother a prostitute in this brothel:

> When I talked to members of his family of what life was like, the stories are so disheartening. They really make your stomach shrivel up. And then I see him taking this thing—and most people would be ashamed of growing up in a family that had these kinds of difficulties, and with this business—and he had the strength to say everyone has perspective on the world, and "I'm going to force America to see this part of itself that it prefers not to look at." And even more, "I'm going to turn this stuff into comedy." And often, he just wanted people to linger in that space and look at stuff that was fascinating and that wasn't funny, which I find interesting as well.

Despite his ambivalence, Scott became increasingly motivated to write his book, in great part because he wanted "to help secure Pryor's legacy" for future generations. "He's an incredible artist who blew open American culture, and he opened all these doors for comedians and performers who followed."

Saul avoided trying to be funny himself—a big temptation for anyone writing about comedy: there's nothing more pathetic than a cultural historian trying to outdo his subject. Taking over the story from the subject is another pitfall. "One of the biggest dangers is bringing yourself into the narrative," Arnold Rampersad said. His friends would ask, "Is that Langston Hughes, or is that you?" He would reply, "Well, I think that it's Langston Hughes"—and he tries to ensure that by being true to his evidence and not his own views: "At every point I try to bring forth evidence." He gave himself the same caution when writing about Ralph Ellison. A lot of readers commented "on how this person who had seemed so Olympian and aloof and accomplished, suddenly he is revealed to have lots of faults and flaws. Well, I made sure that nothing was alleged that was not supported in the immediate vicinity by evidence—preferably evidence that came out of his own mouth or out of his pen, or his wife's pen or mouth."

All of this is the art of receiving documents or doing interviews dispassionately, seeking some level of objectivity. Fred Turner, cultural historian, noted that he learned from his journalism experience ways to craft an authentic story:

> If I listened really hard, and wrote what I heard thoroughly and carefully, I would come out with a story that would be not just my take on something but enough of the thing itself so that people could have their own take on it. One of the things that I really learned as a journalist that I carried into academia is the notion that you're only as good as your material. Your research really is everything.

As part of this, Turner learned how to ask people questions, getting up the nerve to ask about everything, including bad things.

Fred Turner told a story that illustrates the fact that, no matter how good the research or how penetrating the questions, the reader holds all the cards, in the end. He had one experience that affected him greatly to illustrate this point. He was working in Providence, Rhode Island, with the *Providence Business News*, when he interviewed a businessman with Mafia connections who was also a good friend of the mayor. It so happened that this businessman made a large part of his living bilking widows out of their houses. "So I go to the guy's house and spend the afternoon with him, and I found him utterly charming," Turner said. "He was a lovely man. I enjoyed him every minute I was with him. I listened really hard. I asked him everything about how he did this." The next week Turner wrote up the story, explaining in great detail "how he bilked widows out of houses." The businessman's enemies wrote to the paper and called Turner up on the phone, saying, "Wow, that's great! You nailed him! Right on!" But then the businessman's *friends* wrote to say how much they liked the article: "You showed what a great businessman he is!" Fred Turner's lesson from this episode was profound: "If I listened really hard and wrote what I heard thoroughly and carefully, I would come out with a story that would be not just my take on something but *enough of the thing itself* so that people could have their own take on it."

The thing itself—a shady or brilliant businessman, the life of a comic or a poet or a king, the story of an era's political machinations, a startling cultural insight on technology and consciousness, a character in a novel—whatever the thing may be, that thing is taken by the reader, who wrings out whatever truth or conclusion she can, if given the right material. All the writer can do is hand over that material to someone else's brains, and the reader will take it from there.

Clarence Jones

CHAPTER NINE

· · ·

"Tell Them About the Dream, Martin": How Writers Revise

Martin Luther King Jr.'s aide and speechwriter, Clarence Jones, was on the platform when Dr. King delivered his "I Have a Dream" speech at the August 28, 1963 March on Washington. Dr. Jones listened intently to the paragraphs he had originally drafted (including the one with the metaphor of the "promissory note") and then the ones added by Dr. King. Jones was fifty feet behind him when Mahalia Jackson, one of Dr. King's favorite gospel singers—she had performed earlier in the program and was also on the platform—shouted out to Dr. King, *Tell them about the dream, Martin! Tell them about the dream!* Clarence Jones recounted what happened next:

> Dr. King's reaction [was] to take the written text and move it to the left side of the lectern and grab the podium and look at her. And I said to somebody—this is all in real time—I [leaned] over to the person next to me and I said, "These people don't know it, but they're about ready to go to church."

The civil rights leader had been standing very straight as he delivered his speech. But after Jackson shouted her request, he appeared to Jones to become relaxed, "and the rest of the speech from that moment on was completely spontaneous and completely extemporaneous":

> I had heard and [seen] Dr. King speak many, many times—in churches, in labor unions, and so forth. I had never, ever seen him speak the way that I saw him on that day. It was as if some cosmic transcendental force came down and occupied his body. It was the same body, the same voice—but the voice had a timbre;

it had something that I never heard before. It was so powerful. It was spellbinding in its oratorical power.

Dr. King's sudden shift to a very different direction and style is a stunning example of radical revision. Although he had done variations of "the dream" before, this was a remarkable apotheosis. A speech is delivered as a performance in flesh and time, and is not just a simple reading from paper; oratory allows for spontaneity, for instant responses to audience requests or questions, for the cadences of the call-and-response tradition of the Black church. Spontaneous change of the text is not an option regularly available to the fiction writer or essayist, although reality can provoke surprising changes in any piece of prose. There was the example of Shelley Fisher Fishkin feeling the lash of a toy bullwhip on the banks of the Mississippi that provoked a radical re-direction for her book on Mark Twain. That was a sting, but *New York Times* journalist Philip Taubman had an even more frightening experience that radically changed the direction of a book.

Taubman's *Secret Empire: Eisenhower, the CIA, and the Hidden Story of America's Space Espionage* recounts the development of American spy planes and satellites and their deployment against the Soviet Union during the Cold War. I asked him why he'd only written about the space-age espionage carried out by the United States and not also that carried out by the Soviet Union, since it seemed as if he had told only half of the story—that there was a parallel universe, so to speak, that his book hadn't explored. I expected him to answer that it was simply too much to incorporate each country's space-age skullduggery in one volume—that it would be too large, too cumbersome. In fact, he had really set out to write both sides of the story, but "very strange things happened" that intervened.

Taubman explained that, as Moscow bureau chief of *The New York Times,* he knew how to make his way around Russia and find research assistants to work with him, so he had lined one up. The research assistant had been eager to do the project, and had corresponded through email regularly. But all of a sudden the messages had stopped. There had been "radio silence" for weeks on end, but Taubman had kept sending emails to him, asking what was going on:

> Finally, [the assistant] sent a very cryptic message saying, "It is impossible for me to do this work," so I wondered whether someone

had leaned on him. I hired another research assistant and again I don't know what to make of this. He too started out all excited to do this work, and then he was run over by a hit-and-run driver in Moscow. Now maybe it was an accident, I don't know; but at that point I decided it was not worth the trouble.

He knew he had enough material to write a fascinating book about the American side of the equation, so he accepted what could have been a blunt message: "If the Russians were paranoid about their history, I wasn't going to put anybody else at risk." He still doesn't know if these incidents "were the result of a kind of post-Soviet spasm of police state activities or [if] they were just coincidence." But changing the design of that book may have saved someone's life.

Getting a new vision doesn't always amount to dramatic transcendence or spy-thriller mystery. The process of revision is very mundane most of the time—finding the right word, crafting elegant sentences and paragraphs, reorganizing the structure of a text to better reveal your argument or story—yet those changes are often crucial, employing a kind of alchemy to turn crap into gold. What any writer wants is for readers to think that the text has *always* been gold; that the gold had flowed effortlessly from the top of the writer's head—and that the reader would have no idea of the actual dross from which it had been transformed, and wouldn't be aware of the sweat that had gone into making that transformation happen. "The beauty of writing," Welsh poet Gwyneth Lewis observed, "is that you don't have to do it in public. And we don't have to show anything we don't think is okay." It's remarkable how widespread this sentiment is: You can write terrible stuff—but you're free to do so because only you can see it and no one else can. Of course, you have to have the judgment to know whether or not something really is worth being seen in the light of day. Whether it's a poem or a business plan, *you* control the debut—*you* decide if you've achieved the delusion of effortlessness.

John Hennessy, Stanford's president, is also a computer scientist and businessman who insists on very high standards; "not doing it in public" is a principle for him. He was the chairman of the board of a company that had recently gone public, and he had been handed the draft of the prospectus that was going out to the regulators. It was terrible. "We're not sending this out until we fix this writing," he said. "This is an embarrassment." It wasn't grammatically incorrect, but it was sloppy, not good quality. "I knew what they were trying to say, but I felt that an outsider reading it would not know. Particularly in an executive summary, an overview, we should hold ourselves to a higher standard." He had to mark it up and send it back to the lawyers with the comment, "Lawyers should be able to do better than this!"

As Stanford president, Hennessy has a lot of writing brought to him for approval that's been drafted by others, and he follows a piece of advice passed on by a previous Stanford president: "Don't let anything go out that you haven't read and you haven't changed and you haven't made yours." This is especially hard when somebody is in a rush to get out an article or document but it just can't go. He'll send it back, or even revise it himself despite the pressure—although that means making the time to do the revisions. "If I'm not going to get a chance to work on something that's going to go out, I'd rather have it not go out with my name on it," President Hennessy said. If he couldn't change it to his satisfaction, "It should come from somebody else in the University. That's just the view I have about what people expect when they see something that's written by the president of the institution."

Most writers are not at the helm of an institution with a staff producing drafts for review; they create their own drafts, and that can be torturous. Historian Peter Stansky gave the example of writing the first draft of a book review for a journal. When he finished, he liked what he had done. He didn't send it in right away, but looked at it again the next day. Like others, he insists on sleeping on what he writes, never attempting to revise any sooner than the next morning. When he did take another look, he thought, "My God, this is pretty terrible. There were lots of very awkward sentences. How could I think this was satisfactory?" Once again, he rewrote it and thought it was fine, and he put it away to read the next day. Once again he was aghast, and it had to be redone. This went on for several days, and after the fourth revision he exclaimed, "Enough! I'll send it in." Professor Stansky realized he could be cycling around one draft after another forever, always improving it, but he had reached his limit: "You have to let it go. You can never have the perfect manuscript, and maybe I have more errors than I should have, but among many scholars, perfectionism is a terrible enemy because if you say, 'I'm not going to let this go until it's perfect,' you're never going to let it go. At some point you have to let it go."

I've noticed a number of other writers who are also ferocious revisers, even at the very basic sentence level, such as social and cultural psychologist Hazel Markus: "I know each time I start, I'll probably do the first sentence of a manuscript, I don't know, fifty times, a hundred times." While hammering away at the first sentence, she works over the title again and again. "I'll have ten titles there. I look at them—'How do I feel about the title today?'—and kind of rearrange the words, thinking all about the title." Some people think that titles are a last-minute thing, but for Markus it's a guide to her whole project: "To me, the title is trying to capture the whole essence of the book or the article in some way. So I spend a lot of time doing that." It may seem to be an obsession, but she's actually thinking through the full import of whatever she's writing. And Professor Markus isn't the only writer who hammers away for long periods of time. Literary critic Marjorie Perloff also gets into an extended revision loop. "I keep correcting and correcting and going over and over. I'll re-write the first sentence ten times and I still don't like it. Just doesn't sound right. And then I'll write it again," Perloff explained. Melanie Watrous, a fiction writer, is another obsessive: "Maybe no one else notices, but I care." It's not titles or single sentences but entire scenes that consume her. "I'll keep drafting scenes," she confessed, going over each version with a high-lighter to "figure out what I like in each one, what is working, what I'm keeping—and start over," until she settles on the final version.

There are those who edit on the sentence level as they go along through-out their entire manuscript, not just the opening sentence. A lot of writers have reached the level of experience where they don't need to spit out the whole draft before polishing it—the crap unfolds in front of their eyes, so to speak, and they clean up as they go along. The ease of making changes on the computer helps. For older writers, the advent of the word processor radically changed the whole process of revision. "That thing should never have been invented, honestly, because you can just change and change and change," Arnold Rampersad exclaimed. "And do you really make it better? I don't know if you do make it better." Rampersad echoed Peter Stansky's fears of getting caught in an endless merry-go-round of revisions because the writer now has the ability to keep changing the text in a flash. Because the changes may not necessarily be for the better, several writers under-scored how important it is to keep all previous drafts. "You can revise too much," said literary critic Alex Woloch. "I've had the experience of going back to the early file and finding that I had a much better way of saying something."

Donald Kennedy, biologist and science policy writer, also believes that the computer has improved writing, although, as I mentioned before, the text looks so good on the screen "that you're a little, 'I don't want to mess this up. It's so beautiful'—and yet, of course, you should." The computer has made it so much easier "to move paragraphs, to cut and paste." I tell astonished students that in the old days we actually did cut and paste, that it's not a figure of speech or cute computer lingo—that we actually took up scissors and slopped paste or scotch tape on pieces of paper to rearrange text—and then retyped the whole thing. Started typing it all over again, and then again, and yet again. Naturally, anyone would be reluctant to make too many changes with so much labor involved; all that cutting and pasting and typing and retyping was exhausting. But with the ease of computers, according to Kennedy, "You get over your resistance to really moving the pieces around. Then you can do a lot of editing on the screen." But Kennedy observed that the writer can also be tempted to get too incremental, going over the relatively small things to find a better word or reorganize a sentence, "but not get into the guts of it"—avoiding big decisions like opting to delete passages or rearrange the structure of the text.

Writers use a variety of techniques for editing. Eric Roberts, writing computer science textbooks, would go to his local breakfast café and sit at the counter and read his drafts out loud softly to himself to hear how they sounded. Roberts observed that this is what poets do, and you need to do the same for textbooks and other writing: "You will find all the errors, but you will also find the ungainliness." There's the voice and there's the ear; there's the role of writer and the role of editor, and of writer and editor switching back and forth. As cultural historian Fred Turner explained, he splits himself into two personalities as a "practiced habit": "There's the me that produces—sort of a big, gushy guy who will say anything, [a] big teddy bear of words. And then there's the me who edits. And that's the ferociously compulsive, anxious, detail-oriented, fairly unpleasant creature. And they each get their time."

Diane Middlebrook's role-playing got a serious workout through her self-conscious strategy for revision. "If you have a revision strategy, and know what you are looking for, and know that these are typical faults, then you can be confronted with them as problems to be worked on rather than thinking of them as failures, which is so discouraging," she advised. "You should revise with certain purposes in mind. In a biography, I am always finding that the chronology is screwed up: I am anticipating, forecasting; I am clumping things together because it is topical, but it doesn't work yet; I haven't developed enough of an argument for this to work." Middlebrook also suggested that you "outline your own work after it is written, because then you can see where the logic is breaking down or where you repeat yourself. Shrinking it down improves it."

The next step in Diane Middlebrook's strategy would be to review "whether my quotations are too long, whether I have quoted too much. People quote too much anyway. You put more in when you quote because you haven't written the context yet and you don't know how it is going to read. You think, 'This is great,' and you plug it in; then you go back and see that it doesn't fit." Then Middlebrook moved to the next point in her strategy—the thorny question of voice. For example, while writing *Her Husband: Hughes and Plath—A Marriage,* about the marriage of poets Sylvia Plath and Ted Hughes, she had to wrestle with a particularly difficult issue. Ted Hughes's letters were unpublished and were controlled by the poet's estate, which emphatically stated that the letters could not be published. She would be allowed to quote brief passages under the "fair use" rule, but if the quotation was a long passage, she had to paraphrase what it said without using those words. So she developed a unique voice for this quotation-starved biographical narrative, in which the narrator seemed to know a lot without having any anchor in Ted Hughes's own words. She ended up using "signatures of a writing style," modeling her voice on those of other writers; but when her daughter read it, she said it didn't work. "I really didn't believe it at first," Middlebrook confessed. But eventually she came around to her daughter's view, understanding that her approach to creating a general narrative voice was problematic, and she had to change it.

Note that revision can go beyond the writer's use of multiple vantage points or personalities; it can involve interaction with people outside of the bubble of your project—mostly people whom you trust. But it definitely might not concern you alone, no matter how adept you are at playing multiple roles. In Diane Middlebrook's case, even before she reached out to a professional editor, she turned to ... her daughter. Shelley Fisher Fishkin, also a literary scholar, had her father, who she considered to be "a wonderful reader, a wonderful editor." Although he didn't have expertise in her field, he was "a very smart man, a very good writer. And I loved to have him take his green felt-tip pen and mark it up ... I really felt that when my father passed away a few years ago that I lost one of my favorite readers and one of my favorite editors, as well as my father. And I really had no idea who I would turn to." Even though she had many friends who would read her work, it wouldn't be the same. But then there came a surprising development: "I had *grown* my own editor without realizing it." It turned out that her older son was a brilliant editor and would review her drafts from then on.

Of course, accepting advice is not always easy, even from family members. Bill Guttentag is a scriptwriter and filmmaker who won two Academy Awards for the documentaries *You Don't Have to Die* and *Twin Towers,* and also wrote and directed *Soundtrack for a Revolution, Nanking,* and other films. When he made a movie for HBO, there was one section that his wife didn't like. "Get rid of it," she told him—but he didn't. "And then my boss at HBO told me she didn't like it, and she said, 'Get rid of it.' And I didn't get rid of it. I mean, a lot of times they'll tell you, *'Get rid of it.'* In this case, she left it open a little bit, so I didn't get rid of it." Then Guttentag watched the film a year later and he realized they were right; that that scene should have been cut. He went to his boss and said, "You were right about that."

She replied, "You should've listened to your wife."

"Well, you're the boss. Why didn't you tell me to take it out?"

The producer said, "Well, sometimes [you've] got to let the filmmaker make their film."

Other studios would simply have demanded that he edit it out if they thought it had to go, and that would have been the end of the story. HBO gave him leeway to create as he saw fit, even to make his own mistake—to his dismay.

When I asked famed theatrical director JoAnne Alkalaitis if being a director was like being the maestro of an orchestra, conducting actors and lighting technicians and others in one grand ensemble, she took offense, retorting that "maestro" was such a nineteenth-century male concept and that her work as a director was highly collaborative. (I did observe Alkalaitis during script readings and rehearsals and, collaborative as her work may be, she was still the one waving the baton.)

Writing for film, like writing for theater and other media, is a large-scale collaborative enterprise. Bill Guttentag points out that films are basically written three times: first, the original screenplay is written; second, the screenplay undergoes revisions during filming; third, the revised screenplay is edited. "And these are all very distinct and key phases of it, but you really are writing it three times." At each of these three points the script can change—even radically.

A screenplay is supposed to accomplish a lot all at once, he explained. It's a literary work that can make people envision a film; it's an argument to get investors to lay down lots of cash; it's an instruction manual for how costume designers, cinematographers, sound editors, and professionals in many other trades should do their jobs; and finally, it's words chosen to inspire an actor to bring a character to life. "That's a lot to do in 110 pages or so," Guttentag observed. "And unlike other forms of writing, screenplays have little or no value until they're filmed." Only when the script is realized by actors saying the lines and camera people filming the scenes—only then does a screenplay come to life: "It really is born when it's on a screen."

During the early stages of production, a scriptwriter can do a reading with actors—a little field test to "see if it feels natural, if human beings say these sorts of things"—and make revisions then. In the midst of shooting, the actors insert themselves and change things a little bit:

> Sometimes actors will change a script and make it worse; but in my experience, far more often they'll change it in ways that sound better, and you just have to keep track of it. This is a real collaboration, and as shooting proceeds each day, there's a new script—each time printed in different colors to help distinguish one from the other—incorporating changes as the filming proceeds.

But then the work shifts to the editing room, where major changes take place—scenes are taken out or added, lines are cut, shots are rearranged, and anything can be left on the editing room floor. If you're the scriptwriter/director, you're in the editing room "with an assistant editor sometimes, and an apprentice editor," and that's all. It's not the large-scale collaborative environment with actors and many other people that it is on the set. "It's the exact opposite. It's very private, and basically you sit around and you fail all the time." It's one failure after another until it feels right—which is what a lot of rewriting is like.

Theatrical production is similar in many ways to filmmaking, as playwright David Henry Hwang pointed out. Direction, acting—all play into the revision process. But for Hwang, revision really starts after the first time there's a reading of the play, which is the first time a group of actors come together with the director, playwright, dramaturg, and anyone else important to the process, and sit around and say the lines. Out of that, he gets to know what really doesn't work, "and I get a sense of what it is that needs to be changed, at least in the first go-round. Your collaborators are incredibly important to your revision process." Who you chose to work with as a script advisor, who does casting, who ends up as the director: "All those things have a huge impact on your rewriting process. Sometimes the rewriting process can end up going off-track because you don't have the right collaborators." But even if it is going well, that's not the end of it. Revision continues through out-of-town performances and previews, as audiences respond. There's the sense that plays are never finished—they're simply abandoned. At some point it's opening night and the critics are coming, and, with a few exceptions, that's the end of the process.

Hwang used the development of his celebrated play *M. Butterfly* as a good example of this collaborative process. All the time he was working on the play, his producer kept telling him, "It's a great play." Of course, he was producing the play, so he would want to believe in his own investment. "But he also felt that there [was] an emotional hole someplace." Hwang kept mulling over that problem, and when the play opened in Washington, D.C. (before its premier in New York), it got bad reviews. In New York, the literary manager of the theater came to see the show, and told him, "Audiences are liking this, but they're not loving it yet." They concluded that the problem was in the third act, when Song Liling, the Chinese spy who is a man in drag, forces Gallimard, the French diplomat, "to acknowledge his masculinity, that he's actually a man—by dropping his pants, basically." In the Washington version, after that happens, the audience believes "Gallimard is crying and then he's laughing and then he hustles Song offstage and goes on to essentially kill himself." The literary manager in New York responded to this scene with an important observation: "You've got a whole play where you've had these two people interacting, and one of them has been concealing his true identity; he's been pretending to be somebody else. And now, finally, this mask is off. And we never get to see what their relationship is once the mask is off." That particular insight rang a bell for Hwang; there needed to be more of the relationship after the shocking revelation:

> I got very excited about writing a scene where they would have to confront each other, now with Gallimard acknowledging that Song Liling was a man. I actually think it's the best writing in the play. [That scene filled] the emotional hole in the play. That particular way of putting it resonated for me, and I was able to

rewrite the play. There were many other examples of things that got rewritten, but I think that that's the most important rewrite that happened in M. Butterfly.

In this case, the insight of a theatrical veteran was crucial. This kind of editorial intervention can come in many different ways, if a writer is lucky enough to get responses from editors. Few editors today are like the legendary Maxwell Perkins—who could read a manuscript with a deep literary sense and get Thomas Wolfe to cut hundreds of pages from the prolix *Look Homeward, Angel*. What passes for editing today is often just copyediting. It's important to untangle sentence structures, correct grammatical goofs, tab down the appropriate diction, check for inconsistencies, and do other tasks of copyediting—but it's not the kind of surgical operation that can transform a manuscript. However, many of the Stanford writers did have editors who played major roles in their revisions.

Historian Peter Stansky observed that the editors for his book *The First Day of the Blitz* "made very powerful suggestions. More than suggestions; almost demands: We love your book. We absolutely love your book. We're so thrilled with publishing it." And then a pause: *"It does need a little work."* With another book, an editor said, "This book needs to be reorganized." After that judgment the editor continued, "and I'm going to do it for you." And he did, brilliantly. "There's no reason to scorn help," Stansky noted. "It wasn't even all that much rewriting. It was literally the rearranging of text. But the author doesn't necessarily see what needs to be done, so editors can be extremely important." Eric Roberts, writing on computer science, would get a draft returned by a collaborator or an editor filled with red marks, and he would be ecstatic: "Red marks are like gifts from God."

Anne Firth Murray, an activist and not primarily a writer, was the founder of the Global Fund for Women. Women around the world wanted to know how she put together such a successful organization: How did she go from nothing to creating an organization that gave away millions of dollars? How did she do it? So she set about to write what became *Paradigm Found*, and the publisher suggested an editor to help her through her writing process. The editor read through her drafts as Murray produced each chapter, and she would write to her with concrete suggestions.

And that was very helpful; I could respond. We did it by email. So she would say, "Okay, chapter three, page so-and-so, this is what you need. And put 500 words here on this. Oh, I need a story here about that." And to me, that was the easiest thing. I would just read it and I would just write right back to her, on email, immediately.

Murray had no difficulty responding to such requests. It was very helpful "to have a partner who made very specific suggestions. I rise to expectations in that way."

This kind of intervention involves a personal relationship, which can often take on the character of counseling or psychotherapy sessions. This was illustrated by the experience Robert Sapolsky had with one editor from *The New Yorker*, who commented on his article about "why we get less and less interested in novelty as we get older, and we're less open to certain cultural experiences." The article was prompted by a young man named Paul who worked as a secretary for his department; he had just graduated as an English major and needed to make money for a while before going off to graduate school. "So he hung out for a couple years," Sapolsky explained. "And he was irritating the crap out of me because he was great at his work *and* he was pathologically open to new experience."

Every day Paul would sit in his office, each day listening to a radically different style of music—contemporary rock, Gregorian chants, irritating wedding songs. One day he came in with a beard and long hair—and soon after that he shaved everything off to see if people would relate to him differently. He would spend an entire weekend at a festival of twenty back-to-back Bollywood movie musicals just because he had never seen one, and thought that that would be interesting.

"He was just totally depressing me," Robert Sapolsky confessed. "I was sitting there having not done anything new in about fifteen years." So this office worker became a living emblem of this phenomenon of someone changing with ease and gusto—and was the source of Sapolsky's dread. "I started off the piece basically with how he had prompted this and how irritating this was." When Sapolsky made a reference in a sentence about Paul and his thirst for the new, "something with the tone was wrong." He had a conversation with his editor at *The New Yorker* about this one sentence. His editor "was the most frightening thing I had ever dealt with" because he seemed to be "the most knowledgeable, scholarly person on earth. In any subject that comes up, he's read four books on it, including all of my areas of science, which he knows much better than me; and we would have these two-hour phone conversations about three sentences in there. This was completely novel for me." The editor thought about Sapolsky's misgivings with his sentence about Paul, and after a long time he said, "The trouble is, the thing that's the core here, is Paul doesn't want to grow up and be *you*, and you know that, *and it hurts you*."

This was a shock for Professor Sapolsky. "I almost burst into tears. It was like I was having these therapy sessions. And he was right. Paul had betrayed me because he didn't want to grow up and be like me." He immediately called Paul up and told this to him—that Paul had no desire to ever be as narrow or set in his ways as his boss. Sapolsky didn't relate how Paul responded to this news—I imagine Paul was bewildered but glad to help—yet the confused, conflicted portion of the essay was cleared up. This was the only editorial experience Sapolsky had of agonizing over a problem in the text, and "the editor keeping me from becoming an alcoholic by telling me the unresolved issue." This was a highly successful experience, although Sapolsky pointed out that it was just too much for him: "I've been scared of this editor ever since, and never have dealt with him again."

Another type of difficult intervention comes from those close to the book's subject. Jackie Robinson and Ralph Ellison were both dead when Arnold Rampersad wrote biographies of them, but he did get responses from a wife and a literary executor. Jackie Robinson's widow asked him to do the biography rather than a sportswriter because she wanted the author to reveal much more of the man than a sportswriter could. When she began reading the manuscript for the first time, she at first exclaimed that she loved it—that his writing was so beautiful, so moving—and that Rampersad was finally getting to the core of the baseball star and civil rights hero. But then she read the rest of it—and Rampersad reported that "Mrs. Robinson was just so icy over the phone. She's a lovely woman, but …" She exclaimed, *"What have you done to my husband?"* Similarly, Ralph Ellison's literary executor said that if he had known what Rampersad was going to do with the novelist, he wouldn't have allowed him access to his private material.

In each instance, Arnold Rampersad had made sure that only he could determine what went into the book—*legally*. But he didn't want to hurt anyone's feelings. "More than that, I wanted to tell the truth. I wanted to get as close to the truth as possible"—and if anyone had objections, they could be right. In both cases, he said, "Come, let us reason together. Tell me what you don't like. Go through it, mark it up, and we will discuss every point. And if I think you are right, I will change the text. If I think I am right, I will not change the text."

John Callahan, Ellison's literary executor, challenged a lot of the book in an "effervescent, exuberant, slightly boisterous, direct, blunt way." His blunt challenges paid off, because "he made the book a better book." Callahan was afraid that Rampersad was going to become defensive about his writing or his interpretation. "Hell no, I wasn't going to [react that way]," Rampersad thought; and he told Callahan, "You knew the man, you are a professor of English, you were clearly hurt by the portrait. It must mean that something is wrong. So tell me what you think I've done wrong." There were a couple of places where Callahan didn't like quotations from certain people—for example, someone describing Ellison as being "Dickensian mad." "It went down to the wire," Rampersad said, and pointed out that the quotes were accurate, that that's what these people had said—and he insisted that he had to stick to the quotations. But going over each point was important in both cases. "We worked it out, and I think it only improved both books." Arnold Rampersad knew that he could be very severe and stubborn, even self-righteous; and that if he had maintained such a rigid attitude—if he hadn't listened to Mrs. Robinson's and John Callahan's concerns—it would have hurt both books.

David Dunaway wrote a biography of Pete Seeger, and the subject, very much alive at the time, was able to intervene directly. Dunaway started to interview Seeger in 1976, and kept on doing interviews up until the folk singer's death in 2014. The book version of the biography first appeared in 1981 after five and a half years of work. It was an "unauthorized" biography, which means that the person you're writing about doesn't read the manuscript before it comes out, giving the author freedom to say whatever he wants without any self-consciousness or fear of offending anyone. So Seeger didn't read it beforehand, but when it came out he wasn't pleased. Dunaway went over the book paragraph by paragraph with him—much as Arnold Rampersad would do with Jackie Robinson's widow and Ralph Ellison's literary executor—to determine what Seeger thought were its problems. In the end, that tough revision process took two years. He made a number of corrections—a whole new chapter was added, he "rewrote every darn page in that rather large book," and the bibliography grew to be three times longer.

But "the biggest thing that bothered Pete Seeger about the portrayal of his life was that I said that he had a *career*":

Now, he did have eight platinum records and won two Grammys and more medals and awards than most people could think of. He's the most recorded American musician. He also has the distinction—at least it's a distinction in my view—of being the only American musician ever formally investigated by his government for overthrowing the government, and this from a banjo player. But as far as he was concerned, he never did have a "career."

Dunaway thought it through again, trying to understand the folk singer's point. Then he realized that Seeger had come out of a Puritan background. "I studied a little bit about American Puritanism, and I understand they had other words [for 'career']. They had the word 'calling.' And [as] for him—sure, he earned his money recording and singing for people," and most would regard that as a career, but he did not. "He had a *calling*. So I would say that was the biggest change that we had."

After two years of work, David Dunaway published an entirely revised edition of the same book. There have been a few radically revised editions of other books—Walt Whitman's nine editions of *Leaves of Grass* come to mind—but there's rarely been a new edition of a biography. Especially one changed upon the insistence of a banjo player.

Some writers seem to value spontaneity over revision, or at least don't go through the usual procedures for making changes. "I do like the idea, which mathematicians have more than poets, that things get *solved*," Irish poet Eavan Boland said. "I do think that there is some way in which the problems of a poem do get solved off the page." When she was younger, she saw an interview with a British poet she admired who said she never revised a poem: "I just write it as it comes and I'm finished." This perplexed Boland, and she asked other poets in Ireland, "Why would somebody do that?" And they replied, "Because they can do it in their head." In fact, poets have been writing (and rewriting) in their heads for centuries, and many still do. "But in fact, the poetic world has moved more towards revision," Boland observed, "and more towards the page."

"It sounds just like a joke," poet and philosophy professor Troy Jollimore said. "But ... *spontaneity is the kind of thing that you have to work at. It doesn't just happen.*" Jollimore relates the fascination with spontaneity within some literary circles, expressed in Allen Ginsberg's maxim, "First thought, best thought." The idea is that "whatever immediately comes to you, get that down on paper and it is pure and pristine—and you don't touch it, you don't mess with it." However, in Jollimore's opinion, "that is a terrible way to write poems. You will occasionally hit on something really wonderful, but everything else around it is just going to be *dreck*." Jack Kerouac liked to say he wrote *On the Road* in one draft, typing it on a long scroll. But as it turns out, he had actually worked on sketches that went into the novel for years, and produced earlier drafts before he sat down one last time with typewriter and scroll. The *feeling* of spontaneity is something else for Jollimore:

> Some of the poems that I admire the most in terms of apparent spontaneity, in terms of the free flow of thought and genuine surprise—you didn't see this line coming and yet once you read it, it feels inevitable, right, the ideal—you'll find out that the author had to work on that over and over and over until finally it felt spontaneous. And in a way that's a disappointing thing, because romantically we would like to think it's possible to just reach into the wells of your soul and pull out that wonderful poetry. But the reality of it is that if it works for anyone that way, it works for very few people.

When it comes to writing in Troy Jollimore's other field, philosophy, there's hardly any spontaneity. How can there be? If the author changes his argument or decides to bring in different examples, he goes back and rewrites the passage. "But on some level I have to admit I really like the idea of writing philosophy papers that *don't* live up to that. And there are models for it. They've been overlooked and ignored in our tradition." Emerson, for example, did the opposite of what philosophers do now:

> Emerson's essays are wonderful, partly because they're incredibly spontaneous. A philosopher now, if he writes something and then changes his mind, will go back and rewrite that sentence; he'll erase it, right? Emerson would write something, think about it, realize he didn't agree with that, and he would write, "I've just changed my mind. Actually, it seems more like this." So maybe there's a kind of "first thought, best thought" in there in a sense. Emerson has the idea—and he writes about this in "Self-Reliance" and other places—that writing, for him, is going to be this record of thinking as it happens, where he doesn't falsify it by rewriting to make it look more consistent than it was. But he tells you, in fact, what really is going through his mind.

Thinking or composing "as it happens" is something that poet Diane di Prima tried early in her craft. Jack Kerouac stayed at her place in New York on the way to India in February 1957. With Ginsberg, Kerouac, and others in her small apartment, everyone started to read their poems out loud. After she read one of hers, Kerouac asked, "What did it look like when you first wrote it?" She looked at her early draft, and to her surprise she liked it. What she got from that experience was the knowledge that "you could always go back to those drafts and pull something out when you got stuck, you know; and then I got the sense of how your mind worked in the first place, and that was very interesting." She had taken a class on dance composition with a choreographer, who implanted the idea that everything has a form—everything. "He said nothing else. After about ten minutes we all started to go out the door," di Prima said. "We were looking at everything. Oh, *that* has a form; *that* has a form. He was telling us that all forms are okay. Leave your mind alone. Don't mess with everything all the time." As a consequence, she began following her mind in her writing wherever it went: "Write exactly what's happening as closely as you can."

She wanted to write something longer, and she took what she learned from that dance class, "taking a structure and then hanging absolute freedom on the structure." She took the eight trigrams (three-line symbols) that make up the *I Ching*, the Chinese *Book of Changes*, and she would immerse herself in the qualities of each trigram: "I listened to that kind of music. I'd just be in that kind of state for a couple of months. And then I'd start writing. And I'd just write. And I'd write whatever showed up on the wall in front of my big IBM typewriter." In this way, in a kind of mystical state, she wrote *The Calculus of Variation.*

Di Prima was wondering how to revise the book, "how to make it smooth and really hip or kind of avant-garde prose. And I knew that if I did that I would be violating this book, so all of a sudden I decided, 'Hmm, I can't touch this. I'm going to leave all the flaws in it.'" She got an offer from New Directions to publish it, but they wanted to assign her an editor, and she declined, explaining, "This is in the nature of a received text. I can't touch it. And I never did. And so I published it myself. And never did publish with New Directions." For a poet to get published by New Directions was (and still is) a major accomplishment, but given her "calling," her artistic purpose outweighed whatever she would gain for her "career." After *The Calculus of Variation*, Diane di Prima returned to revision in her other works, although much of her poetic method would be to transcribe what she would see before her as a "received text."

Most writers must revise, just as di Prima has for her other works; and many writers produce revised versions of their previously published works—perhaps not changing them as drastically as Dave Dunaway did with his biography of Pete Seeger (or Walt Whitman with his constant rewriting and expanding of *Leaves of Grass*), but almost. Marjorie Perloff described how she wrote an essay on philosopher Ludwig Wittgenstein, published it online, and rewrote it and published it again before it came out in John Gibson and Wolfgang Huemer's anthology, *The Literary Wittgenstein*. Each time the essay would appear, Perloff revised it. Then it was translated into German and she revised it yet again. "Anything I would bring out again, I would probably change again," Perloff explained. "You always find more things to change. You find more footnotes you could add or take away, or that something isn't quite right and you want to re-say it. And so there isn't any one text there; you get a kind of variorum text …" That would be a collection of versions, something that literary scholar John Bryant has termed a "fluid text"—such as a novel with alternate endings, or Whitman's poem "Song of Myself" with its different openings—each version valid.

I tried to get students used to seeing their work with fresh eyes by having them edit each other, training them to be direct but gentle. Diane Middlebrook would show her work to friends she knew who were avid readers, even though they didn't know about her subject. "Passing out the copies made me think of how a reader would see this chapter," she said. "It is so hard to be a reader. One of the ways you can turn yourself into one is by presenting it to other people. The hardest thing of all is to be able to see what needs to be done to a piece you have written."

To provide a model of the editing process, I would offer myself as a sacrificial lamb, passing out a few pages of my own work so my students could practice their critical acumen and etiquette without the risk of hurting each other—and each time I would be shocked and, invariably, humiliated. As soon as I would hand out my manuscript, I instantly noticed a raft of mistakes—the lead paragraphs wrong, the argument screwy, nothing clear, the language sloppy. My students would eagerly confirm my fears and let me know whatever else was weak. Sometimes these were articles I had already sent out to publishers—and I had to reel them back to revise them.

The students were almost always right. Freed of their awe of the teacher, they could light into my work with great vigor. It's hard to take criticism, of course. This is why I would suggest to students that they first offer something positive before diving into shortcomings. Otherwise, the brain latches on to the negative and can't hear anything else. It's cheap dime-store psychology—but I've found it most valuable. When these young critics applied the technique to me—first describing all of what they liked about my draft—I felt comfort that at least some of what I wanted to accomplish had gotten through.

After that came the deluge.

Diane Middlebrook

CHAPTER TEN

. . .

One Last First Draft

THROUGHOUT OUR "How I Write" conversations I felt that each participant knew that what they wrote made a mark on the world. Whatever the field, their writing was charged with purpose and meaning. "Writers shape beliefs," Rebecca Solnit observed. With writing we can know "what it means to be human . . . We are cultural animals and if you make culture you get to make consciousness." Solnit writes essays on culture and politics, so the connection to consciousness may seem more direct in her work, but this connection also happens when writing about physics, biology, or economics. Word acts can create material realities; they can make readers conscious, aware of the world, more willing and able to regard wonders and horrors alike. Political philosopher Robert Reich pointed out that his role as a political philosopher is not to provide a blueprint to improve the world; but his work can help people rethink a problem, can help change the way people view an issue, and from that new understanding they can take action, and as a result government policies and social behaviors can change.

When Shelley Fisher Fishkin felt the sting of the bullwhip on the banks of the Mississippi, she took her book about Mark Twain and American culture in a new direction. Her criticisms in *Lighting Out for the Territory* of the way Hannibal, Missouri, whitewashed the existence of slaves in Mark Twain's boyhood inspired a local historian to open a new museum in Hannibal, known as the Huck Finn Freedom Center: Jim's Journey. The new museum places "the history that the town ignored front and center, rescuing and preserving it for future generations, along with neglected aspects of Mark Twain's involvement with African Americans and his efforts to undermine racism." This is a very dramatic example of the way a book can affect the way someone views the world and, as a consequence, change her actions. But, even when driven by a sense of purpose, most writing discussed here is not a simple tool, not an instrument for something or someone else to employ, but a living world of thoughts, feelings, and words.

Many of the writers in these conversations have no literary pretensions; they just want to communicate their intellectual or scientific findings in a clear and coherent fashion. Writing for them—and for many people—may never really be fun; it may be, as one professor put it, just part of the job description. But they do it anyway, because it's worth it. Dorothy Parker was definitely a literary writer, but she uttered a truth that all kinds of writers can readily agree with: "I hate writing," she quipped. "I love having written."

The "How I Write" conversations revealed a far more diverse range of experiences, techniques, and attitudes about writing than I had expected. But laced through all the observations and stories was the realization that writing is hard work. All the writers in these conversations clearly know that persistent, sometimes painful, labor is what makes writing happen, and nothing can replace hammering away at the task, as frustrating as the work may be.

No matter what hat you wear when you write or how you fashion your argument, no matter how much you've learned from Kafka, Zola, or Hemingway, no matter whether you listen to music as you work or not—you still have to write it down, ugly as the draft may be, and then revise it. At the first "How I Write" conversation, historian Mary Lou Roberts described how she would produce many pages before really understanding what she was writing, then file the draft away and start over. People gasped at the thought of doing so much work and laying down so many words on paper even before "starting."

Ian Morris, archaeologist and historian, participated in the last conversation. He writes sweeping historical narratives of the type made popular by Jared Diamond, discoursing on how human history operates over thousands of years (one of his books is *War! What Is It Good For? Conflict and the Progress of Civilization from Primates to Robots*). Professor Morris described a process similar to that used by Mary Lou Roberts: he often wrote many chapters of a book before realizing what he was really trying to say—and then he would toss those chapters and start all over again. Once again, people in the audience gasped. (His editor at his trade publisher had also gasped, alarmed at the unexpected delay.) A writer must have the will to work, the desire to put up with frustrations and dead-ends in order to make words act in meaningful and fresh ways. Anthropologist and poet Renato Rosaldo summed it up: "hard work, patience, attention."

But writing can be play, too, as numerous participants in these conversations testified. Many of the writers find great delight as they wrestle with ideas and tropes, experiencing that wonderful feeling when everything clicks. There is that moment when Diane di Prima began to receive all the poems of *The Calculus of Variations* as revelation, not revising them at all. What a thrill to be a conduit of a larger wisdom—the joy of being the vehicle for ideas or characters, when your personality recedes and the words take over. "There's a real pleasure of just bringing something into the world," as novelist Thomas Kealey explained that joy. He feels particular delight writing fiction, when he goes into the minds of characters unlike himself and experiences the exhilaration of becoming someone else: "There's a real pleasure with both escaping myself for a while and turning back to myself at the same time."

There's also the pleasure of focus, what Paula Moya characterized as "an absolute and intense engagement with a thought or an idea," that zone where "the world recedes" and only the thought remains. She described a feeling of being taken over by something, perhaps not the revelation Diane di Prima experienced but a heightened consciousness. Ramon Saldivar portrayed this pleasure as extreme concentration, a frame of mind that "goes in a mental, spiritual direction rather than a spatial, temporal one." Bass guitarist Victor Wooten compared such an unfettered yet focused feeling to a kid playing air guitar: without worrying about technique or analyzing the process of playing, the air guitarist delights in acting out what the music feels, playing with pure abandon like a rock star, except that the instrument is invisible. But even when writing is a transcendent experience—and a lot of writers get that joyous feeling of connection and focus regardless of what genre they work in or what spiritual path they pursue—you still have to wrestle with the enormous angel of language.

Once you are finished, and the piece appears in print, you forget all the pain and revel in the product. But after "having written," there are also other adventures that involve forgetting. Some people remember every word they write; their articles, poems, books are etched into their brains. But many writers don't remember; all of that tight concentration of thought begins to unravel as soon as the ink dries or the screen fades. They forget the research that led to a historical piece; they can't recall much of a novel they wrote. They surprise themselves with an argument they don't quite understand or even agree with anymore. For a lot of people, once the intensity of writing fades away, the words and sentences take on lives of their own, and the author watches in wonder or distress or both.

One result is that you can have the experience of reading your own work without recognizing it, as if it's not yours at all. Historian George Fredrickson told the story of an assignment a student handed in to him. The task had been to select a history text and write a review of the book—summarize it, analyze it, evaluate it—a fairly standard assignment. But when Professor Fredrickson read the student's essay, he thought it sounded oddly familiar. Of course, he knew the books that he assigned very well; perhaps, he thought, that could account for the paper's déjà vu feel. It took a while, the familiarity gnawing at him, but then it suddenly dawned on him: *the student had handed in an essay that George Fredrickson himself had written.* The student had had the *chutzpah* to plagiarize his own professor's work and submit it to the author himself, hoping, I suppose, that Fredrickson wouldn't notice. He almost got away with it because, indeed, Professor Fredrickson took a while to awaken to the fact that the familiar words he was reading were actually his own.

How bizarre. But forgetting can also have other characteristics. When you read your own work as something fresh, something strange, it can be very exciting—especially if there's time to make revisions. But then, once published, you almost inevitably discover typos, mistakes, and causes for regret and even remorse. As in a lover's quarrel, sometimes we wish we could take the words back. But it's almost never possible. It's true, David Dunaway was able to revise his biography of Pete Seeger after the folk-singer made his displeasure known, but that's rare. Most of the time the ill-chosen words hang there; if you're lucky, no one reads them and they turn to dust. But sometimes the words act and cause actions, as words do, and some readers may be led down the wrong path or may have terrible thoughts planted in their brains. So far I haven't disowned any of my own writing, although I often cringe at how infantile, wrong-headed, or tone-deaf some passage may be.

I certainly can't disavow my typos. No matter how much the copy editor and I comb the text, at least one goof will slip right through the galleys. For some reason there's an article repeated or a word misspelled or worse. Yet I've come to terms with the stray typo, because the error demonstrates that the work is not perfect, the text is always contingent, always transient, a "draft of a draft," as Herman Melville's Ishmael describes *Moby-Dick.*

I learned from my grandmother that we should welcome imperfection because it wards off the Evil Eye. Although typos may help me avoid the Evil Eye, they can also make me writhe in horror and shame. I had the occasion once of speaking on a college campus about one of my books, and my hosts liked my book so much they printed a passage from it on a banner to drape on the wall behind me. To my dismay, that passage contained the one typo in the book—"again" had been changed to "against"—and I had to speak at a podium in front of the flag of the book's one error. Interestingly, the change made grammatical sense, and the sentence projected a different yet similar meaning. That was a close call I could live with, and I went on, never mentioning to my hosts that the banner was an embarrassment. But shame, failure, despair, utter horror, these are all stations on the journey, even after completing a "draft of a draft."

Over the course of these conversations I've learned a lot about my own writing. All of the books I've written have been motivated by some burning sense of urgency because I needed to discover something about the world and myself and, often enough, because I was pissed off. As Paula Moya explained, anger can be a type of fever "that signals that something is wrong," and it can be "an indicator" of something deeper. There are other "indicators" as well. Many of my writing projects were propelled by a sense of personal discovery, mission, and, more than occasionally, irritation. The writers in these "How I Write" conversations are also deeply driven by some need, sometimes by anger, often by love. I no longer feel strange in my mania because passion, even obsession, is an essential element of any sort of intellectual labor.

In the course of these conversations, as I discovered many of the idiosyncratic ways people work, how they learned to write and revise, their methods of overcoming blocks, the ways they came up with ideas, and all their different approaches to their craft, I came to question my own habits and methods. I discovered new ways of working, new approaches to style, inspired by what these writers shared. At the same time, I felt at ease that my own odd habits were not so bizarre after all, that idiosyncrasy is almost a given, that no one works in the same way as others, though all seek the same goals, all seek readers who will join them in their passion for meaning and consciousness.

Diane Middlebrook knew all of the stresses and terrors along with the joys of writing, and she spoke eloquently about how to keep everything (attitudes as well as research) sorted out. I recently came across her biography in Wikipedia, and I was delighted to find a quote from our "How I Write" conversation prominently displayed. "With a biography, there is no straight line; all is muddled," she said. "You don't know what you know, you don't know what you don't know; if you find anything, you make a note about it, because some day it may find its partner. You have to have very good ways of keeping track of what you have found and where you have put it." This seems to be more than a technique for doing research for a biography; it's an outlook on life.

When I started writing *How We Write,* I didn't know what I knew or what I didn't know about how people write. I thought I did. But as the conversations progressed I came to understand Diane Middlebrook's point. I've muddled along, trying to keep track of what I've found; I may have lost a lot, although the recordings and transcripts of the conversations certainly helped to minimize the losses. I know I must have edited out some great comments or failed to connect valuable observations in this book. But every conversation informed this book, even if I could not quote from all of them.

I'm often at a loss about endings. It's hard to close, to conclude. Too many times I've dragged out my piece of writing with a flourish of the hat or what I've thought was a surprising twist, only to discover that it was a waste of time. I've learned to cut down the filigree and simply stop. In *How We Write: The Varieties of Writing Experience* I believe I've said all that needs to be said, done all that this book set out to do, and that's all that anyone writing a book can hope for.

Except, of course, finding readers. That's up to you.

Profiles of "How I Write" Participants

These short profiles were used to publicize How I Write Conversations. They are not revised to reflect recent work. For example, Adam Johnson's conversation took place before he received the Pulitzer Prize in fiction in 2013. The year of each conversation is noted at the beginning of each profile. There were several conversations held in groups: "Imagining the Lives of Others," with a historian, an anthropologist, and a biographer; student journalists who write for the Stanford Daily; lecturers who teach in the Program in Writing and Rhetoric; and fiction writers currently or formerly in the Creative Writing Program.

Richard Zare

David Abernethy, *Emeritus Professor of Political Science*

2002 | David Abernethy is Emeritus Professor of Political Science. The focus of his research has been on Africa and issues of international development. His articles and chapters in books include "European Colonialism and Post-Colonial Crises in Africa" and "Bureaucratic Growth and Economic Stagnation in Sub-Saharan Africa," and he is the author of *The Political Dilemma of Popular Education: An African Case* (1964). His most recent book, *The Dynamics of Global Dominance: European Overseas Empires, 1415-1980* (2000), has been highly acclaimed as a major advance in the study of colonialism. He received the Lloyd W. Dinkelspiel Award for his contributions to undergraduate education in 2002.

JoAnne Akalaitis, *Theatrical Director, The Public Theater*

2007 | This special conversation is an inside look at the creative process behind the staging (revision) of a classic work, the Bacchae by Euripides with music by Philip Glass. We will have a conversation with famed director JoAnne Akalaitis, along with dramaturg Jim Leverett, who are participating in The Public Theater at Stanford residency, which is part of the Lively Arts' Alchemy series on the nature of artistic collaboration co-sponsored by the Stanford Institute for Creativity and the Arts. JoAnne Akalaitis is co-founder of the critically acclaimed theater company Mabou Mines in New York and the winner of five Obie Awards for direction (and sustained achievement). JoAnne Alkalaitis staged productions at American Repertory Theatre, Lincoln Center Theater, New York City Opera, Goodman Theatre, Mark Taper Forum, Court Theatre, Opera Theatre of Saint Louis, and Guthrie Theater. She has staged works by Euripides, Shakespeare, Strindberg, Schiller, Beckett, Genet, Williams and Philip Glass.

Molly Antopol, *Stanford Creative Writing Program*

2013 | Molly Antopol is a recent Wallace Stegner Fellow and current Draper Lecturer at Stanford University. Her debut story collection *The Un-Americans* is forthcoming from W.W. Norton in February 2014. She received her M.F.A. from Columbia University, and her writing has appeared or is forthcoming on NPR's *This American Life* and in *One Story, Glimmer Train, American Short Fiction, Mississippi Review Prize Stories* and elsewhere. She lives in San Francisco and is at work on the novel, *The After Party*, which will also be published by Norton.

Donald Barr, *Professor of Sociology and Human Biology*

2003 | Donald Barr is a physician and is Associate Professor of Sociology and Human Biology, and is the founder and director of Stanford's undergraduate curriculum in health policy. His research has included health policy and health care reform in the former Soviet Union and the effect of the organizational structure of the U.S. medical care delivery system on the quality of primary care. More recently he has begun to study cultural and linguistic barriers to health care access for low-income patients, and factors associated with higher rates of attrition from pre-medical studies among minority students at Stanford and other universities. His book *Introduction to U.S. Health Policy: The Organization, Financing, and Delivery of Health Care in America* was recently published by Pearson Education. In June 2003 Dr. Barr was awarded the Lloyd W. Dinkelspiel Award for Distinctive Contribution to Undergraduate Education at Stanford University. This conversation will focus on writing for medicine and social science.

Joel Beinin, *Professor of Middle East History*

2007 | Joel Beinin has taught Middle East history at Stanford since 1983. His research deals primarily with the social history of the modern Middle East, with a focus on workers, peasants, and minorities. He has also written and lectured extensively on Israel, Palestine, and the Arab-Israeli conflict. His books include *The Struggle for Sovereignty: Palestine and Israel, 1993-2005* (with Rebecca Stein), *Workers and Peasants in the Modern Middle East*; *Political Islam: Essays from Middle East Report* (co-edited with Joe Stork), *The Dispersion of Egyptian Jewry: Culture, Politics and the Formation of a Modern Diaspora, Was the Red Flag Flying There? Marxist Politics and the Arab-Israeli Conflict in Egypt and Israel, 1948-1965*. He served as President of the Middle East Studies Association of North America in 2002. He is also director of the Middle East Studies Program at the American University in Cairo.

Eavan Boland, *Professor of English and Bella Mabury and Eloise Mabury Knapp Professor in Humanities*

2004 | Eavan Boland has published nine volumes of poetry, including *Against Love Poetry, The Lost Land, In a Time of Violence*, and *An Origin Like Water: Collected Poems 1967-87*. She has received the Lannan Award for Poetry and has published a volume of prose called *Object Lessons: The Life of the Woman and the Poet in Our Time*. She is regarded as one of the outstanding Irish poets of our time.

David Brady, *Professor of Political Science*

2004 | David Brady, Chair of the Public Policy Program and Associate Director of the Hoover Institution, has written extensively on the political process. His books include *Party, Process, and Political Change in Congress* (editor), *Revolving Gridlock* (co-author), *Change and Continuity in House Elections* (editor), and *Public Policy in the 1980's* (co-author). His many articles range from "One Man, One Vote – So What?" in 1969 to "Out of Step Out of Office: Voting and Election in the U.S. House of Representatives" (co-author) in 2002.

John Bravman, *Professor of Materials Science and Engineering and Vice Provost of Undergraduate Education*

2003 | In addition to his dissertation, "Morphological Aspects of Silicon," Prof. Bravman has produced numerous technical papers, often in collaboration with other scientists and engineers. He has also reviewed the dissertations and research essays of numerous graduate and undergraduate students. In addition to scientific writing, Prof. Bravman, in his administrative capacities, produces much day-to-day writing, such as reports and memos, the equivalent of "business writing" in the corporate world, so we will be able to explore this often over-looked area of composition.

Terry Castle, *Professor of English, Walter A. Haas Professor of the Humanities*

2009 | Terry Castle specializes in the history of the novel, especially the works of Defoe, Richardson, and Fielding, and in the study of eighteenth-century popular culture. She has written seven books: *Clarissa's Ciphers: Meaning and Disruption in Richardson's 'Clarissa'* (1982), *Masquerade and Civilization: The Carnivalesque in Eighteenth-Century English Culture and Fiction* (1986); *The Apparitional Lesbian: Female Homosexuality and Modern Culture* (1993), *The Female Thermometer: Eighteenth-Century Culture and the Invention of the Uncanny* (1995), *Noel Coward and Radclyffe Hall: Kindred Spirits* (1996), *Boss Ladies, Watch Out! Essays on Women, Sex, and Writing* (2002), and *Courage, Mon Amie* (2002). She is the editor of *The Literature of Lesbianism: A Historical Anthology from Ariosto to Stonewall* (2003). She has received a number of awards and writes regularly for the *London Review of Books*, the *New Republic*, and other magazines and journals. Terry Castle's book of autobiographical essays, *The Professor and Other Essays,* will be appearing this year. She also produces a visual art blog, Fevered Brain Productions, at http://terry-castle-blog.blogspot.com

Harriet Scott Chessman, *Novelist*

2014 | Harriet Chessman is the author most recently of the acclaimed novel *The Beauty of Ordinary Things*, the story of the unexpected love between a young Vietnam veteran and a Benedictine nun. Her other books include the novels *Someone Not Really Her Mother, Lydia Cassatt Reading the Morning Paper,* and *Ohio Angels,* as well as *The Public Is Invited to Dance,* a book about Gertrude Stein. Her fiction has been translated into ten languages. She has taught literature and writing at Yale University, Bread Loaf School of English, and Stanford University's Continuing Studies Program.

Diane Di Prima, *Poet*

2013 | Feminist Beat poet Diane di Prima was born in Brooklyn, New York, a second generation American of Italian descent. She began writing at the age of seven, and made the decision to live her life as a poet at the age of fourteen. After attending Swarthmore College for two years, she moved to Greenwich Village, becoming a writer in the emerging Beat movement. She edited the literary magazine *The Floating Bear,* first with Amiri Baraka (LeRoi Jones) from 1961 to 1963 and then solo until 1969. She co-founded the Poets Press and the New York Poets Theatre and founded Eidolon Editions and the Poets Institute. After joining Timothy Leary's intentional community in upstate New York, she moved to San Francisco in 1968.

Di Prima has published more than 40 books. Her poetry collections include *This Kind of Bird Flies Backwards, Revolutionary Letters*, the long poem *Loba* (hailed by many as the female counterpart to Allen Ginsberg's *Howl*), *Seminary Poems,* and *Pieces of a Song: Selected Poems.* She is also the author of the short story collection *Dinners and Nightmares,* the semi-autobiographical *Memoirs of a Beatnik,* and the memoir *Recollections of My Life as a Woman: The New York Years.*

A practicing Buddhist since 1962, she also co-founded the San Francisco Institute of Magical and Healing Arts. Di Prima was named Poet Laureate of San Francisco in 2009, and she was awarded the National Poetry Association's Lifetime Service Award, the Fred Cody Award for Lifetime Achievement and other honors.

David Dunaway, *Oral Historian and Radio Documentarian*

2009 | David Dunaway is the co-author of *Oral History: An Interdisciplinary Anthology*, and he has for many years employed oral history and audio techniques in his work. For the last thirty years, David Dunaway has documented the work of famed folk singer Pete Seeger, resulting in *How Can I Keep From Singing? The Ballad of Pete Seeger*, published by McGraw Hill in 1981 and revised, updated, and republished by Villard/Random House, 2008. A companion radio series *Pete Seeger: How Can I Keep From Singing?* was broadcast nationally in 2008. It was recently awarded BEA awards for Best Documentary and Best Audio. He is the co-author of *Huxley in Hollywood* (1990), *Aldous Huxley Recollected* (1996), and *Writing the Southwest* (1995, 2003). His most recent book *Singing Out: An Oral History of America's Folk Music Revivals* with Molly Beer will be released this spring. Dunaway has also been active in radio since 1972, focusing on presenting folklore, literature, and history. Over the last dozen years he has been Executive Producer of award-winning national radio series for Public Radio International, including *Writing the Southwest* (1995), *Aldous Huxley's Brave New Worlds* (1998), *Across the Tracks: A Route 66 Story* (2001), and *Pete Seeger: How Can I Keep From Singing?* (2008). He is currently a DJ for KUNM-FM, a professor at the University of New Mexico in Albuquerque and San Francisco State University in California.

Paulla Ebron, *Associate Professor of Cultural and Social Anthropology*

2006 | Paulla Ebron is the author of *Performing Africa*, a work based on her research in The Gambia that traces the significance of West African praise-singers in transnational encounters. A second project focuses on tropicality and regionalism as it ties West Africa and the U.S. Georgia Sea Islands in a dialogue about landscape, memory and political uplift. This project is entitled, "Making Tropical Africa in the Georgia Sea Islands."

Penelope Eckert, *Professor of Linguistics, Cultural and Social Anthropology, and Director of Feminist Studies*

2003 | Penelope Eckert describes herself as a "Second Wave Feminist" and a "Third Wave Variationist," focusing her research on the social meaning of linguistic variation, the role of gender and sexuality in sociolinguistic variation, and adolescents and pre-adolescents as "the movers and shakers in linguistic change." Prof. Eckert has written numerous articles, such as "Vowels and Nail Polish: The Emergence of Linguistic Style in the Preadolescent Heterosexual Marketplace," and several books, including *Gender and Language Practice* (with Sally McConnell-Ginet), *Linguistic Variation as Social Practice*, and *Jocks and Burnouts: Social Categories and Identity in the High School*.

Harry Elam, *Professor of Drama*

2004 | Harry Elam is the Robert and Ruth Halperin University Fellow for Undergraduate Education, Professor of Drama, Director of Graduate Studies in Drama, Director of the Institute for Diversity in the Arts and Director of the Committee on Black Performing Arts at Stanford University. He is author of *Taking it to the Streets: The Social Protest Theater of Luis Valdez and Amiri Baraka* and *The Past as Present in the Drama of August Wilson,* and co-editor of *African American Performance and Theater History: A Critical Reader, Colored Contradictions: An Anthology of Contemporary African American Drama, The Fire This Time: African American Plays for the New Millennium* and *Black Cultural Traffic: Crossroads in Black Performance and Popular Culture.* His articles have appeared in *American Drama, Modern Drama, Theatre Journal, Text and Performance Quarterly* as well as several critical anthologies, and he is the co-editor of *Theatre Journal,* and on the editorial board of *Modern Drama* and *Comparative Drama.*

Nancy Etchemendy, *Fantasy and Horror Novelist for Children and Young Adults*

2008 | Nancy Etchemendy's novels, short fiction, and poetry have appeared regularly for the past 25 years, both in the U.S. and abroad. Though she is best known for her children's books, she has also published several dozen stories for adults, mostly dark fantasy and horror. Her work has earned a number of awards, including two Bram Stoker Awards for children's horror, a Golden Duck Award for excellence in children's science fiction, and an Anne Spencer Lindbergh Prize silver medal for excellence in children's fantasy. Her books include the novel *The Power of Un* and *Cat in Glass and Other Tales of the Unnatural,* a collection of short dark fantasy for young adults. She leads a somewhat schizophrenic life, alternating between unkempt, introverted writer of weird tales and requisite gracious wife of Stanford University's Provost.

Shelley Fisher Fishkin, *Professor of English, Director of American Studies*

2005 | Shelley Fisher Fishkin is one of the leading scholars in American culture and literature, particularly on the work of Mark Twain. She is the editor of the Oxford edition of Twain's work, and she most recently edited and published Twain's play *Is He Dead?* Her other books include *Lighting Out for the Territory: Reflections on Mark Twain, Was Huck Black: Mark Twain and African-American Voices,* and *From Fact to Fiction: Journalism and Imaginative Writing in*

America. She is also a co-editor of *Encyclopedia of Civil Rights in America* and *Listening to Silences: New Essays in Feminist Criticism,* and the editor of *People of the Book: Thirty Scholars Reflect on their Jewish Identity.* She is currently president of the American Studies Association.

Richard Thompson Ford, *George E. Osborne Professor of Law*

2009 | Richard Thompson Ford's work has focused on the social and legal conflicts surrounding claims of discrimination, on the causes and effects of racial segregation, and on the use of territorial boundaries as instruments of social regulation. Methodologically, his work is at the intersection of critical theory and the law. He has written the books *The Race Card: How Bluffing about Bias Makes Race Relations Worse* (2008) and *Racial Culture: A Critique* (2005), and contributed chapters to *The Legal Geographies Reader: Law, Power and Space* (2001) and other collections. His articles have appeared in the *Harvard Law Review* and other law journals, as well as the *Washington Post, San Francisco Chronicle, Christian Science Monitor* and *Slate,* where he is a regular contributor.

George Fredrickson, *Professor Emeritus of U.S. History*

2003 | George Fredrickson is one of the most eminent historians of the United States and of comparative studies of racism and racial identity in the U.S., South Africa, and Nazi Germany. His most recent book, *Racism: A Short History,* has been hailed as a major breakthrough in the analysis of racial oppression. Professor Fredrickson's other books include *The Comparative Imagination: On the History of Racism, Rationalism, and Social Movements, Black Liberation: A Comparative History of Black Ideologies in the United States and South Africa,* and *The Black Image in the White Mind: The Debate on Afro-American Character and Destiny.*

Amy Freed, *Artist in Residence, Drama Department*

2006 | Amy Freed is the author of *The Beard of Avon, Freedomland* (both commissioned by South Coast Rep), *The Psychic Life of Savages,* and other plays. Her work has been produced at SCR, New York Theatre Workshop, Seattle Repertory, American Conservatory Theater, the Goodman Theatre, Playwright's Horizons, Woolly Mammoth, and other theaters around the country. Her recent play, *Safe in Hell,* another SCR commission, received its premiere production in April 2004, and was presented at Yale Rep in the fall of 2005. Her newest play, *Restoration Comedy,* debuted at Seattle Repertory in December

2005, and received its Bay Area premiere at the California Shakespeare Festival. Amy has been the recipient of the Joseph Kesselring Award, The Charles MacArthur Award, is a several times winner of the LA Drama Critics Circle Award, and was a Pulitzer finalist for *Freedomland*.

Estelle Freedman, *Professor of History*

2003 | Estelle Freedman specializes in U.S. women's history, particularly the role of women in movements for social reform. She has also written extensively on the history of sexuality in the U.S., as well as lesbian history. Her most recent book, *No Turning Back: The History and the Future of Women*, has been widely praised as one of the most comprehensive and analytical studies of feminism to date. Her other books include *Maternal Justice: Miriam Van Waters and the Female Reform Tradition*, *Intimate Matters: A History of Sexuality in America*, and *Their Sisters' Keepers: Women's Prison Reform in America, 1830-1930*.

Albert Gelpi, *Emeritus Professor of English*

2015 | From 1968 through 2002 Albert Gelpi taught American literature, particularly American poetry, from its Puritan beginnings to the present day. Gelpi has written *Emily Dickinson: The Mind of the Poet* (1965) and *The Tenth Muse: The Psyche of the American Poet* (1975), which centers on American Romantic poetry; its sequel, *A Coherent Splendor: The American Poetic Renaissance 1910-1950* (1987) continues the historical argument by relating American Modernist poetry to its Romantic antecedents. He is also the author of *Living in Time: The Poetry of C. Day Lewis* (1998) and has edited *The Poet in America, 1650 to the Present; Wallace Stevens: The Poetics of Modernism; Denise Levertov: Selected Criticism; The Blood of the Poet: Selected Poems of William Everson*, and (with Barbara Charlesworth Gelpi) *Adrienne Rich's Poetry and Prose*. With Robert Bertholf he edited *The Letters of Robert Duncan and Denise Levertov* (2004) and the collection of essays, *Robert Duncan and Denise Levertov: The Poetry of Politics, The Politics of Poetry* (2006). His latest book is *American Poetry After Modernism: The Power of the Word* was published this year, and his next project is the selected prose of C. Day Lewis, *The Golden Bridle*.

Bill Guttentag, *Screenwriter, Director, Producer,*
Lecturer, Graduate School of Business, Stanford University

2011 | Bill Guttentag is a two-time Oscar-winning documentary and feature film writer-producer-director. He also wrote and directed *Nanking*, a theatrical documentary that premiered at the 2007 Sundance Film Festival and features Woody Harrelson, Mariel Hemingway, and Jürgen Prochnow. In 2008 he wrote and directed *Live!*, a dramatic feature starring Eva Mendes and Andre Braugher. *Soundtrack for a Revolution* had its international premiere at the 2009 Cannes Film Festival. He is currently in post-production on *Knife Fight*, a film he wrote and directed about a Democratic political consultant, starring Rob Lowe, Jamie Chung, Julie Bowen, Carrie-Ann Moss, Eric McCormack, Jennifer Morrison, and Saffron Burrows, will be released in 2012.

In 2003 Bill Guttentag won an Oscar for the documentary *Twin Towers*. He has also received a second Oscar, three additional Oscar nominations, a Peabody Award, three Emmy Awards, two additional Emmy nominations, two Writers Guild Award nominations, a Producers Guild Award nomination, and a Robert Kennedy Journalism Award. His films have been selected for the Sundance Film Festival three times and have played and won awards at numerous American and international film festivals. They have also received a number of special screenings internationally and in the US, including at the White House.

His first novel, *Boulevard*, was published in 2010 and the paperback version was released in 2011.

He is a lecturer at the Graduate School of Business at Stanford University, teaching a class on the film and television business.

Thomas Hare, *Stanford Humanities Center Marta Sutton Weeks Fellow 2011-12; Comparative Literature, Princeton University*

2012 | Thomas Hare is Professor of Comparative Literature at Princeton. Trained at the University of Michigan, he taught first at Stanford, moving to Princeton in 2001. His interests range from the interaction of Buddhism with the arts in traditional Japan to the representational systems of ancient Egypt. His books include *Zeami: Performance Notes* and *Zeamis Style: The Noh Plays of Zeami*, offering translations and critical analysis of works by the important Noh dramatist. He has also published *ReMembering Osiris: Number, Gender, and the Word in Ancient Egyptian Representational Systems*, examining the texts and visual arts of ancient Egypt. His current project is *Performance and Practice in Buddhist Japan* looks closely at the interaction between Buddhist practice and the performance of four quintessentially Japanese arts during the medieval and early modern period in order to better understand how "practice" is conceived outside a monastic context.

John Hennessy, *President of Stanford University*

2004 | President John Hennessy produces speeches, memos, articles, and other types of writing as university president. But the president is also a professor, a highly regarded computer scientist. He has been the author or co-author of over one hundred scientific papers, as well as the co-author of two textbooks: *Computer Organization and Design: The Hardware/Software Interface* and *Computer Architecture: A Quantitative Approach.* Professor Hennessy initiated a project at Stanford to develop a simpler computer architecture known as RISC (Reduced Instruction Set Computer), and he has played a key role in taking this technology to industry, serving on several boards of directors. He is an experienced writer in the realms of science, business, administration, and educational policy, and we will gain unique insights on how he approaches such diverse writing tasks.

Scott Hutchins, *Novelist, Lecturer, Stanford Creative Writing Program*

2013 | Scott Hutchins is a former Truman Capote fellow in the Wallace Stegner Program at Stanford University. Set against the backdrop of San Francisco's hi-tech industry, Hutchins' debut novel *A Working Theory of Love* has been widely reviewed. His work has appeared in *StoryQuarterly, Five Chapters, The Owls, The Rumpus, The New York Times, San Francisco Magazine* and *Esquire.* He is the recipient of two major Hopwood awards and the Andrea Beauchamp prize in short fiction. Hutchins teaches courses on fiction writing in Stanford's Creative Writing Program.

David Henry Hwang, *Playwright in Residence, The Public Theater*

2007 | Celebrated playwrite and screenwriter David Henry Hwang graduated from Stanford in 1979. Most of his plays have focused on Asian American themes, such as his acclaimed play *M. Butterfly.* Hwang's other works include *FOB* (first developed at Stanford), *The Dance and the Railroad, Rich Relations, Face Value,* and an updated version of *Flower Drum Song.* He has also written opera librettos and screenplays for film and television. He has won Tony, an Obie, a Drama Desk, and a Circle Awards, along with fellowships from the Guggenheim and Rockefeller foundations and the National Endowment for the Arts. At Stanford he is working on a new play, *Yellow Face.*

Adam Johnson, *Novelist, Associate Professor of English in Creative Writing*

2012 | Adam Johnson's novel *The Orphan Master's Son* was published this year to great acclaim. He is also the author of *Emporium*, a short-story collection, and the novel *Parasites Like Us*, which won a California Book Award. He is a Whiting Writers' Award winner, and his fiction has appeared in *Esquire, Harper's, Playboy, Paris Review, Granta, Tin House* and *Best American Short Stories*. His books have been translated into thirteen languages. Johnson was a 2010 National Endowment for the Arts Fellow, and he is Associate Professor of English in Creative Writing.

Troy Jollimore, *External Faculty Fellow at the Stanford Humanities Center, Philosopher and Poet*

2007 | Troy Jollimore writes poetry and philosophy, so this discussion will encompass two very different types of work. His first book of poetry, *Tom Thomson in Purgatory*, won the 2006 National Book Critics Circle Award and was selected by Billy Collins for the 2005 Robert E. Lee and Ruth I. Wilson Poetry Book Award. His poems have appeared in journals, including *Ploughshares, PRISM International, The Malahat Review,* and *Exile*. In philosophy, he has written *Friendship and Agent-Relative Morality*, as well as a number of articles, such as "Morally Admirable Immorality" and "Why is Instrumental Rationality Rational?" As a fellow at the Humanities Center this year, he is working on a book entitled *The Nature of Loyalty*. He is currently Associate Professor of Philosophy at California State University, Chico.

Clarence B. Jones, *Scholar in Residence, The Martin Luther King, Jr. Research and Education Institute*

2013 | As the 50th anniversary of the March on Washington approaches, we have the opportunity to talk with a key speechwriter and counsel to Martin Luther King, Jr. From 1960 until his assassination in 1968, Clarence Jones worked closely with Rev. King, assisting him in drafting the celebrated "I Have a Dream" speech that Rev. King delivered August 28, 1963. Through his work in the civil rights movement, Dr. Jones has dramatically impacted the course of American history. For example, in April 1963, he drafted the settlement agreement between the City of Birmingham and Rev. King to bring about the end of demonstrations and the desegregation of department stores and public accommodations. In September 1971, he again found himself at the center of historic events when, at the request of Governor Nelson A. Rockefeller, he helped in the attempt to negotiate an end to the historic Attica prison inmate rebellion. Dr. Jones also had a successful career in an investment banking firm, and was the "first Negro" on Wall Street. He has founded successful financial, corporate and media-related ventures. He is the co-author of *What Would Martin Say? Behind the Dream: The Making of the Speech That Transformed A Nation*, and *Uprising: Understanding Attica, Revolution and the Incarceration State*. He is currently co-writing a book, *Where Were You?* for the 50th Anniversary of the Assassination of President John F. Kennedy. Dr. Jones posts a regular column in the Huffington Post. He is also writing his autobiography: *Memoirs of A Winter Time Soldier.*

Journalists for *The Stanford Daily*
James Hohmann, Julie Klein, Daniel Novinson, Emma Trotter

2008 | Every day we read *The Stanford Daily*, but who are the people who bring you the news, film reviews, sports analysis, and everything else you read in the paper and on line? Now we can have a roundtable conversation with award-winning journalists and editors who work for the newspaper to find out how they investigate stories, cover events, meet intense deadlines, write with an engaging style, and more.

James Hohmann is the web and multimedia editor for *The Stanford Daily*, and has been Editor-in-Chief and President. He won the James Robinson Award for his incisive coverage of organized labor. He's worked on the city desk of the *San Jose Mercury News*. Over the summer, he interned on the national desk at *The Dallas Morning News*, and he continues to write for the newspaper. He will begin a reporting internship at *The Washington Post* in June 2008.

Julie Klein is a junior majoring in history. She has worked at *The Daily* since her freshman year, when she was a staff writer for news. Last year Klein worked as a news desk editor once per week, and this fall she worked as the managing editor of news.

Daniel Novinson has been the football and men's basketball beat writer for three years, the managing editor of sports and a news desk editor. He won the James Robinson Award for breaking the story about Azia Kim posing as a Stanford student. He's interned at Detroit TV and radio stations. He's a senior, a public policy and economics dual major who recently became pre-med, and a returning resident assistant in Roble.

After serving as features and news editor on her high school newspaper staff, **Emma Trotter** began writing for *The Stanford Daily* during fall quarter of her freshman year. She writes for news and *Intermission*, and she is the Tuesday night desk editor for news this volume.

Terry Karl, *Political Science*

2004 | Terry Karl, the Gildre Professor of Latin American Studies, was the director of Stanford's Center for Latin American Studies from 1990-2001. She has published widely on transitions to democracy; problems of inequality; human rights and civil wars; contemporary Latin American politics; and comparative politics and international relations, with special emphasis on the politics of oil-exporting countries. Her work includes such books as *Bottom of the Barrel: Africa's Oil Boom and the Poor* and articles such as "Economic Inequality and Democratic Instability," "Reflections on the Paradox of Plenty," "The Hybrid Regimes of Latin America," and "Dilemmas of Democratization in Latin America."

Tom Kealey, *Lecturer, Creative Writing Program*

2006 | Tom Kealey is the author of *The Creative Writing MFA Handbook*. His stories have appeared in *Best American NonRequired*, *Glimmer Train*, *Story Quarterly*, *Prairie Schooner*, the *San Francisco Chronicle* and elsewhere. His nonfiction has appeared in *Poets and Writers* and *The Writer*. His novel in progress is entitled *The Winged Girl*.

David Kennedy, *Donald J. McLachian Professor of History*

2005 | David Kennedy received the Pulitzer Prize for *Freedom from Fear: The American People in Depression and War, 1929-1945*. His other books include *Over Here: The First World War and American Society*, *The American People in the Depression*, and *Birth Control in America: The Career of Margaret Sanger*, in addition to many articles. He is also a co-author of a highly influential textbook *The American Pageant: A History of the Republic*, now in its 13th edition.

Donald Kennedy, *Bing Professor of Environmental Science and Policy, Emeritus, and President Emeritus of Stanford University*

2005 | Professor Kennedy writes extensively on science, policy, and education, and he is currently editor of *Science*, one of the leading scientific journals in the world, as well as a former president of the university. He can share insights about writing for scientific, public policy, and administrative and educational purposes. His books include *Valuing Nature* (co-author), *U.S. Policy and the Global Environment* (co-author), *Academic Duty, Academic Misconduct, Agricultural Production, Innovation, and Biological Diversity* (co-author).

Susan Krieger, *Feminist Studies Program*

2011 | Susan Krieger is the author of *Traveling Blind: Adventures in Vision with a Guide Dog by My Side* (2010). This book is a romance, a travel adventure, an emotional quest, and a deeply reflective description of coming to terms with lack of sight. It reveals the invisible work of navigating with a guide dog while learning to perceive the world in new ways. Krieger's writings are highly personal and in recent years have focused on disability. We will talk with her about innovative writing in the social sciences, including her latest work in progress, *The Art of the Intimate Narrative: Unconventional Academic Writing*. Her other books include *Things No Longer There: A Memoir of Losing Sight and Finding Vision* (2005), *The Family Silver: Essays on Relationships among Women* (1996), *Social Science and the Self: Personal Essays on an Art Form* (1991), *The Mirror Dance: Identity in a Women's Community* (1983), and *Hip Capitalism* (1979). She is a sociologist and writer and teaches in the Program in Feminist Studies.

Jim Leverett, *Dramaturg, The Public Theater*

2007 | Jim Leverett began his career as an actor on Broadway and beyond. He was the first director of Literary Services at Theatre Communications Group, where he helped to initiate many publications, including *American Theatre* magazine. In 1988, he received the first Literary Managers and Dramaturgs of the Americas award for services to the field. He wrote introductions to Harvey Fierstein's *Torchsong Trilogy* and Spalding Gray's *Swimming to Cambodia*, along with numerous pieces in other national and international publications, including Yale's *Theater* for which he is a contributing editor. He has worked as dramaturg throughout the United States, most recently Shaw's *Mrs. Warren's Profession* at Berkshire Theatre Festival. He is Associate Professor of Dramaturgy and Dramatic Criticism at the Yale School of Drama and visiting professor in the Theater Division of Columbia University's School of the Arts.

Gwyneth Lewis, *Arts Practitioner/Writer Fellow at the Stanford Humanities Center, Poet and Nonfiction Author*

2011 | Gwyneth Lewis published six books of poetry in Welsh and English. Her first collection in English, *Parables & Faxes* (Bloodaxe, 1995) won the

Aldeburgh Poetry Festival Prize and was short listed for the Forward Poetry Prize, as was her second book, *Zero Gravity* (Bloodaxe, 1998). *Chaotic Angels* collects her first three books of poetry in English. Lewis' first non-fiction book, *Sunbathing in the Rain: A Cheerful Book on Depression* (Flamingo 2002), was shortlisted for the Mind Book of the Year and was recently broadcast as a play on BBC Radio 4. She is also a librettist and an award-winning playwright. Her current project is *Poetry and the Body*, a scholarly survey of prosody, drawing on Celtic, English, and American poetry from earliest times to the present day, exploring the effect of meter and rhyme on poets' and readers' bodies. The whole project argues that prosody is far more than literary ornament – it's fundamental to how we learn and develop language and an essential part of our ongoing health as creators of poetic discourse. She was appointed the first National Poet of Wales in 2005.

Andrea Lunsford, *Professor of English and Director of the Program in Writing and Rhetoric*

2003 | Andrea Lunsford is a scholar of rhetoric and composition studies. She writes about writing – from college writing handbooks to scholarly analyses of women's rhetoric, collaborative writing, and other topics. Her books include *The St. Martin's Handbook, Everything's an Argument, The Everyday Writer, Reclaiming Rhetorica: Women in the Rhetorical Tradition, The Presence of Others,* and *Singular Texts/Plural Authors: Perspectives on Collaborative Writing.*

Liisa Malkki, *Associate Professor of Anthropology*

2008 | Liisa Malkki's research interests include: the politics of nationalism, internationalism, cosmopolitanism, and human rights discourses as transnational cultural forms; the social production of historical memory and the uses of history; political violence, exile, and displacement; the ethics and politics of humanitarian aid; child research; and visual culture. Her field research in Tanzania explored the ways in which political violence and exile may produce transformations of historical consciousness and national identity among displaced people. This project resulted in *Purity and Exile: Violence, Memory, and National Cosmology Among Hutu Refugees in Tanzania* (University of Chicago Press, 1995). In another project, Malkki explored how Hutu exiles from Burundi and Rwanda, who found asylum in Montreal, Canada, imagined scenarios of the future for themselves and their countries in the aftermath of genocide in the Great Lakes Region of Africa. Malkki's most recent book is *Improvising*

Theory: Process and Temporality in Ethnographic Fieldwork (with Allaine Cerwonka). Her current book-length project (based on fieldwork from 1995 to the present) examines the changing interrelationships among humanitarian interventions, internationalism, professionalism, affect, and neutrality in the work of the Finnish Red Cross in cooperation with the International Committee of the Red Cross.

Hazel Markus, *Davis-Brack Professor in the Behavioral Sciences*

2005 | Hazel Markus' work is concerned with how gender, ethnicity, religion, social class, cohort, or region or country of national origin may influence thought and feeling, particularly self-relevant thought and feeling. She is a co-author of the forthcoming *Well-being, American Style*, along with *Engaging Cultural Differences: The Multicultural Challenge in Liberal Democracies*, and *Emotion and Culture: Empirical Studies of Mutual Influence*. She is co-author of numerous articles and empirical studies.

Scotty McLennan, *Dean of Religious Life*

2003 | Rev. Scotty McLennan is the author of *Finding Your Religion: When the Faith You Grew Up with Has Lost Its Meaning* and *Church on Sunday, Work on Monday: A Guide to Reflection* (with Laura Nash). Writing about religious faith and ethics presents many questions of thought, approach and tone. As Dean of Religious Life, Rev. McLennan will also offer insights into the very particular genres of the sermon and other forms of oratory, in addition to the rhetoric involved in ceremonial and spiritual occasions. Plus, as Doonesbury's "Dude of God," he has the unique experience of living a parallel life as a fictional character himself.

Thomas McNeely, *Jones Lecturer, Creative Writing Program*

2006 | Thomas McNeely has published stories in *The Atlantic Monthly*, *Ploughshares*, and other journals. His story, "Sheep," has been included in *Best of the South: The Best of the Second Decade*. He is currently working on a novel.

Diane Middlebrook, *Emerita Professor of English*

2002 | Diane Middlebrook is the author of *Suits Me: The Double Life of Billy Tipton*, *The Poetry of Anne Sexton and Sylvia Plath*, *Anne Sexton: A Biography*, and, forthcoming, a book on Ted Hughes and Sylvia Plath and a biography of Ovid.

Abbas Milani, *Director of Iranian Studies*

2011 | Abbas Milani is the Hamid and Christina Moghadam Director of Iranian Studies at Stanford, Research Fellow and Co-director of the Iran Democracy Project at the Hoover Institution, and Visiting Professor in the Department of Political Science. He is also one of the most knowledgeable commentators on Iranian politics and culture, and is in constant demand by media, governments (both the US and foreign), and universities for his interpretation of the latest events in Iran and their significance. Milani is the prolific author of over twenty books, most recently *The Shah,* which is acknowledged as the definitive biography of a man Milani finds immensely complicated, intriguing, and finally tragic. He's also the author of a memoir, *Tales of Two Cities,* which narrates his life as a student in the United States and as a politically active young man who returns to Iran and spends a year in the Shah's prison. *Kirkus Reviews* calls it "a breathtaking example of the quiet, selfless, gorgeousness of the memoirist's art."

Valerie Miner, *Novelist, Artist-in-Residence at the Clayman Institute for Gender Research; Consulting Professor of English and Feminist Studies*

2008 | Valerie Miner is the award-winning author of twelve books. Her most recent novel, *After Eden,* was published in the "Literature of the American West Series" by the University of Oklahoma Press in Spring, 2007. Other novels include *Range of Light, A Walking Fire, Winter's Edge, Blood Sisters, All Good Women, Movement: A Novel in Stories,* and *Murder in the English Department.* Her short fiction books include *Abundant Light, The Night Singers,* and *Trespassing.* Her collection of essays is *Rumors from the Cauldron: Selected Essays, Reviews and Reportage.* In 2002, *The Low Road: A Scottish Family Memoir* was a Finalist for the PEN USA Creative Non-Fiction Award. *Abundant Light* was a 2005 Fiction Finalist for the Lambda Literary Awards. Her stories and essays are published in more than sixty anthologies. Her collaborative work includes books, museum exhibits as well as theater.

Ian Morris, *Jean and Rebecca Willard Professor of Classics*

2015 | Ian Morris is Jean and Rebecca Willard Professor of Classics and a Fellow of the Archaeology Center at Stanford University. He grew up in Britain and studied at Birmingham and Cambridge Universities before moving to the University of Chicago in 1987 and on to Stanford University in 1995. He has published thirteen books and more than a hundred articles in academic journals and newspapers. His book *Why the West Rules—For Now: The Patterns of*

History, and What they Reveal About the Future won three literary awards, was named as one of the best books of the year by *The New York Times* and other newspapers and periodicals. His follow-up book *The Measure of Civilization* appeared in January 2013, and his latest book *War! What is it Good For?* came out in April 2014. The next, *Foragers, Farmers, and Fossil Fuels: How Values Evolve,* will be published in 2015.

Paula Moya, *Associate Professor of English*

2004 | Paula Moya is the director of the undergraduate program of CSRE. She writes on Chicana/o culture and literature, minority and feminist theory, and American literature. Her books include *Learning from Experience: Minority Identities, Multicultural Struggles* and *Reclaiming Identity: Realist Theory and the Predicament of Postmodernism* with Michael Hames-Garcia.

Anne Firth Murray, *Consulting Professor in Human Biology*

2006 | Anne Firth Murray, New Zealand-born, has worked for the United Nations as a writer and spent several years as an editor with university presses. For the past 25 years, she has worked in the field of philanthropy. She founded the Global Fund for Women in 1987 and served as its President until she retired in 1996. She is now a Consulting Professor in the Human Biology Program at Stanford University. Professor Murray also serves as a consultant on civil society and other issues to many foundations and is on numerous boards and councils of nonprofit organizations. Her book, *Paradigm Found: Turning your Dreams into Positive Action*, will appear 2006. She is currently working on a new book on international women's health and human rights.

Nancy Packer, *Emerita Professor of English*

2011 | Nancy Packer has published six books: *Small Moments,* which received the California Commonwealth Club Award for fiction, has been called "moving, amusing, touching, and even frightening." *In My Father's House* is a non-fiction work in stories, about Packer's growing up among boisterous siblings and a strong-willed father who was a Member of Congress. *The Women Who Walk* chronicles the lives of women in mid-life travails; as one critic said, "It's hard to see how these stories could be better." In a lighter mood, *Jealous-Hearted Me,* which received the Alabama Library Association Award, tells the story of the opinionated, outrageous Momma and her long-suffering daughter and son-in-law. Packer's stories have been widely anthologized, including in *O. Henry Prize Stories* and *Best American Stories*. She has also co-authored two textbooks, *The*

Short Story: An Introduction and *Writing Worth Reading*, both published in multiple editions.

Packer was a professor in the Stanford English Department, teaching creative writing, and received both the Dinkelspsiel Award and the Dean's Award for excellence in teaching. Twice she served on the Pulitzer Selection Committee for fiction. Packer is the widow of the late Herbert Packer, who was a Professor of Law and Vice Provost at Stanford. Their two children, Ann and George, are both writers.

Marjorie Perloff, *Emerita Professor of English*

2006 | Marjorie Perloff writes on contemporary and avant-garde poetry and poetics, as well as on intermedia and the visual arts. Her many books include *The Poetics of Indeterminacy: Rimbaud to Cage, The Futurist Moment: Avant-Garde, Avant-Guerre, and the Language of Rupture,* and *Wittgenstein's Ladder.* Professor Perloff has recently published her cultural memoir *The Vienna Paradox,* which has been widely discussed. She has written widely for periodicals, such as *TLS* and *The Washington Post,* as well as major scholarly journals. She is a member of the American Academy of Arts and Sciences and is the current President of the Modern Language Association.

Program in Writing and Rhetoric (PWR) Faculty Roundtable:
Christine Alfano, Kevin DiPirro, Alyssa O'Brien, Susan Wyle

2005 | Writers who teach writing can give us unique view off the writing process, so this special roundtable features four Program in Writing and Rhetoric faculty whose writing includes composition textbooks, plays, fiction, and literary criticism.

Susan Wyle is author of *Revisiting America: Readings in Race, Culture, and Conflict,*

Christine Alfano and **Alyssa O'Brien** co-authored *Envision: Persuasive Writing in a Visual World.*

Alyssa O'Brien is also author of articles in visual rhetoric, literary modernism, feminist criticism, and film theory.

Kevin DiPirro is a playwright, author of *Through Shite to Shannon* and *Mobl'd Queen's Good,* along with poetry, fiction and essays.

Arnold Rampersad, *Sara Hart Kimball Professor in the Humanities, Department of English*

2007 | Arnold Rampersad has just published the biography of the novelist Ralph Ellison. His books include *The Art and Imagination of W.E.B. DuBois, The Life of Langston Hughes* (2 vols. 1986, 1988), *Days of Grace: A Memoir,* co-authored with Arthur Ashe, and *Jackie Robinson: A Biography.* In addition, he has edited several volumes including *Collected Poems of Langston Hughes,* the Library of America edition of works by Richard Wright, with revised individual editions of *Native Son* and *Black Boy,* and *Slavery and the Literary Imagination* (with Deborah McDowell) He was also co-editor, with Shelley Fisher Fishkin, of the *Race and American Culture* book series published by Oxford University Press. From 1991 to 1996, he held a MacArthur Foundation fellowship. He is an elected member of the American Academy of Arts and Sciences and the American Philosophical Society.

Dr. David Rasch, *Director of the Stanford Help Center*

2003 | *What's writer's block? Do I have it? Why do I wait to the last minute before writing? Why do I get so nervous whenever I have to write?* This is a special session with David Rasch, who regularly deals with such questions. Dr. Rasch is a psychologist and the director of the Stanford Help Center, a counseling service for the faculty and staff of the university. He has assisted writers with productivity problems for the past 15 years through classes, workshops, support groups and individual sessions. Dr. Rasch teaches a class entitled "Overcoming Writing Blocks and Procrastination" through Stanford Continuing Studies, and has presented on his group work with tenure-track junior faculty at state and national conferences. He authored a chapter on assisting university faculty and staff through organizational changes in the book *Process and Organizational Redesign.* He is currently writing a book designed to help writers who are struggling with blocks, anxiety, procrastination, and related difficulties.

Rob Reich, *Associate Professor of Political Science*

2009 | Rob Reich is director of the Ethics in Society Program and co-director of the Philanthropy and Civil Society Center. His books include *Bridging Liberalism and Multiculturalism in Education* (2002) and, co-authored with Debra Satz, *Toward a Humanist Justice: The Political Philosophy of Susan Moller Okin* (2008), and he is currently completing *Ethics, Public Policy, and Philanthropy: The Normative Basis of Private Activity in the Public Interest.* He has written numerous journal articles and chapters in books, including "When Adequate Isn't: The Retreat from Equity in Education and Policy and Why It Matters," "Philanthropy and its Uneasy Relation to Equality," "The Failure of Philanthropy: American Charity Shortchanges the Poor, and Public Policy is Partly to Blame," and "Why Homeschooling Should Be Regulated."

John Rickford, *Martin Luther King, Jr. Centennial Professor of Linguistics and Director of the program in African and Afro-American Studies at Stanford*

2002 | John Rickford is one of the world's experts on African American Vernacular English and West Indian Creole. He received an American Book Award from The Before Columbus Foundation for *Spoken Soul: The Story of Black English* (2000). His other books include *Style and Sociolinguistic Variation* (with Penelope Eckert) (2001), *African American Vernacular English: Features, Evolution and Educational Implications* (1999), *Dimensions of a Creole Continuum* (1987), *Sociolinguistics and Pidgin-Creole Studies* (Editor) (1988), and *A Festival of Guyanese Words* (Editor) 1978).

Eric S. Roberts, *Charles Simonyi Professor and Senior Associate Dean in the School of Engineering*

2002 | Eric Roberts is the author of *Programming Abstractions in C, The Art and Science of C,* and *Thinking Recursively.*

Mary Lou Roberts, *Professor of History*

2002 | Mary Louise Roberts is an historian of France who focuses particularly on women and gender dynamics in the late nineteenth and early twentieth centuries. Her latest book is *Disruptive Acts: The New Woman in Fin de Siecle France* (2002). She is also the author of *Civilization Without Sexes: Reconstructing Gender in Post-War France, 1918-1928* (1994).

Richard Roberts, *Frances and Charles Field Professor of History*

2008 | Richard Roberts is the author of *Two World of Cotton: French Colonialism and the Regional Economy of the French Soudan, 1800-1946, Cotton, Colonialism, and Social History in Sub-Saharan Africa* (with Allen Isaacman), *Law in Colonial Africa* (with Kristen Mann), *The End of Slavery in Africa* (with Suzanne Miers), *Warriors, Merchants, and Slaves: The State and the Economy of the Middle Niger Valley, 1700-1914.* He is currently interested in the social history of everyday life during the 25 years surrounding French conquest of the interior of West Africa. He examines how colonial conquest and the establishment of colonial rule ushered in changes in African societies and economies. His current project examines the life of Faama Mademba Sy, who became an African king under French colonial rule in 1899.

Paul Robinson, *Professor of History, Director of Interdisciplinary Studies in Humanities*

2002 | Paul Robinson writes extensively on intellectual, cultural, and sexual history, engaging in a wide range of topics, interdisciplinary approaches to research, and writing styles. His books include, *Gay Lives: Homosexual Autobiography from John Addington Symonds to Paul Monette, Freud and His Critics, Opera and Ideas: From Mozart to Strauss, The Modernization of Sex: Havelock Ellis, Alfred Kinsey, William Masters, and Virginia Johnson,* and *The Sexual Radicals: Wilhelm Reich, Geza Roheim, and Herbert Marcuse.*

Terry Root, *Senior Fellow at the Woods Institute for the Environment and Professor of Biological Sciences*

2008 | Terry Root primarily works on large-scale ecological questions with a focus on impacts of global warming. She actively works at making scientific information accessible to decision makers and the public (e.g., being a Lead Author for IPCC Third and Fourth Assessment Reports). She is the author of numerous scientific articles for such journals as *Science, Climatic Change, Biodiversity and Conservation,* and *Nature.* She has written numerous chapters in books, as well as being the author of *Atlas of Wintering North American Birds: An Analysis of Christmas Bird Count Data* and co-author of *Wildlife Responses to Climate Change: North American Case Studies.*

Richard Rorty, *Professor of Comparative Literature and Philosophy*

2004 | Richard Rorty is one of today's most celebrated philosophers and social commentators. His books include *Contingency, Irony, and Solidarity, Objectivity, Relativism and Truth: Philosophical Papers I, Essays on Heidegger and Others: Philosophical Papers II, Achieving Our Country: Leftist Thought in Twentieth Century America, Truth and Progress: Philosophical Papers III,* and *Philosophy and Social Hope.*

Renato Rosaldo, *Lucie Stern Professor in the Social Sciences, Professor of Cultural and Social Anthropology*

2002 | Renato Rosaldo is one of the world's leading anthropologists. He has done field research among the Ilongots of northern Luzon, Philippines, and he is the author of *Ilongot Headhunting: 1883-1974: A Study in Society and History* (1980). He is also the author of *Culture and Truth: The Remaking of Social Analysis* (1989). He is the editor of *Creativity/Anthropology* (with Smadar Lavie and Kirin Narayan) (1993), *Anthropology of Globlization* (with Jon Inda) (2001), and *Cultural Citizenship in Island Southeast Asia: National and Belonging in the Hinterlands* (2003), among other books. He has been conducting research on cultural citizenship in San Jose, California since 1989, and contributed the introduction and a chapter to *Latino Cultural Citizens: Claiming Identity, Space, and Rights* (1997). He is also a poet. Professor Rosaldo has serves as President of the American Ethnological Society, Director of the Stanford Center for Chicano Research, and Chair of the Department of Anthropology.

Ramon Saldivar, *Professor of English and Hoagland Family Professor of Humanities and Science*

2007 | Ramon Saldivar is author of the books *Figural Language in the Novel: The Flowers of Speech from Cervantes to Joyce* and *Chicano Narrative: The Dialectics of Difference.* His most recent book, titled *The Borderlands of Culture: Américo Paredes and the Transnational Imaginary,* is a study of the modern American borderlands, transnationalism and globalism and their role in creating and delimiting agents of history.

Robert Sapolsky, *Professor of Neurology and Neurological Sciences*

2003 | Robert Sapolsky is one of the leading neuroscientists in the world, a research associate with the Institute of Primate Research Museums of Kenya, and a recipient of a MacArthur Fellowship. At the same time, he has been called "one of the best scientist-writers of our time" by Oliver Sacks and "one of the finest natural history writers around" by *The New York Times.* Robert Sapolsky has produced, in addition to numerous scientific papers, books for broader audiences, including *A Primate's Memoir: A Neuroscientist's Unconventional Life Among the Baboons, Why Zebras Don't Get Ulcers: Stress Disease and Coping,* and *The Trouble with Testosterone.*

Debra Satz, *Associate Professor of Philosophy*

2004 | Debra Satz is director of the Ethics in Society Program. Her writing focuses on social and political philosophy, philosophy of economics, and feminist philosophy. She is the co-author with John Ferejohn of *Rational Choice and Social Theory* and her articles and chapters include "The Limits of the Market: A Map of the Major Debates," "Equality of What Among Whom?: Thoughts on Cosmopolitanism, Statism and Nationalism," and "Markets in Women's Sexual Labor."

Scott Saul, *Associate Professor of American Studies and English, UC Berkeley*

2011 | Scott Saul is currently a fellow at the Stanford Humanities Center, working on *Becoming Richard Pryor*. Built on a foundation of archival research and well over a hundred hours of interviews with those who befriended, loved and collaborated with Pryor, the book aims to be the first full-dress biography of the legendary comedian. Saul's first book, the American Book Award-winning *Freedom Is, Freedom Ain't: Jazz and the Making of the Sixties*, offered a new account of "the Sixties" by putting the music of jazz at the center of that story. He writes frequently for magazines such as *Harper's*, *The Nation*, and *Boston Review*, covering the interplay of American culture and politics.

Carol Shloss, *Affiliated Professor of English*

2008 | Carol Shloss is the author of four books: *Flannery O'Connor's Dark Comedies*, *In Visible Light: Photography and the American Writer*, *Gentlemen Photographers*, and *Lucia Joyce: To Dance in the Wake*, which was nominated for the Pulitzer Prize in Literature and was a finalist for the National Book Critics' Circle Award. She continues on the editorial boards of the Joyce Studies Annual and College Literature. She is currently at work on her next book about Ezra Pound and his daughter Mary de Rachewiltz: *Treason's Child: Mary de Rachewiltz and the Real Estate of Ezra Pound*. In the early 2000s, along with the Stanford Center for Internet and Society, she successfully sued the Estate of James Joyce for the right to restore deleted materials from her biography of Lucia Joyce, winning $240,000 from the Estate.

Rebecca Slayton, *Lecturer in the Science, Technology and Society Program and Affiliate of the Center for International Security and Cooperation*

2009 | Rebecca Slayton researches and writes about the sociological history of science and technology. She conducted her doctoral research and writing in physical chemistry, and has worked as a science journalist, so our conversation will range across very different types of writing. Her current research focuses primarily on how technical judgments are generated, taken up, and given significance in international security contexts. She is currently working on a book *Proving Improbability: Physics, Computing, and Missile Defense, 1949-89* and an article "Laser-Sharp Visions? Precision, Futurism, and Laser Development in the United States, 1958-1988." Publications in Science and Technology Studies (STS) include "Speaking as Scientists: Computer Professionals in the Star Wars Debate," "Discursive Choices: Boycotting 'Star Wars' Between Science and Activism," and "Revolution and Resistance: Rethinking Power in Computing History." As a physical chemist, she developed ultrafast laser experiments in condensed matter systems and published several articles in physics journals.

Rebecca Solnit, *Activist, Historian and Writer*

2010 | Rebecca Solnit is a remarkably versatile, politically engaged, and erudite writer who has taken on subjects ranging from nineteenth century photography to Nevada nuclear test sites, from Yosemite to a social history of walking, in a career spanning twenty years. In her latest book, *A Paradise Built in Hell: The Extraordinary Communities That Arise in Disaster,* she describes the spontaneous moral communities of care and compassion that emerge in the wake of disasters like 9-11 and Hurricane Katrina. Whatever her subject, her writing is poetically invigorating, and no reader walks away unchanged. Her many books include *Storming the Gates of Paradise, A Field Guide to Getting Lost, Hope in the Dark: Untold Histories, Wild Possibilities, Wanderlust: A History of Walking, As Eve Said to the Serpent: On Landscape, Gender and Art, River of Shadows: Eadweard Muybridge and the Technological Wild West* (for which she received a Guggenheim, the National Book Critics Circle Award in criticism, and the Lannan Literary Award). A contributing editor to *Harper's,* she frequently writes for the political site Tomdispatch.com and for *Orion* magazine.

Peter Stansky, *Frances and Charles Field Professor of History, Emeritus*

2010 | Peter Stansky has been an extraordinarily productive author of British history and biography, and he is a vibrant intellectual presence on the Stanford campus. As one critic put it, "Stansky's writing, like his conversation, is full of color, personality, flair and the Higher Gossip." He has produced studies of some of the seminal figures in British political and cultural history from the mid-nineteenth to the mid-twentieth century: William Gladstone, William Morris, George Orwell, Henry Moore, Benjamin Britten. His books include *Sassoon: The Worlds of Philip and Sybil, Gladstone: A Progress in Politics, Redesigning the World, William Morris, the 1880s, and the Arts and Crafts,* and *On or About December 1910: Early Bloomsbury and its Intimate World.* He has also edited and co-authored many books, including *Journey to the Frontier: Two Roads to the Spanish Civil War.* His most recent book, *The First Day of the Blitz: September 7, 1940,* was published in 2008.

Claude Steele, *Professor of Psychology*

2004 | Claude Steele is chair of the Psychology Department. His work focuses on social psychology, investigating such areas as racial and sexual stereotyping. He has worked on numerous studies, producing such journal articles and chapters as "How Self-Esteem Influences the Assessment of Our Abilities," "Young Gifted and Black: Promoting High Achievement among African-American Students," and "The Role of Standardized Testing in Race-Sensitive Admissions."

Leonard Susskind, *Felix Bloch Professor in Physics*

2007 | Leonard Susskind studies theoretical physics, particularly the field of string theory and quantum field theory, and he is widely recognized as one of the fathers of the String Theory model of particle physics. His current research includes models of internal structure of hadrons, quark confinement, instantons, and quantum cosmology. He has won both the Pregel Award from the New York Academy of Science and the J.J. Sakurai Prize in theoretical particle physics. In addition to his scientific research, Prof. Susskind has written two books for broader audiences: *The Cosmic Landscape: String Theory and The Illusion of Intelligent Design* and *An Introduction to Black Holes, Information and The String Theory Revolution: The Holographic Universe.*

Philip Taubman, *Consulting Professor at the Center for International Security and Cooperation (CISAC)*

2009 | Philip Taubman is author of *Secret Empire: Eisenhower, the CIA, and the Hidden Story of America's Space Espionage.* He is currently working on a book project about nuclear threats and the joint effort of Sid Drell, Henry Kissinger, Sam Nunn, William Perry and George Shultz to reduce nuclear dangers. Professor Taubman worked at *The New York Times* as a reporter and editor for nearly 30 years, specializing in national security issues, including intelligence and defense policies and operations. At *The Times*, Taubman served as Washington correspondent, Moscow bureau chief, deputy editorial page editor, Washington bureau chief and associate editor. Taubman was a history major at Stanford, Class of 1970, and served as editor-in-chief of *The Stanford Daily* in 1969. Before joining *The New York Times*, he worked as a correspondent for *Time* magazine and was sports editor of *Esquire.*

Sean Kicummah Teuton, *Associate Professor of English and Indigenous Studies at the University of Wisconsin-Madison*

2013 | Sean Kicummah Teuton is the author of *Red Land, Red Power: Grounding Knowledge in the American Indian Novel* and *North American Indigenous Literature: A Very Short Introduction* (forthcoming, Oxford). Teuton is a citizen of the Cherokee Nation. As a fellow at the Stanford Humanities Center he is working on *Cities of Refuge: Indigenous Cosmopolitan Writers and the International Imaginary.* The book proposes a theory of Indigenous internationalism through the example of nineteenth-century North American Indigenous writers, who embrace a critical cosmopolitanism their present-day descendants too often reject.

Fred Turner, *Assistant Professor of Communication*

2007 | Fred Turner's research and teaching focus on digital media, journalism and the intersection of media and American cultural history. He is the author of two books: *From Counterculture to Cyberculture: Stewart Brand, the Whole Earth Network and the Rise of Digital Utopianism* (2006) and *Echoes of Combat: The Vietnam War in American Memory* (1996; Revised 2nd ed. 2001). His essays have largely explored questions of media and cultural change and have tackled topics ranging from the rise of reality crime television to the countercultural roots of the idea of virtual community. He also worked as a journalist for ten years. His news stories, features and reviews have appeared in a variety of venues, including the Pacific News Service, the *Boston Phoenix* and the *Boston Sunday Globe Magazine*.

Abraham Verghese, *MD, Novelist, Senior Associate Chair and Professor for the Theory and Practice of Medicine, Stanford University School of Medicine*

2011 | A graduate of Madras University, Abraham Verghese is an acclaimed physician, one of the founding directors of the Center for Medical Humanities and Ethics at the University of Texas Health Sciences Center, San Antonio, where he was the founding director of the Center for Medical Humanities and Ethics. In 1990-91, Dr. Verghese attended the Iowa Writers Workshop at the University of Iowa where he obtained a Master of Fine Arts degree. His first book, *My Own Country,* about AIDS in rural Tennessee, was a finalist for the National Book Critics Circle Award for 1994 and was made into a movie. His second book, *The Tennis Partner,* was a *New York Times* notable book and a national bestseller. His third book, *Cutting for Stone,* was published by Knopf and is a *New York Times Book Review* bestseller. He has published extensively in the medical literature, and his writing has appeared in *The New Yorker, Sports Illustrated, The Atlantic Monthly, Esquire, Granta, The New York Times Magazine, The Wall Street Journal* and elsewhere.

Malena Watrous, *Jones Lecturer, Creative Writing Program*

2006 | Malena Watrous received an MFA in fiction from the University of Iowa Writers' Workshop. Her stories have been published in *Triquarterly, The Massachussetts Review,* and the *Alaska Quarterly Review,* and she has received prizes from *Glimmertrain* and the Faulkner Society. She is currently working on a novel, and reviews fiction for the *San Francisco Chronicle.*

Alex Woloch, *Assistant Professor of English*

2002 | Alex Woloch works on the history of the novel and literary theory. His teaching is focused on nineteenth-century British literature and covers the broad development of the European and American novel. He is particularly interested in narrative realism and the question of representation in its literary, rhetorical and political dimensions. He is the author of *The One vs. the Many: Minor Characters and the Space of the Protagonist in the Novel* (Princeton University Press, 2004) that attempts to reestablish the centrality of characterization — the fictional representation of human beings — within narrative poetics. He is also the co-editor, with Peter Brooks, of *Whose Freud? The Place of Psychoanalysis in Contemporary Culture* (Yale University Press, 2000). Professor Woloch is currently working on a study of George Orwell.

Victor Wooten, *Bass Guitarist and Author*

2010 | Victor Wooten has been hailed as an innovator, composer, arranger, producer, author, teacher, vocalist, and multi-instrumentalist. Known for his solo recordings and tours, and as a member of the Grammy-winning Béla Fleck & The Flecktones, he was voted "Bassist of the Year" by Bass Player Magazine three times, and is the only person to have won the award more than once. His solo projects, such as the Grammy-nominated Yin-Yang album continue to garner him accolades as both an instrumentalist and composer, and he has collaborated, recorded and performed with such artists as Branford Marsalis, Chick Corea, Dave Matthews, and Prince. In 2008, Wooten surprised critics with *The Music Lesson*, a book that contains many of the lessons, ideas, and ways of thinking about music that have made him famous but in the form of a story about a struggling young musician who wanted music to be his life and wanted his life to be great.

Irvin Yalom, *Professor Emeritus of Psychiatry*

2012 | Dr. Yalom's most recent novel is *The Spinoza Problem*. He is the acclaimed author of stories and novels related to psychotherapy, including *Love's Executioner, When Nietzsche Wept, Lying on the Couch, Momma and the Meaning of Life*, and *The Schopenhauer Cure*. He is also the author of numerous non-fiction works and textbooks, such as *Staring at the Sun: Overcoming the Terror of Death* and *The Theory and Practice of Psychotherapy*.

Marilyn Yalom, *Senior Scholar at the Clayman Institute for Gender Research*

2014 | Marilyn Yalom is the author of numerous books and articles on literature and women's history, including *Maternity, Mortality, and the Literature of Madness, Blood Sisters: The French Revolution in Women's Memory, A History of the Breast, A History of the Wife, Birth of the Chess Queen, The American Resting Place* and her most recent book, *How the French Invented Love: 900 Years of Passion and Romance*. She has been a professor of French and is presently a senior scholar at the Clayman Institute for Gender Research at Stanford University.

She has been married to the psychiatrist and author Irvin Yalom for fifty years and is the mother of four children and the grandmother of five.

Richard Zare, *Marguerite Blake Wilbur Professor in Natural Science and Chair of the Department of Chemistry*

2008 | Professor Richard Zare is renowned in the area of lasers applied to chemical reactions and to chemical analysis. He has authored or co-authored four books, is the author or co-author of over 800 peer-reviewed publications, and he is deeply involved in publishing, being Chair of the Board of Directors of Annual Reviews. Annual Reviews publishes authoritative, analytic reviews in 37 focused disciplines within the Biomedical, Life, Physical, and Social Sciences. Professor Zare is the recipient of many awards including the National Medal of Science (1983), the Welch Award in Chemistry (1999), and the Wolf Prize in Chemistry (2005).

Steven Zipperstein, *the Daniel E. Koshland Professor in Jewish Culture and History, Co-Director of Jewish Studies*

2005 | Steven Zipperstein writes modern Jewish history and has published widely in professional and popular publications including *The New York Times, The Washington Post, New Republic, Partisan Review* and *Dissent.* His books include *The Jews of Odessa: A Cultural History, Elusive Prophet: Ahad Ha'am and the Origins of Zionism, Imagining Russian Jewry: Memory, History, Identity,* and *Assimilation and Community: The Jews in Nineteenth-Century Europe.* He is currently writing a cultural history of East European and Russian Jewry from the eighteenth century to the present, which will be published by Houghton Mifflin. His biography of the American Jewish novelist and essayist, Isaac Rosenfeld, will be completed soon.

Hilton Obenzinger writes fiction, poetry, history, and criticism. His books include *Busy Dying, Running Through Fire: How I Survived the Holocaust by Zosia Goldberg*, and *American Palestine: Melville, Twain, and the Holy Land Mania*. *New York on Fire*, a history of the fires of New York in verse, was selected by *The Village Voice* as one of the best books of the year and was nominated by the Bay Area Book Reviewer's Association for its award in poetry. His sequence of poems and sketches *This Passover or the Next I will Never be in Jerusalem* received the American Book Award.

Born in 1947 in Brooklyn, raised in Queens, and graduating from Columbia University in 1969, Hilton Obenzinger has taught on the Yurok Indian Reservation, operated a community printing press in San Francisco's Mission District, coedited a publication devoted to Middle East peace, and worked as a commercial writer and instructional designer. He received his doctorate in the Modern Thought and Literature Program at Stanford University. He directed honors and advanced writing from 1998 to 2010 at what is now the Hume Center for Writing and Speaking, and he's taught in the English Department, the American Studies Program, and Continuing Studies at Stanford. He is currently Associate Director of the Chinese Railroad Workers in North America Project at Stanford. For more, see www.obenzinger.com

Photo: John Todd